TWEENS

ALSO BY MICHELLE MITCHELL

Books for parents:

Everyday Resilience: Helping kids handle friendship drama, academic pressure and the self-doubt of growing up

Self-Harm: Why teens do it and what parents can do to help

Parenting Teenage Girls in the Age of a New Normal

What Teenage Girls Don't Tell Their Parents

Books for tweens:

The Everyday Resilience Journal

A Guy's Guide to Puberty

A Girl's Guide to Puberty

TWEENS

What kids need NOW, before the *teenage years*

Navigating friendships, moods, technology, boundaries, body image and the road ahead

MICHELLE MITCHELL
foreword by Maggie Dent

LIFE

The information contained in this book should not substitute medical and/or professional advice, or personal judgement. The author and publisher accept no responsibility for any action taken as a result of this material.

PENGUIN LIFE

UK | USA | Canada | Ireland | Australia
India | New Zealand | South Africa | China

Penguin Life is part of the Penguin Random House group of companies whose addresses can be found at global.penguinrandomhouse.com

Penguin
Random House
Australia

First published by Penguin Life in 2023

Cover design by Christabella Designs
Internal design by Post Pre-press Group, Australia
Typeset in 11.5/16.5 pt Berkeley Oldstyle by Post Pre-press Group, Australia

Printed and bound in Australia by Griffin Press, an accredited ISO AS/NZS 14001 Environmental Management Systems printer

 A catalogue record for this book is available from the National Library of Australia

ISBN 978 1 76104 989 7

penguin.com.au

We at Penguin Random House Australia acknowledge that Aboriginal and Torres Strait Islander peoples are the Traditional Custodians and the first storytellers of the lands on which we live and work. We honour Aboriginal and Torres Strait Islander peoples' continuous connection to Country, waters, skies and communities. We celebrate Aboriginal and Torres Strait Islander stories, traditions and living cultures; and we pay our respects to Elders past and present.

To my kids, now 24 and 20. May these words
be a reflection of my heart towards you.

CONTENTS

FOREWORD
MAGGIE DENT

Every age and stage of child development has its unique gifts and challenges. Every child is different, and the massive transformational journey of adolescence that happens in late childhood as our child changes into an adult has become longer over time. In traditional kinship communities, the transformation began later and finished earlier, and now in the twenty-first century it is starting well before the teen years and lasting often until the late twenties! The window of early adolescence, commonly known as 'the tweens', has been largely ignored. That is why this book from the wise and passionate Michelle Mitchell is so incredibly timely for parents and those who work with children aged 9 to 12.

Things have changed a lot since I was a high school teacher. To start with, tweens were still primary school children who were a long way off from typical teenage issues, and the digital world was just a possibility. There are many reasons why our tweens are maturing earlier. Social researcher Mark McCrindle calls tweens Generation Alpha – the cohort born since 2010 who have been moulded by unique times and massive social and cultural change. Sadly, we are becoming aware that many of these Generation Alphas are struggling to thrive in our busy, chaotic and unpredictable world.

Science now shows that it is around the age of 8 that adrenal androgens start getting busy, making subtle but distinctive changes to the emotional and cognitive world of our tweens. This signals the earliest beginnings of puberty and often happens invisibly, and yet it can impact our tweens in very confusing ways. They can begin to compare themselves to others in unrealistic ways and to feel the pressure of conforming to impossible cultural standards. This process is happening well before it did for previous generations, and it's happening before our children have the cognitive capacity to fully understand helpful and healthy ways of being a tween.

Our school systems have become far more competitive, and the endless testing is putting undue pressure on all of our children, particularly those about to step into high school. Without supportive guidance, this can create negative mindsets that can inhibit our tweens' potential to grow to be capable, confident and resilient. Some of our tweens are still very child-like and uncomplicated, while others have begun displaying many of the behaviours commonly associated with tweens. This may include moodiness, pulling away from parents, seeking more privacy, and of course the beginning of rolled eyes and the occasional slammed door. Girls tend to begin this process around 18 months before boys, however nothing is set in stone. Be prepared for anything, and be prepared to become informed about the importance of this stage of development, as it is very important in the shaping of your son's or daughter's life.

That's where Michelle comes in, as your sage guide. Not only has she explored the research, but from her own survey you will have the voices of parents of tweens and, best of all, you will hear from tweens themselves informing you of their concerns and what they want from you.

This guide is not only informative, it is packed full of practical suggestions that can and will help parents to be what their tweens really need. Michelle carefully explains that tweens are not teens, and that they have particular needs and wants that need to be addressed. Every now and then she drops an insight so powerful it will see parents taking a deep breath. Take this one for example: 'If you aren't ready to talk to your child about pornography and paedophiles, you aren't ready for them to be online. Preventive education and a clear "what to do" are essential.'

Much has been written about the importance of parents being the rails on the bridge to adulthood, and this book will show you how you can be just that for your tween. With warmth, humour and clarity, Michelle explores all of the key areas of concern: starting high school; body image; emerging sexuality; screens; healthy boundaries; and tweens' big emotional worlds.

What I have discovered during my education and parenting career, is that the number one fundamental need for every child of every age is to know that they have at least one safe, reliable grown-up who cares deeply for them and who will always have their back. Our tweens need grown-ups who can be a safe base, who they can approach easily, who will listen without judgement and who will help them land on hope rather than despair. Not only can parents make a huge difference, significant adult allies, whom I call 'lighthouses', can also make a world of difference for a young person who is struggling to find their way. Please watch out for other people's tweens and shine a light of consideration and caring.

The two strongest drivers for tweens on this journey to adulthood are working out their own sense of identity and finding where they belong. This excellent book will help you guide your child, whatever their gender, through this interesting stage of development with more confidence and awareness.

Thank you, Michelle, for yet another wonderful book on such an important topic, a book full of wisdom, compassion and guidance that I believe will help families, schools and communities everywhere take better care of our tweens. With a stronger foundation before the teen years, I believe we will see more young people find a pathway to thrive rather than struggle.

Maggie Dent is a bestselling parenting author and host of the ABC podcast *Parental as Anything*.

A QUICK DEFINITION

I originally intended to write a book for parents of both tweens and teens. However, the more I looked at age-specific research and considered the experiences of those who participated in my survey, the more I felt compelled to narrow my message. Before you turn the page, know that we will be exploring the lives and needs of those aged between 9 and 12 years old, whom I will refer to as 'tweens'. The term 'teenager' will be used to describe those aged 13 to 19, while the word 'adolescence' will be used to describe the transition from childhood to adulthood, which typically spans the ages of 10 to 24.

ABOUT THE SURVEY

I've been on a mission to see where the voices of those between the ages of 9 and 12 are showing up in research, media, sports, the arts and our local communities. I've immersed myself in popular culture and trawled through television shows, books, the fashion industry and a diverse range of social media and gaming platforms in order to get some insight into their world.

This is what I have found. For the most part, relatable and healthy role models are missing in action. Tweens are either depicted as goofy, silly children or as overly grown-up and sexualised adolescents, with very little in between. We are encouraging tweens either to continue to view content that is void of substance or to jump into the adolescent world head-first before they are ready for it.

Throughout my entire career I have only ever known tweens to live in the shadow of teenagers and their cute, but demanding, younger brothers and sisters. Tweens have always flown under the radar, and, by default, received the dregs of education initiatives, research budgets, media coverage and at times their parents' attention. Time and time again I have seen programs and resources dedicated to parenting tweens and teens as a single entity, without acknowledgement of the significant developmental differences between these age groups.

For this reason, it has been particularly important for me to gather data in my 2020 survey of not only 1603 parents, but also 567 tweens. I ran this survey through my community over the course of several months, posing 24 questions to parents and 17 to tweens. Some questions were multiple choice and others asked for open-ended answers. The survey focused on life circumstances, current challenges, upcoming concerns and significant relationships in tweens' lives. My team and I have spent hours organising, discussing and digesting the important messages that families shared. Thank you to everyone who responded with honesty on topics such as technology, communication, anxiety, body image and friendships, and to those who spoke personally with me. I hope to aptly amplify your thoughts in this book.

My most important finding is that tweens gravitate towards those who are approachable, who help them overcome challenges and who listen to them. Collectively, they voiced a strong desire to be taken more seriously by the world around them and not to be overlooked or dismissed because of their age. Overwhelmingly, tweens wished they were better understood and had more avenues to contribute to the world meaningfully.

I look forward to sharing my findings in the breakout sections in this book, so look out for them. They will speak far more insightfully than my words ever could. Please note that names have been changed to protect privacy, while original grammar and spelling have been retained in some places in order to safeguard authenticity. In a few instances, quotes have been edited for length or clarity. It is my hope that these examples help us deeply listen to tweens, because without a stronger understanding of the real needs, concerns and desires of this age group, I'm not sure we are going to be able to show up for them in the way they need us to.

INTRODUCTION
A CHANGE IN CONVERSATION

For the last 25 years I have been listening to parents in my role as a primary school teacher and then as the founder of Youth Excel, a charity I established to support young people and their families. Over time I have witnessed a saddening change in the conversation. In years gone past, I rarely heard about tweens struggling with significantly poor mental health. Nor was there a recognised need to talk to primary school children about anxiety, anger management, consent or any number of wellbeing-related topics that we discuss with them today. Tweens were known as the compliant, manageable, sweet-and-innocent ones who didn't give parents too much trouble.

Nowadays, I get calls and emails from parents about tweens stumbling across pornography, sending nudes, vaping, becoming physically violent or self-harming, issues we have predominantly only ever seen in high school. I meet upper primary school teachers and principals who are deeply concerned about their students' obsession with YouTube superstars and sexy dance moves. I hear about sass and mood swings that are surprisingly teenage-like and difficult to handle.

On a very sad and serious note that must be mentioned, Kids Helpline reports a clear trend of increasing calls relating to suicide from children under 14. Records show children start making contact as young as 7 years old, with numbers rapidly increasing between the ages of 11 and 14.[1,2,3] On the topic of non-suicidal self-harm, a large Australian study found that approximately 7.6 per cent of 10- to 12-year-olds reported using this coping strategy, which I find heartbreaking.[4]

The people I interviewed for this book were far more apprehensive about parenting a tween than I remember being when my children were that age. Siobhan, mother of 12-year-old Ellie, says, 'The biggest challenge is parenting in a way that is different from the way you were parented. I am a product of the '70s and '80s Catholic household. As parents, we are called to build a bridge from the way we were parented to how this generation needs us, but this is really stretching us. It's like Brené Brown says: "My heart is covered with stretch marks."'

Most parents I have spoken to identified with being stretched and many expressed a deep lack of confidence. Charmaine shared, 'It's hard for us parents too. In our day we were told what to do, and that was it. Now we are meant to allow them to feel and express themselves, which sounds good in theory, but it's hard to know where the line is.' Jennifer offered a similar sentiment when she said, 'I don't know if I am doing it well or not well, and I often feel like I have such limited experience and resources myself. I don't know how to judge this or gauge this. I like to think that I am doing it well, and sometimes I do, but mostly I don't.'

It takes courage to parent this generation of tweens. It's courage that will drive parents into the needed places of their kids' lives, and it is courage that will enable us to do things differently than we have seen them done before. Regardless of whether your tween is still playing with dolls and cars (or the iPad equivalent), or enjoying more teen-ish activities, they need you in their lives. Their wellbeing is reliant on both your deliberate presence and the management of external influences, including technology. I know this is an incredible challenge when our modern-day lifestyles involve long work hours or shift work, or unforeseen obstacles such as homeschooling during COVID-19 lockdowns, but we must try.

At the heart of this book's message is that tweens are *not* the new teenagers, despite the real challenges they are experiencing.[5] They embody a very specific stage of development that is unlike anything that has come before or after. Even when tweens encounter teen-like issues, they surface completely differently because tweens are confined to childlike cognition, and they have greater trust in adults' ability to guide them. I am so looking forward to unpacking the latest research on tweens' brain development in Chapter 1, 'Almost a Teenager'.

As I've walked through schools and viewed kids in supermarkets, restaurants, parks, playgrounds and gaming arcades, I've seen diversity at its finest. The differences between tweens are as wide as they are deep. Capturing this diversity has been my greatest challenge while writing this book. This book isn't directed at a stereotypical family – in fact there is no such thing. Instead, I hope my words speak to the varied experiences of many families, and you are able to see and hear your household in its words. I imagine you will have moments where you say to yourself, 'My child is nothing like that!' and other moments where you say, 'Gosh, that sounds like my young one!' Take both responses as an insight into your unique child's world.

Think of this book as an operating manual rather than an academic research paper. I hope to unpack the question, What is life like for those between the ages of 9 and 12, and how can we best support them? Some parts of this book will resonate more strongly with you now, and others will resonate with you in the months and years to come, because tweens' development can be incredibly fast-moving. Each strategy will contain new meaning as it becomes relevant to your home, so continue to dip in and out of these pages as your experience catches up with them. My hope is that this book will support you for many years to come.

To begin, we are going to dig into the developmental drivers that are impacting your tween and undercover why these are different than the ones they are likely to experience in their teenage years. This is critical reading that includes ground-breaking new research from the Murdoch Children's Research Institute, which will help you understand the key opportunities at this stage of development.

Next, we will get super practical. I aim to help you navigate the issues that matter in your home, now. We will discuss friendships, moods, confidence, healthy tech habits, identity exploration, puberty, sex, body image, sibling relationships, mental health and high school. In many instances I'm going to offer you the exact language I have used in my presentations at schools over the past 20 years. Towards the end of the book we will review some beautifully insightful messages directly from tweens themselves. Each of these findings will give you a better understanding of their world. I will also offer you a sneak peek into the years ahead, and what will matter most as you approach this transition.

As you read, I hope you feel like you are walking through the pages of this book with me. Let's stroll and chat . . . and occasionally stop for a deeper conversation. Borrow my foresight. That's what I am here for. Listen to other families and let them be a catalyst for your own reflection. Consider the latest research and statistical data I will offer you and glean knowledge from the work of people who are adding value to the conversation.

Like you, my greatest responsibility in life is my children. Although my boys are now young adults, it wasn't that long ago that we were worrying about friendship choices, manoeuvring around moods, adjusting to ever-changing hobbies and responding to fights about who was cheating in backyard cricket and who was not. I have endeavoured to share stories from my own home throughout this book to remind you that we all walk the journey alongside our kids – none of us escapes its painful moments.

I am very grateful for the community that helped us along the way. Extended family, friends and teachers all embraced my kids and taught them what they couldn't learn solely within the four walls of our home. I especially want to acknowledge the significant role my dear parents played. Like so many others, my kids felt like their grandparents' home was an extension of ours. We have some hilarious memories of times when my kids acted up while staying with them and I was called to come salvage the situation.

If you are putting your hand up to guide this generation of tweens, thank you. Whether you are an educator, a therapist, a sports coach, a dance instructor, a youth worker or a parent who opens their heart and home to their child's friends – thank you. We all remember those who stepped into our world at key moments and shone a light on the way forward. They are people we will never forget. I hope I can, in some way, lean in for your family and be a part of the community that supports your child. I desperately want all our tweens to transition into adulthood wiser, safer and surrounded by trusted adults. They deserve that.

Chapter 1

ALMOST A TEENAGER

Key Message: The best way we can invest in the future is to be present today.

I was standing in the foyer of my then psychology clinic, casually chatting to a mum and her daughter who were both waiting to see their regular practitioner. During our conversation, the mother described her 10-year-old as 'almost a teenager'. I looked closely at the little person in question. She had a tiny frame, with a big scrunchie decorating her pigtail. I had watched her and her mother walk hand in hand into the clinic moments before. Her mascara-free eyes smiled at me. *Almost*, I thought, *but not quite.*

If your child is between the ages of 9 and 12, you are in the throes of the 'between' years. You are parenting a young one who is not quite a child and not quite a teenager, but the exciting news is that nor are they aimlessly caught in limbo. Tweens embody a very specific stage of development that, once understood, will revolutionise the way you parent, educate and support those in your care. Right now you have a window of opportunity that can change the trajectory of adolescence and beyond.

Until quite recently, the information I am about to share with you has been missing from the developmental picture. Research has largely neglected our tweens, with interest focusing on the early years and late adolescence once problems have surfaced. Only a few decades ago many assumed that development was complete between the ages of 7 and 8 because brains had reached their adult size. Others hypothesised that the brain was taking a nap before it commenced further changes during adolescence.[1]

However, thanks to the groundbreaking work of researchers and world-first studies such as CATS (Childhood to Adolescence Transition Study) initiated by the Murdoch Children's Research Institute, we now understand that the tween years are anything but quiet or latent.[2] Instead, we know they are a time of rapid change, with significant reorganisation and restructuring of the brain being undertaken in preparation for adolescence. Our kids experience not only the obvious physical and biological changes associated with puberty, but also a whole range of unique cognitive, social, sexual and emotional changes in the same life-altering way.[3] Although we haven't always recognised it, the time between 9 and 12 years of age is the most rapid period of development since toddlerhood.

Dr Lisa Mundy, Senior Research Fellow at the Murdoch Children's Research Institute, describes the tween years as a transformative phase of life that is critical to setting children on the best possible path for adolescence.[4] In my interview with Dr Lisa, I felt her passion for data that suggests children are not set in stone but are particularly mouldable. She explains, 'The tween years are a reorientation to what comes next. Our research tells us that it is over and above as important as what has already come. Along with the early years, it is the best possible time to intervene and reset developmental trajectories.'

Research now refers to the tween years as a developmental 'switch point'.[5] When I look at a 10-year-old, the words 'switch point' pull a sense of responsibility out of me. Tweens are ready to be 'switched on' to their potential, and every trusted adult in their lives can be a part of that process. It's during these years that kids will be most responsive and adaptive to the environment around them. The right support, administered at this opportune time, can make the world of difference. Although some young people indeed find the intensity of change during these years overwhelming, there is so much we can do to safeguard their journey.

As I interviewed parents for this book, they offered me a compelling rationale for embracing the tween years as a switch point. Many shared sincere and deep concerns about their tween's wellbeing. If I am honest, it was beyond what I was expecting to hear. Very few parents talked about small or insignificant issues, and I got the feeling that current research was only scratching the surface of the problem. 'Exhausted', 'overwhelmed' and 'scary' were words I repeatedly heard parents use. One mum bluntly told me, 'Age 11 is not what I expected – it is hard.' My interviews contained both joyful and teary moments as parents shared their fond memories, greatest fears, current struggles and hopes for the future.

'Gosh, he is acting like I was acting when I was 15,' Christine explains. 'He is only 10 – moody, big emotions. He has always been a sensitive boy and we have always been close.' Siobhan, mother of 12-year-old Ellie, expounds, 'I didn't see this coming. We had a really tough two or three years with anxiety, which showed up as school refusal. We did everything we could – changed schools and then COVID-19 happened. Parenting a tween is 100 times harder than parenting a toddler.' And finally, Tony, dad to 11-year-old Kristy, jokingly says, 'If this is any sign of what is to come, I'm moving out . . . or at least building a shed to escape!'

All parents felt an urgency to invest in their tween before the full pressures of high school hit. There is such wisdom in this, and I share your desire to build a strong foundation to work from. Caroline, mother of two tweens and a teen, shared, 'I'm trying to get on the front foot, knowing how extreme I was as a teenager. I want them to know they are supported and loved, and that they have that support and love within themselves – they just have to believe that.' If you, like Caroline, want to maximise the benefits and developmental potential of the tween years, this book is going to be life-changing for you.

Climbing Mountains

To help you understand more about your tween's stage of development, I want you to imagine you are climbing a mountain with your child. It's not the first mountain you have climbed with them, but it is unlike any other. This mountain is called Tween Kingdom – a typically playful, diverse and expansive place where development is on high speed. While I acknowledge the view from Tween Kingdom is different for every family, it's common for parents to feel a sense of pride or relief as their child gains more skills and independence while spending time on this mountain.

Know that your tween's brain is working overtime at the top of the mountain, and we need to be careful not to patronise, dismiss or minimise the important work that is being done. What is trivial in our world is big in theirs. Although conversations about friendships and school might feel repetitive and laborious to us, huge internal work is being undertaken to master the skills they need for life.

It's on this mountain climb that they will begin to develop more complex reasoning, problem-solving and deduction skills than they had as a child and, at times, show remarkable maturity and insight. They will fine-tune their ability to deeply understand others' minds, which we will talk more about in Chapter 2, 'Speaking Tween'. Their concept of self, including gender and sexual feelings, will expand, and so will the way they relate to you. You might feel a sense of uneasiness about this, but I hope to put your mind at rest. It's essential that the whole family shifts to accommodate this change.

While climbing this mountain they will experience 'windows of opportunity', times where their brain is open for accelerated growth. These windows are specific to this age group and will never be repeated in quite the same way. You can liken them to the windows of opportunity from previous mountain climbs. For example, you may remember many years ago your 6-month-old baby beginning to take note of the world; this was because the neurons associated with their vision began developing rapidly at 2 to 4 months old and peaked at 8 months.[6] This time, as tweens, their growth is more likely to be centred around social and emotional learning.

It's no surprise that sensitivity is characteristic of this age group, and it's not just hormonal changes that will bring them to tears. There will be times when they feel deeply uncomfortable about the pace of this mountain climb, and the view from where they stand. Interestingly, some parents have told me that it's gotten easier as their kids entered the teenage years, which is worth taking note of if your tween is currently struggling.

I absolutely loved this statement by Jacqueline, mum of a now 13-year-old, because it offers a bit of hope for those who are finding the tween years tougher than they imagined. She explains, 'When my daughter was 9 it was starting to play out big time. She was coming home and crying herself to sleep. In some ways, it has gotten easier as she has gotten older. She is now starting to understand her own emotions and how to deal with them, and that allows us to have better conversations. Even though we know that we are still in for a bumpy ride, our girl has more experience to draw on and we can have more grown-up conversations.'

Facts Neuroscientists Agree On

It's a once-in-a-lifetime collision. There are so many factors that distinguish your child from other tweens. Fundamentals like genetics, IQ, temperament (a big one!) and innate talents and abilities have defined them since they were born. Life experiences, birth order, gender and of course their relationship with significant adults have also played a critical role in their development. Who your child is right now is going to intercept with a cascade of hormones and brain changes, with the fundamental purpose of forming their unique identity and preparing them for a life independent from you. Think of puberty as a once-in-a-lifetime collision that will truly make them stand out from classmates and siblings.

It starts earlier than you realise. Tweens experience 'under the bonnet' changes long before they grow their first pubic hair. Dr Lisa Mundy explains, 'It is important that we don't look at puberty and the transition to adolescence as a "unitary event", which happens around the ages of 11 and 12. Instead, we need to see it as a cascade of hormonal changes that takes place over time, with a significant rise around 7 to 8 years of age where there is a huge rise in hormones called adrenal androgens, which then continues into our early twenties. We now know that huge growth is happening even when we don't see it.' In fact, the first menstrual cycle (termed menarche) is the very last event that occurs in the process of the female pubertal transition. Spermarche, the development of sperm in boys' testicles, is the male counterpart.[7]

It's smudgy. When it comes to development, the lines are blurry and the overall picture is smudgy at best. Research offers us a general guide, but it can't expressly talk about your unique child – you can. Your tween's physical, cognitive, social, sexual and emotional development is likely to be progressing at different paces. They may be an absolute mismatch of experiences that is incomparable to their peers. A typical example of this is when a tween is externally showing signs of maturation, while cognitively they may still be childlike.

Timing and tempo can impact mental health. Pubertal timing refers to how a tween's development compares to same-sex peers of the same age. Puberty tempo refers to how quickly a person completes these sets of pubertal changes. Research clearly tells us that the timing and the tempo of puberty both have a big impact on children's mental health and resilience, as does the feeling of being in sync (or out of sync) with peers.[8] Those who start puberty earlier or later than the majority of their peers need our wholehearted support. We will be continuing this conversation in a practical way in many sections of this book.

Gender impacts experience. On average, girls are likely to experience hormonal and physical changes about 12 to 18 months earlier than boys, who then quickly catch up.[9] Despite this, research suggests that neither gender escapes challenges, although there is definitely more research on our girls' experiences.[10] In very general terms, our boys are more likely to experience behavioural challenges, while our girls are more likely to experience social challenges.[11]

Hormones are only part of the story. The hormones responsible for puberty have always been in our tweens' bodies, so they aren't 'new'. What is new is that they are now being released in adult doses. Karen Young, a specialist in neurodevelopment and author of the internationally acclaimed website Hey Sigmund,[12] explains, 'These new levels of hormones often feel like an aggressive ambush of their existing systems. We must realise that brains produce behaviour, not hormones.' So much of the tricky behaviour tweens exhibit gets blamed on hormones, but we must realise that hormones aren't the whole story, which makes both brain health and genetics important factors to consider.

Synaptic pruning adds another layer. Although typically more dominant during the teenage years, synaptic pruning – also known as brain remodelling or downsizing – can begin at the onset of puberty. Synaptic pruning will signify a slow loss of 15 to 20 per cent of grey matter over the course of adolescence.[13,14] This happens because the brain no longer needs to grow diversely but instead wants to specialise and centre itself around things that make it unique, moving tweens into a different stage of development.

Almost a Teenager

Here's the reality of tween life: place a couple of 11-year-olds side by side and the developmental chasm between them can place them in different universes. It's a very clear juxtaposition. I'll use Charmaine and Kerry as an example, as they both have 11-year-old sons. Charmaine describes her son Harry as steady and easygoing, compliant and childlike. Kerry shares a very different experience when she speaks of her son, Ethan, 'It feels like overnight he had a deeper voice, slept in more in the mornings, struggled to go to sleep at night and wanted to spend much more time with friends. Even though he is very close with his younger brother, he wants to separate from him when he is around his friends. It's changed everything. For many years the kids have been able to choose one television show together, and now he wants to choose a different show than his younger siblings.'

I've noticed that parents of tweens also fall into two camps. The first camp is for parents whose tweens are exhibiting 'almost teenage' behaviours. Parents might notice an unexpected door slam (just to add emphasis) or a statement like 'you can't tell me what to do', which brings a novel atmosphere to a usually playful home. I remember the first time I tried on my big girl boots and told my mother to 'shut up'. That did not go down well! The second camp includes parents who often proudly say, 'Thank God they aren't at that stage yet!' Once your tween does cross this threshold, you might notice some or all of the following behavioural changes:

- backchatting more than normal
- idolising those older than them
- trading hobbies they once loved for new-found interests

- a greater appetite for risk-taking
- trying many types of extracurricular activities until they find the right 'fit'
- an increased need for sleep
- increased friendship challenges and a desire to fit in
- a heightened feeling of being embarrassed in front of others
- more intense mood swings
- increased attention to body weight and physical appearance.

In the days to come, some young adults will recall a slow slide into adolescence and others will feel like their childhood literally disappeared overnight. While writing this book, my eldest son, who is now 24, thoughtfully weighed in on its content and his experience as a tween. He particularly remembers experiencing 'almost a teenager' behaviours around 11 years old, which were a huge shock to his quickly growing person. Crossing this threshold impacted every decision he made and how he saw us as parents. He gorgeously recalls, 'I woke up one morning feeling that you didn't understand me at all. I couldn't work out why *you* had changed overnight. I thought something weird had happened to you. Looking back, it makes me laugh, but that's just how I felt at the time.'

He went on to recall the day he fervently defended the idea that dinosaurs were 'not real', an idea he heard from his dad who was the all-knowing, superior intelligence in his world. The funniest part of this story is that his dad never said dinosaurs weren't real but perhaps questioned some of the hypotheticals my son was being taught. Armed with this black-and-white interpretation of my husband's words, my son adamantly, fanatically and publicly called the teacher wrong and argued with any classmate who opposed him. Before long he had the teacher on the backfoot, believing his dad must be some type of palaeontologist. The class ended up swaying in his favour, rather than the teacher's, probably because of my son's passion and trust in his father's words. Only months later did he think, 'What is dad on about? Of course, dinosaurs are real! That has now become the most embarrassing moment of my life!'

At about the same age, I remember he wanted to listen to death metal. Apparently, the guitar riffs were beyond amazing! We explained that the language used in this genre of music was inappropriate for his age and responded to his request with a gentle 'no'. He was totally okay with our response, and we had a rational conversation about the reasons behind our decision. I remember giving him credit for his incredible maturity! Only weeks later, he recalls thinking to himself, 'What are these lunatics on about? I want to listen to that music and it's not like I don't hear swear words at school! What's the big deal?' So, my son put the music on his iPod. When we found it, we said, 'I thought we agreed you wouldn't listen to that?' And he replied, 'I've thought about it some more and changed my mind.'

You might find that your tween attempts some 'almost teenage' moves and then retreats back into the safety of childhood. The dance back and forth is completely normal and gives parents time to warm up to the transition. Most tweens can be both defiant and profusely sorry at the same time, which reminds us how tender and young they still are. They can be cute one minute, a little moody the next and just as confused by the contradiction as we are. Some children do make a big, bold leap into adolescence, which shocks both them and the world around them, but many tweens will 'try before they buy'.

What's comforting to remember is that even when they do cross the line, they have only *just* crossed over – they are still reachable. They are still open to our influence and the influence of the environments we place around them. I guess that is why the tween years are often seen as a low-stakes training ground to teach kids the key skills they'll need in the future. You have the chance to teach them to swim while they're still near the shoreline, rather than out in the waves. The precious thing about tweens is that they will easily absorb your values without question or much experimentation, despite having 'almost teenage' moments. The good news is that for a while longer your tween will only look towards adolescence in anticipation, so you have time to figure this out.

While tweens can have challenging moments, there is one big difference between the tween and the teen years – their desire to follow your lead. With tweens the door is still open. Most tweens are keen to embrace every ounce of time and energy parents have to offer, and they still believe that their parents have superhero qualities. I regularly hear about tweens requesting endless goodnight tucks, cherishing every moment of their parents' attention before the end of the day. I've often spotted tweens routinely holding their parent's hand without the slightest hesitation, and smiled. The connection is ever so tangible.

Learning to Flip It

We often talk about how much we love our children. I can only hope that your love is as unstoppable as the sea. However, I want to take a moment to flip the experience. Let's assume that your child also has a deep love for you. They are as invested in you as you are in them. They cannot fathom life without you. They fear losing you just as much as you fear losing them. In my survey, I noticed how much tweens don't want to disappoint their parents. They don't want to hurt you and are incredibly apologetic about their difficult moments. I also noticed that they worry about becoming the disapproved of, sassy, rude, mood-swinging teenager who they know is going to irritate you.

This heartfelt story from Melinda, mother of Mitchell, is an excellent example of our tween's desire to protect us from their more difficult moments. Melinda had taken her son to their GP because he admitted to feeling depressed. She explains, 'It was very confronting when the GP asked my son, "Do you talk to your mum about stuff?" and my son answered, "Sometimes I talk, but I don't want to bother her about everything. Because she gave birth to me, I don't want her to worry." He knew I was busy and he felt like he didn't want to add another thing to the already full plate.'

Tweens don't choose the timing of puberty, or its associated ups and downs – it's chosen for them. This is an uncomfortable starting position for some of our tweens. Sadly, in my survey 26.8 per cent of tweens said they *weren't* looking forward to the transition to adolescence. Their associated comments suggested that tweens were largely concerned about disconnecting from their parents and losing the things that are synonymous with their childhood, including a sense of security and protection. Some don't feel ready to let go or explore life beyond you. Children who feel this way need twice as much reassurance as others.

Of tweens surveyed, 26.8% weren't looking forward to becoming a teenager. When asked why, these were some of their responses:

- ◢ Not sure what to expect.
- ◢ I don't want to be like my brothers and sisters and hurt my parents.
- ◢ I don't want to have hormones.
- ◢ I don't want to start acting rude towards my parents and arguing.
- ◢ I don't want to become sassy and rude.
- ◢ I don't want to get angry.
- ◢ I don't want to become unreasonable.
- ◢ I don't want to go through mood swings.
- ◢ I don't like change.
- ◢ I don't want to grow up.
- ◢ I don't want to go through puberty.
- ◢ I don't want to get my periods.

Growing up demands that our children let go of something. If you think about it, childhood is pulled from them inch by inch without their consent. They have no control over the arrival of puberty, or the mood swings they start to experience. They are treated like teenagers from the moment they enter high school, and that is not their choice either. Understandably, that might bring an element of grief that we should wisely meet with compassion. One mother I interviewed shared a very personal conversation she had with her 12-year-old daughter who was an only child. Her daughter had said, 'I just worry that if I start spending more time with my friends, we won't be as close. I want to stay little and stay with you.'

Time has proved that you love your child. They have heard you brag about how cute and adorable they are. They have seen you patiently tie their shoelaces and pack their school lunches. They know you keep their paintings and craft projects in a special box because they are precious to you. However, they need to discover that your love will stay strong as they begin to change. They need to know that your love will grow with them and for them as they enter a new season of their lives.

While interviewing for this book, one mother shared a memory from her own tween years, which has relevance for us all. She and her mother were driving past a local high school, filled with loud and excitable teenagers. Her mother turned and sternly said, 'I hope you aren't going to be a difficult teenager.' She remembers thinking, *What's a difficult teenager?* She didn't have any older brothers or sisters as reference points, and no clue as to what her mother was inferring. Point being – it is very easy to unknowingly allow our uneasiness to stand in the way of the important developmental work our kids have to do as they grow, and to give them the impression that we want them to bypass that stage of development.

Please realise that your tween will be more likely to grow into their own person safely and constructively when you *back their journey*. We have a big role to play in reassuring our kids that we want them to grow up and find their own way. Don't underestimate the courage it takes for parents to open the door to adolescence and communicate that change is not only okay but celebrated.

The Next Mountain Climb

Before we move on, I'd like to revisit the example of climbing mountains that we used earlier in this chapter. In the not-too-distant future, you and your tween will reach the pinnacle of what you can experience together in this stage of development. However, just as you are setting up the picnic blanket to settle in for a lengthy lunch, your tween may begin to look for greener pastures. They may catch sight of Teen Kingdom before *you* are ready to start the climb. This is right about the time when parents think, 'Why can't we stop the clock, so life doesn't get any more complicated? Why can't we just settle here and enjoy the view for a while?'

When parents of tweens mention how difficult their kids are, there is usually a parent of an adolescent who pipes up, 'You just wait. There is plenty more to come!' Please feel free to offer a big eye roll to the doom and gloom you hear about the teenage years. The days to come will not necessarily be worse, but they will be different. However, don't be fooled into thinking that what you are experiencing now even comes close to resembling the full adolescent experience. The terrain of the next mountain climb will be completely different and will require a new parenting skill set, which is another discussion for another day.

In my survey of over 1600 parents of tweens, I noticed that 93.5 per cent answered with a big *yes* when asked if they were concerned about the upcoming teenage years. That caught my attention! If you are putting up your hand to join this group of worried parents, you will align with the overwhelming majority who care deeply about their kids. You are invested and in exactly the right frame of mind to prepare for the next mountain climb. What I don't want you to do is continue to look to the future with dread.

> **Of parents surveyed, 93.5% felt concerned about the teenage years. When asked why, these were their top three responses:**
>
> ◢ I don't want them to choose risky behaviour.
> ◢ My tween is already struggling.
> ◢ I don't feel prepared.

Promise me this: each time you find yourself worrying about the years ahead, remind yourself that while foresight is helpful, living in the future is not. Nathan Wallis, an inspirational New Zealand–based neuroscience educator,[15] suggests, 'If we aren't careful, our children can easily find themselves caught in a never-ending loop of preparation.' Think about it. In kindergarten, we prepare them for primary school. In upper primary, we prepare them for high school. In high school, we prepare them for the 'real world'. Among all the preparation, please don't forget to support the important work that is happening within them now. The best way we can invest in the future is to be present today.

Chapter 2
SPEAKING TWEEN

Key Message: Lighthouses don't just shine a light on the way forward, they shine a light on their soul.

When tweens seek me out to chat about their life's challenges, they bravely open their hearts to someone who they sense will understand them. They follow a hunch, with the hope of having what I call a 'high-quality' conversation, one where they feel heard, seen and empowered. For me, these conversations typically happen after a school presentation, when kids linger or line up to speak to me. I've got limited time, as do they. There are multiple eyes on us while we are speaking, so the pressure is often tangible. It's not dissimilar to the times when my own kids have wanted to ask me something personal at an inconvenient time, except at schools I don't get to reschedule – I've got one shot at it and then I'm gone.

To be effective, I've had to become really good at dialling in to what tweens need – very quickly. Over the years, I have noticed that there are certain pathways that lead me directly to high-quality conversations. Understanding these pathways can mean the difference between 'getting through' to your child or not.

It can mean the difference between your tween simply hearing you or actually understanding you. It can mean the difference between your tween coming to you with their troubles or turning to someone else. In this chapter, I hope to show you how to shape your words to better reach your tween's heart.

> **Survey responses from tweens when asked, 'What is the biggest challenge in your life at the moment?' Tweens could select multiple answers:**
>
> ◢ Handling big, sad or nervous feelings – 37.92%
> ◢ Getting along with brothers and sisters – 36.16%
> ◢ I am not very confident – 33.16%
> ◢ Wanting to be on technology all the time – 28.57%
> ◢ Learning my schoolwork – 26.62%
> ◢ Fighting with friends – 22.57%
> ◢ Problems at home – 18.52%
> ◢ No challenges; life is easy! – 13.58%

To start, I'd like to draw on the work of Jean Piaget, a developmental psychologist born in 1896 who proposed that children moved through cognitive stages as they developed. He suggested that all children go through the same stages, in the same order, but not at the same rate – and that the process is largely fuelled from within rather than manipulated by external influences. He believed that each stage reorganised, matured and changed how kids thought, explored and figured things out. In his opinion, kids weren't just little people with less knowledge than grown-ups – they thought differently to adults. There were types of thinking they were capable of and incapable of depending on their stage of development.[1] Of note is that children who are neurodivergent, a term that acknowledges that brains can function in ways not considered typical, may have either delayed or accelerated cognitive development.

The two stages of Jean Piaget's cognitive development that are evident in tween years are concrete thinking and formal thinking. Both stages are used to describe a time in a child's life when certain types of cognitive growth take place. As a general guide, kids aged 7 to 11 are concrete thinkers, and from the age of 11 they are formal thinkers. To be able to fully comprehend each stage, it's important to understand the difference between them.

Concrete thinking:

◢ They focus on their physical, tangible world.
◢ Their interpretation of the world is literal, concrete and often rigid.
◢ They link new information to their immediate reality or pre-existing knowledge – and often try to link it to their parents' values and ideas.
◢ They become less egocentric and begin to think about how others see them.
◢ They realise that their thoughts are unique to them and that someone else can think something different than they do.
◢ They are developing the ability to see a situation from someone else's point of view.

Formal thinking:

◢ They apply new information to hypothetical scenarios.
◢ They can take a piece of information and apply it to another piece of information.

◢ They take in multiple perspectives at once, including those of friends and adults.

◢ They may argue different points of view to see things from another angle.

To me, each of these stages represents a different pathway that leads to a child's heart. They are life-changing for my relationship with kids! Follow the pathway that best relates to your tween, and the connection will be tangible. When communicating with a tween, I always ask myself, Which stage are they currently experiencing? Are they predominantly thinking concretely or formally? The quicker I am able to answer that question, the quicker I can offer tweens what they came for. If I am not attentive to the individual and what is going on inside of them, I might mistakenly pitch my language beneath or beyond a tween's comprehension, neither of which leads directly to their heart and mind. If my language is beneath them, they feel I am treating them like a 'baby' or simply telling them what to do. If my language is beyond them, they feel lost and inadequate.

Cognitive development often gets overshadowed by the more obvious physical changes that occur during puberty, so it's easy to miss the mark – be mindful of this. Also, be mindful that developmental stages typically overlap. That's why I find it helpful to create a third pathway in my mind, one that incorporates both concrete thinking and formal thinking. I often initially speak to tweens in a concrete way and then deliberately extend into more formal thinking. Challenge yourself to flip between them as often as needed.

Connecting with Concrete Thinkers

As I walked into a Year 5 classroom to present a sexual health lesson, I overheard a girl say to the boy next to her, 'My mum told me they used a vacuum to get me out!' I watched as her classmate's eyes doubled in size. 'A vacuum?' he exclaimed, loudly. I'm sure he was visualising his family's Electrolux vacuum cleaner. 'I'll take it from here!' I suggested. Moments like these have given me insights into concrete thinking, which is an important base from which tweens build towards formal thinking. Because one stage builds on the next, the more firmly established concrete thinking is, the better. We can help by understanding and investing in what our tweens' brains need at this stage of development. Here are some key tips to help parents do this:

Enjoy using language. When I walk past families in shopping centres, I often notice tweens nattering on and on and on, almost clueless as to whether their parents are listening or not. What makes me laugh is that tweens' detail-infused, long-winded stories almost always end in the linking word 'and'. That three-letter word is often followed by a cautious pause, hinting at the potential to lead in to another story if parents show the slightest interest. You can see kids scrambling to find something else captivating to talk about. Precious! While it may appear that tweens are simply wanting attention, I'd like to suggest there is another driver at play – language development. The more our kids practise speaking, reading, writing and listening to language, the better. You might also notice they are intrigued by, or even obsessed with, using new, cool or rude words. These can be quite a show-off point.

Understand the daily debrief. Tweens often practise organising their thoughts and using logic by giving their families a blow-by-blow run-down of their day. After hearing me speak at a conference about this, one mother had a lightbulb moment. She shared, 'Just yesterday I asked my daughter how her day was. She went and got a pen and paper and literally wrote out a play-by-play account of everything that happened, including correlating times. I was stunned. She used highlights for emphasis and colour coding. I just didn't get it. Now it makes sense!'

Be the source. Concrete thinking is characterised by logic, so tweens see the world in very literal and rigid ways. I remember asking a Year 5 boy to 'hop up' and help me clean the whiteboard. To my surprise, he actually hopped towards me! While concrete thinking makes for some very cute moments, it also has the potential for tweens to feel confused and wounded by the complexities of this world. They rely heavily on us to help them interpret the messy issues they encounter and to be the 'source' of information. If they ask you a direct question, know they are relying on you to answer it or provide them with a framework for thinking, which we will talk about more in Chapter 3, 'Tricky Friendship Days'. If we don't do this, they will find another source.

Help them join the dots. Tweens rely on us to help them make sense of abstract concepts by using objects, events and issues they already demonstrate an understanding of. Know that they will always try to link new knowledge to their immediate reality or to their parents' point of view. This is their starting point. When speaking to tweens I always ask myself, Where are they linking this information? Through careful discussion, we help tweens expand their vocabulary and consider variables and the different applications of information. This not only supports their development towards formal thinking, but also helps them thrive in a world that often demands they apply knowledge before they are cognitively ready to do so.

Encourage questions. Asking questions confidently, especially in front of others, is something that typically challenges tweens. When tweens put up their hand and begin a sentence with, 'So, does that mean . . .?' they risk sounding uninformed or overly simplistic in front of peers who may be more advanced than they are. It's high risk at this age because children's developmental progress differs so dramatically. I often respond, 'That's one of the most common questions tweens ask me,' because I want them to know they are not alone and that their thought process deserves to be honoured, respected and treasured rather than just tolerated.

Capitalise on lists and images. Right now, your tween might struggle to complete substantial tasks on their own without relying heavily on you to direct them. Any undertaking that requires multiple tasks or ways of thinking may feel insurmountable (to the point of meltdown) if they are left to tackle it by themselves. That is because they aren't fluent in organisational skills. I often find myself writing key concepts and drawing diagrams on whiteboards when I am teaching this age group. Why? The simpler the information is laid out, and the more sequentially it is broken down, the easier it is for them to engage with.

Support their expanding world view. Before the age of 8, our children are grounded in their own perspective. They may be unable to consider how someone else feels and may believe that everyone has the same thoughts and feelings that they do. It is hard for them to put themselves in someone else's shoes, including their siblings'. Adjusting to the amount of feedback they can now absorb can be overwhelming. One big learning curve is realising that their thoughts are exclusive to them. It can be a shock for them to discover their friends' parents do things differently than you do! They may screw their nose up at these differences, as anything outside of their worldview is still perceived as 'weird' or 'wrong'. We will continue to unpack this in Chapter 5, 'Sturdy Self-esteem'.

Connecting with Formal Thinkers

From about 11 years old, tweens may be sliding away from concrete thinking towards formal thinking. Sometimes I feel like I am seeing their minds stretching into new territory before my eyes. Their brains are linking, sorting and categorising an array of new thoughts, ideas and feedback. Here are some key tips for parents of formal thinkers:

Accept a shift in conversation. If your tween begins to talk more about moral, philosophical, ethical, social and political issues, they are progressing to formal thinking. They may be more interested in talking about a topic of interest than recounting what happened in their day.

Leave more time. Chances are that you will need to spend more time listening and asking deeper questions as your tween's thinking becomes more complex. Now is the time to encourage diversity of thought and realise that yours will not be the only opinion they are considering. They will no longer be asking you to be *the* source but *one* source of information. It's always good to remember that tweens may take longer than normal to process their thoughts because this way of thinking is new to them, so you'll need to be patient!

Listen for new ideas. Formal thinkers will be able to take in different points of view, including that of their friends and other adults in their lives. They may begin to argue different positions to see things from new angles and begin to challenge their parents' ideas. In time, they will be able to adapt to environments based on the data their brain collects. What may have once been rejected is now able to be accommodated. For example, they might have once said, 'Jimmy's parents are so weird. They let him eat in the lounge room!' But now they are saying, 'Jimmy's parents let them eat in the lounge room. That's such a good idea!'

Step back. Watch for signs that your tween can now take new information and apply it to another piece of information, without you being the middleman. This is your cue to step back from being the source – a role you get to enjoy during the concrete thinking stage. They will now create their own links between new and old information, and change their existing point of view after gaining new knowledge. As they do this you will have to be mindful you don't hinder their emerging thought processes.

Keepsake Moments

In a few short years, you will have a teenager on your hands. Hard to believe, right? The road that leads you to their hearts and minds now won't be the same road you take when they are teenagers, so I want you to treasure these tween moments. Do yourself a favour and buy a keepsake notebook or set up a special 'memories' file on your computer. I promise that you will forget how precious these years were if you don't write down the glorious moments you've had together. I'm so glad that I've kept a record of funny moments I've had with my own kids; I read them every now and then when I need to smile.

Here are a few of the keepsake moments that parents have sent to me:

I couldn't stop laughing at my 12-year-old son. I asked him to hang out the washing while I was at the shops. When I came home, I found a washing machine still full of clothes. I asked him why he didn't hang them out, and he said, 'Mum, I hung out all the clothes.' To my shock, my son had hung out the clothes that were dry! The clean clothes in the basket, ready to be folded, not the wet clothes in the washing machine!

When I asked my daughter if she knew how babies were made, she said, 'Of course! I've seen the ads, Mum.' When I asked what ads she had seen, she said, 'The vitamin ads. Couples take a vitamin and that makes them have babies.' It took me a minute to realise she had seen the prenatal vitamin supplement ads and assumed they were the source of life.

Last year I asked my son to take the toilet rolls upstairs and put them in the toilet. As in, restock the loo rolls. You know what happened? Yep – three whole toilet rolls thrown in the toilet bowl. When I questioned him about it, he said, 'But you said to take these toilet rolls and put them in the toilet.' I guess I did!

My 11-year-old daughter desperately wants a part-time job. In the school holidays, she sneaked my phone into her room and called three different department stores to ask for a job. She asked to speak to the manager each time! When she was told she had to be at least 13, she asked if she could put her name down in advance, so she'd be first on the list after her thirteenth birthday.

While grocery shopping for Year 6 camp, I decided to check in to see how my daughter was feeling. I told her she could ring me anytime, to which she replied, 'I'm not nervous, Mum. I can't wait to leave home. My friends and I are already planning for it.' She's not leaving home any time soon!

Testing the Waters

It's normal for tweens to experiment with language. They are only just gaining the ability to sense their own inner real estate. The more self-perception they gain, the more they will be able to judge what language is appropriate for the environment they are in, and what is not. Our kids need to learn to piece together what is going on internally with the feedback they are receiving externally. While they are learning this, they are going to go through some weird and wacky moments!

I recently had a boy tell me that a scam email he received came from the email address info@catdogbumpoowee. The fact that he had found a way to say all those words in one sentence, to a teacher figure, at school, without getting into trouble, totally empowered him! He was beaming. I'm sure he thought he was set to become the next international comedian, but from where

I stood he had goofily launched into a world where some day he'd get knocked down a couple of pegs.

Tweens don't always realise that humour that might slay 8-year-olds may fall flat in front of another audience. Although there will be many times when you choose to explain the inappropriateness of language in a certain setting, there may also be times when you just need to let it go!

Banter is another area where tweens can innocently miss the mark. A quick tussle of words can end up being taken as seriously as an MMA cage fight. Tweens can test the waters with adults too, which is again an experiment to find out how big and tough they are. At times I look at a child speaking to their parents and think, *That might go down okay with your peers, but not so much with your parents. Back the truck up!* The first time a child swears, tells their parent to shut up or whispers 'I hate you' are moments that usually give parents a chuckle, followed by a mental note to remind their child who they are speaking to.

Who Tweens are Turning To

I want to finish this chapter by offering some insights about who tweens are turning to and why, insights which come directly from my survey. I'm thankful that kids consistently told me that home was their safe place. They acknowledge that their parents know them the best. Comments like these showed the real connection they share: 'Well, my parents are a massive influence on me, and I love them very much. They are always there when I need them.'

Your tween's family is a blend of people who love and provide for them and can comprise biological parents and parental figures. Whether a tween is being raised by single parents, same-sex parents, foster or adoptive parents, grandparents or other guardians stepping into a parenting role, all are irreplaceable. A massive 86.5 per cent of tweens told me they were most likely to talk to their mums when they needed support. When I looked at the comments, I realised that tweens appreciate their mum's accessibility, listening ear and practical help in conquering life's challenges. Sadly, only 8.32 per cent were most likely to turn to their dad. It is hard to share these findings, as I don't think they reflect the intentions of most fathers. Dads, if your kids turn to you for support, they are incredibly lucky to have you in their lives, as so many miss out on a father's perspective as they grow up. Given these comments from our tweens, it may be helpful for all dads to actively remind their kids that they are always ready to emotionally support them.

Even amid the COVID-19 pandemic, grandparents were a big feature in the comments from tweens in my survey. I personally loved hearing about their mischief-making moments, such as eating junk food together or staying up later than normal when tweens had a sleepover at their grandparents' house. Many, many tweens felt that they had common interests with their grandparents, such as playing computer games, cooking, drawing or caring for a pet. Some of these interests were shared in person, and others were more commonly shared over Zoom and FaceTime. Importantly, I noticed that tweens felt needed or helpful while with their grandparents, which can be seen in comments like this from Maria, parent of a 12-year-old. 'Colby loves Nan, and Nan loves Colby. He gets anything he wants when he stays there, but he also feels grown up and looks after her.'

Grandparents also play a very practical role in family life, offering transportation, homeschooling and the occasional home-cooked meal while parents meet the demands of work.

One grandma shared, 'My granddaughter is suffering lately. She is desperate to be away from her single-parent mum (my amazing daughter) and her 9-year-old brother, who has ADHD, and who can be non-compliant and very demanding. The family are rallying to help out with a few sleepovers.'

I also found that regular activities that included all three generations or extended family, had a big impact on kids' lives. A great example of this was the Lakeland family, who all went motorbike riding on Saturday mornings. Even Grandad was able to be a part of the action by watching on, accompanied by his flask of coffee and some biscuits. Another example was the Chouraria family, who planned a camping holiday each year with their extended family, meaning there was a tribe of cousins to both play and fight with and a diverse range of trusted adults for kids to spend time with.

Survey responses from tweens when asked, 'Who has a big influence on your life?':

- My grandpa because he's always writing me emails and asking me about my education, and I love beating him at Monopoly.
- My grandmother is so kind, and she teaches me the most important lessons, like making friends or being polite.
- My grandparents because they send us crosswords and take us bike riding and camping.
- My nanna because she makes me feel happy and I can tell her everything and we can play together. She likes the way I do stuff and she's interested in the things I make.

> ◢ My grandparents always support me with my school and sport, and I look up to my grandma especially because she has so many friends and is one of the kindest and bravest people I know. She turned 60 and to celebrate she went skydiving!

For a variety of reasons, many parents I spoke to didn't have extended family or partners on call for support. Although I could hear the real strain this caused, so many of them were doing a remarkable job at building a community to fill this gap. There seemed to be a lot of emotional and practical support happening between families, including hosting regular sleepovers, taking turns carpooling and organising food drop-offs during COVID-19 lockdowns. Most parents I spoke to saw help-seeking behaviour as a sign of strength rather than weakness, and they were very open to leaning on each other.

Other Influences

Survey responses from parents when asked, 'Does your tween have any other role models who have a significant influence in their life?' Parents could select multiple answers:

- ◢ Extended family member – 47.47%
- ◢ Family friend – 37.2%
- ◢ School teacher – 26.8%
- ◢ No one outside of parents and carers – 21.19%
- ◢ Sports coaches – 20.16%

▲ Online personality – 14.47%
▲ Counsellor – 6.8%

When parents were asked about other role models who had significant influence on their tweens, it was family, extended family members and family friends who trumped. Although other influences such as school teachers and sports coaches still showed up in tweens' lives, they did not rate as highly as those who came through the front door of their home. The tribe around your child is present because *you* allowed them to be. This tells me one thing – parents are still (rightly so) the gatekeepers of their child's world. One wise mum explained, 'I have given him people who he can talk to if he is not comfortable talking to me as his mum – his godfather, his uncle. I'd prefer him to talk to people I choose.' The tween years are an opportunity to set them up with a variety of support options in preparation for a time when they may begin to pull away from us and look for a broader scope of influence. We will talk about this more in Chapter 11, 'The Road to Independence'.

We also can't ignore the influence that online personalities are having on tweens. When my survey asked tweens what they enjoy doing online, watching YouTube dominated. I read hundreds of comments from tweens who idolised people they have never met, usually because they shared a common interest or they seemed 'cool' or 'inspiring'. Interestingly, my survey showed that 31.39 per cent of tweens identified an online personality as a major influence in their lives. When parents were asked the same question, only 14.47 per cent felt that there was an online personality who held such an important place in their child's life. That means approximately twice as many tweens identified their online life as more significant than their parents did. This perhaps indicates we are not considering the impact of technology in the way we should.

Survey responses from tweens when asked to comment further about online influences:

- ◢ YouTubers give me entertainment.
- ◢ I watch YouTube to cool me down and it's a very good pastime.
- ◢ Authors make books for me to read to supply me with educational fun and a fun way to improve your mind. It gives a lot of entertainment when you're in bed and are super bored.
- ◢ Billie Eilish because she writes amazing music that reflects on my life. How she was sad as a child and as an adult.
- ◢ I love YouTube. Norris Nuts, the LaBrant Family and the Rybka Twins are my favourites.
- ◢ There are some YouTubers who are really good and funny people who help you get through your rough times.
- ◢ I love Oddly Satisfying. It's my life!
- ◢ Maddie Ziegler is so important in my life because she motivates me to never give up in my dream to become a professional dancer. She always says to always be confident and to believe in yourself.

Hugh van Cuylenburg, former classroom teacher and founder of the Resilience Project, whose mission is to teach positive mental health strategies to help people become happier and more resilient, often shares these words: 'We learn from people we like.' As parents, we must be aware of who our tweens 'like' and why. The fact that tweens are so influenced by people they share a common interest with often leaves them vulnerable, which we must be mindful of. While I have no doubt that online personalities can be a positive influence in tweens' lives, I'm also sure they can have the opposite impact. We will talk more about this in upcoming chapters, but, for now, I'd like to share my thoughts about who qualifies to be an online or offline lighthouse in our tweens' lives.

The Heart of a Lighthouse

Of tweens surveyed, their greatest concerns were:

- ◢ What people think of me
- ◢ That people will judge me
- ◢ Being embarrassed
- ◢ People not liking me
- ◢ Losing connection
- ◢ Whether I will be good enough
- ◢ Disappointing people I loved
- ◢ Being a disappointment to my parents.

Now is the right time to intentionally build a safe tribe of adults around your tween, knowing your child won't draw on you for everything in the years ahead. Teenagers usually swap out connection with parents for connection with other significant allies – which is incredibly normal, but incredibly hard for parents. It's important for you to get your head around this now. They won't come to you for everything, and they won't necessarily heed your voice when making decisions. Ouch! But get ready to open the door to other trustworthy adults.

There will be special people in your tween's life whose input they will be forever grateful for. My own children speak of a few of our family friends in the most affectionate way. My eldest attributes his 'sanity' to them when he says, 'I don't know what I would have done without Ben. He just got me. He was another responsible adult, but he had a different perspective than you – my parents. He didn't have such a strong view about some of the stuff I was thinking about.' It melts my heart to hear him talk about these people's faithfulness to him. They loved him unconditionally, kept a sense of humour and normalised the challenges he was facing in a way that we, as parents, can't do in the same way. Look for these people now and foster the connection your child has with them.

I'd like to share a few special words from Maggie Dent, a loved mentor, parenting educator and author of many parenting titles, including the wildly successful books *From Boys to Men* and *Girlhood*. She has long championed the role of lighthouses in adolescents' lives. These words help define the very heart of a lighthouse, and the irreplaceable impact they can have:

> *It takes only one adult who can hold the light in a young person's life to make a significant difference to the life outcomes for that young person. The most important things that lighthouses bring are unconditional acceptance, unconditional positive regard (regardless of any perceived sense of failure on the young person's part), no judgement, and no unheeded advice or lectures. Essentially, lighthouses lean in with compassion and act as a safe base and place to regroup, recover, replenish and grow.*[2]

Lighthouses are allies for our tweens. They don't just shine a light on the way forward, they shine a light on their soul. And if they have a choice, they always choose the latter. Lighthouses aren't so much about wanting our tweens to succeed at doing but at being. I am personally so grateful for the teachers, sports coaches and youth pastors who showed me how to care for myself, to follow my gut instincts, to speak out and to be brave. If you get a chance to shine a light on a child's way forward, say yes. If you get a chance to shine a light on their soul, say, 'I'm all in.' It's an honour one shouldn't bypass.

Chapter 3
TRICKY FRIENDSHIP DAYS

Key Message: We want our kids to commit to the invisible, unpaid work of understanding themselves and how they connect with the world.

Over the past two decades I have witnessed a deterioration in young people's social skills and relational satisfaction. Although our kids are 'talking' to each other more than ever before, the National Youth Mental Health Survey indicates that 54 per cent of them feel lonely.[1] This statistic stopped me in my tracks, especially when I notice teenagers putting more effort into their online status than close friendships. If we are to make a dint in the overall wellbeing of this generation, we have to help them prioritise genuine face-to-face connections. I would love to see our kids move from wanting to be popular to having the skills and character needed for forging strong, meaningful relationships.

The science is very clear about the measurable benefits of deep relationships. Just as we need food, water and shelter, human beings *need* to be seen, heard and loved within a community. Years of research confirm that belonging has a significant impact on our mental health, and that the health benefits outweigh that of diet and exercise.[2]

Given this, I want to be very practical and arm you to help tweens work through small tensions that so often stand in the way of belonging. At this current moment in their lives, making and maintaining friendships require many skills that our tweens are still developing, such as perspective-taking, problem-solving, communication and setting boundaries to name a few. They do still need us, which is obvious when we see how overwhelmed they are after a tricky friendship day at school. However, they need us as a consultant rather than a 'hands-on' manager or magic fairy who fixes everything. If we can help them move through low-level tensions to build wisdom and trust, they will be all the better for it.

Survey responses from parents when asked, 'Which option describes your tween's closest friendships?':

- ◢ Rock solid and stable – 28.94%
- ◢ Friendly, but not close – 37.86%
- ◢ Full of conflict – 4.91%
- ◢ Possessive and manipulative – 4.26%
- ◢ Disinterested – 1.29%
- ◢ Physically aggressive – 0%
- ◢ Other – 22.74%

The Tiny Voice

Before we get started, I would love to introduce you to Willow, a young person I had the opportunity to meet while preparing for an episode of *You! Who?*, my online show for tweens. Although we only met over Zoom, she made quite an impression on me! Willow is an articulate, thoughtful and caring 10-year-old girl who was keen to resolve her friendship predicament at school. She approached me the way most tweens do – quite literally with pen and paper in hand, ready to write down (word for word) exactly what she should say or do to fix things. Her wonderful mum quietly sat in the background while Willow led the conversation based on a series of questions she had prepared earlier.

Willow was in a friendship group of four, but two of her friends had started to turn 'mean'. When I asked her what 'mean' looked like, she said, 'They pretend I am not there, and they go off and hide so I can't find them.' *Hard stuff*, I thought. Willow was both scared and sad to let the relationship with these girls go, as it had once brought her so much joy. Her impulse was to convince them to like her by doing something impressive. She wanted to defy the odds and turn things around. If we are honest, we've all been there – wishing a relationship was something it wasn't. Hoping that if we tried hard enough, or jumped through enough hoops, we would change people's view of us.

I've learnt a lot about myself by listening to tweens. Their raw honesty is often deeply profound, and surprisingly relatable. During our conversation, Willow said something so insightful that it will always stay with me: 'Most days I run after them,' she explained. 'But some days there is this tiny voice that says, "Why are you doing this? Why don't you just go and play on the oval with your other friends?"' Time and time again, I've come unstuck when I did not give my tiny voice the attention or expression it needed. On more than one occasion, I second-guessed myself and missed vital opportunities. Too often I allowed someone else's opinion to overshadow my own. At times, I deliberately buried my better judgement underneath disappointment or pain, and my guess is that you have too.

There is no greater gift than the tiny voice. It guides our tweens if they are prepared to sit with it as their teacher. It often talks to them about the most uncomfortable and confronting truths – truths that even us as parents can't share with them in the same way. Intentionally listening is a starting point for problem-solving. Only once our inner truth is seated at the discussion table can we incorporate the wisdom and support of others. I think of my tiny voice as the home base that I run to and run from.

How We Can Help

If our tweens are going to feel the benefits of belonging to a community, they have to commit to the invisible, unpaid work of understanding themselves and who they are in this world. This means tuning in to their tiny voice, which is no small job – but it is their job, not ours. The problem with childhood conflict always being followed by adult intervention is that tweens can easily get into the habit of projecting their wishful thinking onto someone else who they perceive as being more powerful than they are. If tweens are focusing their energy on recruiting support from either adults or peers (or both), they don't learn to advocate for themselves and to move from passive ways of working with the world to active ones.

When your tween first shares their friendship struggles with you, deliberately *pause*. I know it's tempting (and much quicker) to be prescriptive, but it won't help them in the long term. Once you've listened to them, ask, 'Are you wanting me to help with a strategy or do you just need me to listen?' This question, right there, is the key to truly being helpful. Most kids need us to patiently, and compassionately, hear their friendship issues out. We can make things worse by offering unsolicited advice.

If they are looking for a strategy, I use a set of 'ten guiding principles for friendships' to guide the conversation. Each principle represents a different option available to them, and I encourage tweens to choose the principle (or principles) that resonates the most with them at that time. This way, I offer them a framework to think within. I don't leave them alone, but nor do I take the reins. I stand firmly in the consulting position with my magic fairy wings out of sight. When any of us encounter chaos, we seek ways to structure it and gain clarity. That's the goal of these principles – to bring clarity.

Below I have chosen to expand on five of my guiding principles, but you can find a full list on my website. They have been so helpful that teachers often place them on their classroom walls and some kids choose to put them in their bedroom to refer to. You will notice I mention concrete and formal thinking within some of these explanations, because our tweens are often moving between the two stages. If you missed that information, you can find it in Chapter 2, 'Speaking Tween'. Know that these principles apply to all tweens, not just girls. In both research and my observations anecdotally, girls' friendship issues tend to be more sophisticated and emotionally intense, which is most likely due to earlier onset of puberty and differing brain structures to boys their age.[3] Please also note that while these principles are ideal for common friendship challenges, I want to talk more specifically about targeted meanness and bullying at the close of this chapter.

> **Top five survey responses from tweens when asked, 'What is your biggest friendship concern?':**
>
> ◢ Being rejected
> ◢ Losing my friends
> ◢ Being lonely
> ◢ Not fitting in
> ◢ Being replaced.

Principle 1: We Are All Learning

The price we pay for connecting with people is that there will be moments of disappointment and pain. If we accept this, we operate under the premise that we are all learning. If we don't accept this, we leave no margin for error, and we may be quick to judge, assume, separate and divide to protect ourselves at the first sign of our expectations not being met. The moment we widen the possible outcomes that we find acceptable is the moment we open our hearts to more friendships.

I use Channel 9's television show *Snackmasters* to help me illustrate this concept to tweens.[4] The premise of the show is that a pair of Michelin-starred chefs compete to see who can best replicate an iconic snack. In series 1, episode 1, pasta chef Mitch Orr and pastry chef Anna Polyviou strive to replicate the perfect Hungry Jack's Angry Whopper Burger. As the story goes, Mitch accidentally leaves his tomatoes off his burger. The whole episode is based around the question, How essential is tomato to the burger? And will Mitch's exceptional bun and meat patty be strong enough to carry him through to victory? Spoiler alert for those who haven't watched the show – of course, he wins!

Just like burgers, friendships have key ingredients – trust, respect, joy, honesty, generosity and clear boundaries help them taste great. However, because of the developing nature of tweens, they quite often unmaliciously leave off one of these ingredients. When this imperfection meets tweens' high expectations, it often leaves them feeling like they don't have 'true' friends, when what they do have is 'good' friendships. I tell them that it is possible for people to forget a tomato (or two) and still have a winning friendship.

If your tween is wondering if someone is a good friend or not, have them answer the questions below. Each question has three possible answers – most of the time, some of the time or none of the time. If they can see evidence of healthy ingredients in their friendship most of the time, they can be assured they are on the right track. You might notice I have left off the words 'all of the time', to avoid setting unrealistic targets for them to shoot towards.

- ◢ 'Are there signs that you are enjoying each other, such as laugher or unforced chatter when you are together?'
- ◢ 'Can you be yourself around them?'
- ◢ 'Do they ask for and value your opinion?'
- ◢ 'Do they care about your feelings?'
- ◢ 'Do you apologise to each other when necessary?'
- ◢ 'Can you say no to each other without the relationship falling apart?'

As our tweens grow, formal thinking will allow them to identify toxic friendships, understanding that their relationships shouldn't be characterised by ongoing betrayal with a few happy moments in between. It will allow them to define what 'most of the time' actually means and help them discern the difference between a one-off incident and a repetitive pattern of poor behaviour. We want our tweens to gravitate more closely towards those who have good intentions, even when their thinking skills are still developing. We don't want them to be overly accommodating of deliberately or consistently hurtful behaviour.

Principle 2: People Don't Come with Remote Controls

Emily is another beautiful tween soul I met at a school. Emily trustingly shared these honest words with me: 'I think my friend has replaced me with someone else.' I could tell she barely believed the words coming out of her own mouth. I could hear her shock and hesitancy, so I compassionately leaned in. I asked her to repeat it again, and then again, until I could hear the penny dropping as she realised it is possible for people to not like us, and it is also possible for people to behave in hurtful ways, and we have very little – if not zero, zip – control over it!

I used an example of a remote control to help Emily accept the situation and separate herself from the choices of others. In this instance, I encouraged Emily to imagine each of her friends came with a remote control. This remote control could allow her to fast forward an awkward moment, rewind a misunderstanding or pause a nasty comment that she didn't know how to respond to. Fortunately, Emily saw the funny side to this analogy, and she realised that the only remote control she had was the one that controlled her own actions. The more we all learn to turn the remote control inwards, the better.

When tweens turn the remote control inwards, it builds trust. The simple act of owning our actions, instead of blaming others, makes people around us feel safe. It defines character. The very first time an argument takes place, the 'clean-up process' matters most. The way tweens accept responsibility, apologise or simply reassure their friend that they still value the relationship, speaks volumes. It provides the perfect opportunity for them to hold true to themselves, and it encourages others to do the same.

Principle 3: Space Solves Most Things

When friendships experience tension, our tweens may be tempted to make strong decisions. They may aggressively want to be 'in' or 'out', 'besties' or 'enemies'. They may be tempted to give someone the death stare or to renounce their friendship. Jordie explains, 'I have people I don't like who I was friends with from the start, and then we broke our relationship as friends, and then we gave each other death stares and I accidentally hit them.'

When it comes to friendships, tweens have far fewer options and much less mobility than we do as adults, which makes transitions more sensitive. That's why I highly recommend avoiding big break-ups or announcements. One bold statement such as 'I am never going to play with you again!' can be impossible to repair. Josh, a 10-year-old who is in the middle of a friendship drama at school, tells me, 'It can explode across the whole grade and get out of hand if the gossip starts.'

I find that space solves most things. Space, quietly executed, might look like saying 'no' to an invite, being cautious about sharing deeply personal things, not texting quite so often, or hanging out with other people during break times. Tweens might need to create space for a few hours, a day, a week or a few months – or forever. Space allows for a friendship to naturally evolve or change as needed.

Space often feels counterintuitive because tweens, just like adults, often cling to their position tightly in the hope of remaining in control. The hardest part about space is that it often requires you to stand alone, which can make you feel vulnerable and weak. Although standing alone might seem impossible to face, I want to offer these wise words from Chloe, who is now in Year 7. Reflecting on her Year 5 friendship drama, she says, 'The advice I would give is to walk away earlier, even if it means you have to go to the library alone at lunchtime. It's not worth all the crying, and when I ended up walking away, I made new friends.'

The tween years are well known for transitions among friendships. Although it's natural for relationships to move and change, the diversity and quickly changing nature of tweens intensifies that shift. This is hard for them. In time, they will more easily understand and accept that all friendships come for a reason or a season, and that people can change over time. Formal thinking will help them understand they can both like someone and need space from them. Similarly, they can like someone and choose to not be like them, because they are their own person.

Principle 4: Stay the Boss of You

While our tweens are working on their terms and conditions for friendships, they learn so much about their personal boundaries and what they are okay and not okay with. We want their first 'yes' to be to themselves and their own instincts. Before a tween finds the words to express a boundary, they need to ask themselves, 'What are you trying to protect – your sleep, peace of mind, belongings?' This type of clarification often helps them speak their mind with confidence, knowing why the boundary is needed.

The first sign of a tween saying 'no', or setting a boundary, may sound clumsy and awkward. As our tweens grow, they will better know their own mind and communicate boundaries more easily. Remember that home is the practice ground, so that means giving your tween a lot of opportunities to speak for themselves and to make decisions. It is easy to give our tweens the impression that setting boundaries is selfish, dramatic, weak or unfriendly. We must be careful not to undermine their voice or consistently put other people's needs before theirs.

I'd like to share a practical example of this that most of us have experienced. Bella had invited 20 friends to her previous birthday party, which ended up being a nightmare to manage. This year she didn't want the drama, so she decided to invite only two close friends for a sleepover. Bella's mum was soon contacted by another mum, whose daughter was not invited. She didn't outright ask for an invitation, but she did offer her best wishes for the event. After the call, Bella's mum began to pressure her daughter to extend an invite to this girl, despite Bella explaining to her mum that they were not close friends at all.

Setting boundaries is very difficult to execute well. Even when we have the best intentions, people can get hurt or feel overlooked. Only with practice comes the ability to communicate with ease and grace. Most tweens need to rehearse their words to get the execution right. That way, they can be confident and clear. I like to help tweens condense their boundaries into portable messages – short, snappy, memorable statements. If tweens are able to 'carry' an idea with them, they are able to deliver their message more confidently.

Here are a few ways tweens might communicate a boundary:

- ◢ 'I can't give you an answer now.'
- ◢ 'I'd like you to just listen.'
- ◢ 'Please don't share my work.'
- ◢ 'I don't want to look at that.'
- ◢ 'That's a very personal question that I'm not comfortable answering.'
- ◢ 'I don't watch scary movies.'

▲ 'I can't stay overnight.'

▲ 'I'm not the right person to talk to about that.'

▲ 'I'm not a hugger.'

▲ 'I can't give you money.'

▲ 'That's not happening.'

▲ 'I don't think so.'

▲ 'No, thank you!'

▲ 'I'm not interested.'

▲ 'You need to stop.'

▲ 'That's not my style.'

▲ 'You are on your own with that one!'

Principle 5: Handle with Care

Helping our kids understand what personal boundaries should sound like can be a game changer for them. To help, I use the PDP sandwich, which is based on a concept in William Ury's book, *The Power of a Positive No.*[5] I suggest to tweens that we put the disappointing news between two slices of bread (or wrap it in a burrito). When tweens don't use the PDP sandwich, they might sound like a police officer or a grumpy teacher. Unless they have to 'arrest a friend' (which is sometimes necessary), the PDP sandwich is the way to go. Here's how it works:

P – Positive always leads the way with kindness.
D – Disappointing news is how we say no without damaging a friendship.
P – Positive news makes sure we end well.

An example of how the PDP sandwich can be used to say no to a sleepover is, 'I love spending time with you. I can't come for a sleepover, but how about we do something on a Saturday afternoon and mum picks me up at 9.30 pm?' If your tween can provide an alternative that works for both of them, great! Another example of how the PDP sandwich can be used for saying no to gossip online is, 'Hey [insert lots of emojis]. How about we talk about something more fun? Look at this funny cat video.' By sending them a funny cat video, your tween is giving their friend a 'hint' that they don't want to gossip. Friends are often pretty good at listening to hints.

In general, tweens can be strikingly unaware of how their behaviour deeply impacts others. I love this typical tween statement, which was anonymously submitted in my survey, 'I am really sporty, so sometimes I get too stuck with my sport friends and forget how my other friends feel.' As tweens grow, they will be able to be more deliberate about moving from an egocentric position, which is very fixed, and ask themselves, 'How do other people experience me?' In doing so, they'll strike a more helpful tone when interacting with their friends.

Prepare Yourself for Change

Year 6, Term 1
Dad: 'Bye.'
Harry, his son: Slight nod and half wave.

Year 6, Term 2
Dad: 'Bye.'
Harry: Half wave, head down with no eye contact.

Year 6, Term 3
Dad: 'Bye.'
Harry: 'Do you have to park so close to the school to drop me off?'

Year 6, Term 4
Dad: 'Bye.'
Harry: 'Can you wait half an hour after the bell to pick me up?'

The need to belong will become increasingly important in your tween's life, and they will begin to search for greater intimacy in relationships outside of the home. Be prepared for this shift. It is a big one that often leaves parents and younger siblings feeling dislodged or replaced. As tweens set their sights on exploring the world beyond you, they also often get a crash course in disappointment. You might feel like you are watching every heartbreak you have ever experienced play out again in slow motion (on repeat), which can be difficult.

Over the years I have noticed that young people who establish healthy relationships understand the three things below. I wish I had understood each of these points when I was younger. It would have made my social experiences so much better! The good news is that we have a chance to communicate them to our kids now.

You choose the level of intimacy. Please teach your tweens that they get to choose the level of intimacy within a friendship – no one should choose that for them. Just because someone wants to be close friends with them does not mean they have to feel the same way. While I support the idea that 'more is best', and that tweens should surround themselves with a variety of people, we must also help our kids understand that friendship is a loosely used word that can be assigned many meanings. When it comes to deeper connections, not everyone is a good fit for them, and nor are they a good fit for everyone else! I like to explain that there are special times and places where it is safe to completely let your guard down and be yourself. As our tweens grow, they can more easily determine the appropriate intimacy level in a friendship and ask themselves:

- ▲ 'How will this play out?'
- ▲ 'Can I trust someone with this information?'
- ▲ 'How would this information make someone else feel?'
- ▲ 'Are they a good fit for me right now?'

You can change your mind. I want to empower every child who is developing their sense of self and personal boundaries to get a clear message that it is okay for them to change their mind. As we encourage flexibility, we help tweens listen to their intuition in the moment. Tweens are learning, and having the intuition and the confidence to move with the moment is so essential during this period of change. That is why I always ask tweens to decide on a plan A and a plan B, knowing that there is not just one way to deal with life's problems. Questions like these might help your tween be flexible:

- ▲ 'Is this working the way you thought it would?'
- ▲ 'Do you think there might be a better way?'
- ▲ 'Do you have another idea?'
- ▲ 'Do you want to give it a few days, and then assess it again?'

You need to look after yourself. At about the age of 8, our kids can feel two emotions at the same time.[6] They can feel happy that they are going to dance that afternoon *and* sad that they had a fight with a friend. They can feel lonely at school *and* supported by their non-school friends. They can wake up nervous about going to school *and* go on to have a good day. There are many positive things that our tweens can experience at the same time as friendship challenges, but it takes maturity to realise this. Using the word 'and' also gives them the opportunity to ask the question, 'How can I look after myself?' Understandably, when things aren't going well, we all probably want to focus on the most pressing issue at hand. The problem with this is that things look much more intense when they are carefully examined. Talking about their daily challenges is only one step in the process they need to rebalance themselves for the next day.

About Blatant Meanness

If your tween is going through a very difficult friendship season, please know they are not alone. It's not unusual for tweens to experience a horrendous year, full of heavy-duty social learning that makes parents' stomachs churn. However, we must be clear about the line between friendship drama and flat-out, consistent meanness, which is commonly referred to as bullying. Let's face it – kids can be really, really mean when they want to be. Power very easily goes to their head, and, if left unaddressed, it gathers momentum quickly.

I am sure you can think of bucketloads of examples, but here is an example from Jess, the parent of an 11-year-old girl. She writes, 'I have noticed some concerning dynamics with my daughter's friends at school, and this came to a head when my daughter and her friends created a "burn book" and wrote nasty things inside it about other children.' The burn book concept is commonplace on social media too, with tweens asking questions in group chats such as, 'Who is the most hated person in the group?' Another mum shares, 'A few girls at school are picking on my son. They are relentlessly calling him names, stealing his stuff, laughing at him . . . one girl even kicked him.

I'm not sure what to do or how to help him. I've been to see the teacher, but they said they would look into it and I don't seem to be getting anywhere fast enough.'

When confronted with this type of obvious, blatant meanness, most kids crumble, unless we really give them permission to use their voice. I want you to be aware that things can get a lot worse than a burn book, even in primary school, and our kids need to be prewarned. During my career, I have seen some horrible incidents of bullying and physical assault. I particularly remember an 11-year-old girl who had her head flushed in a toilet regularly. She had been drying her hair with the toilet hand dryer to hide the incidents. She disclosed her experience to a psychologist working for Youth Excel at the time. As the story unfolded, I could not believe the pain this girl had endured without telling a soul. Her trusting, open heart had not been able to comprehend that the people she called friends really intended to hurt her, so she became paralysed.

Parents, I want you to know that the words 'please stop' don't always work in the playground. Strong words have their time and place. There are times when it is totally appropriate to be impolite. In my book *The Everyday Resilience Journal: A tween's guide to friendships, schoolwork and growing up*, I talk about teaching kids to push back with the truth as an alternative to pushing back with meanness. Strong comeback lines aim to safeguard who they are, so their soul stays immovable. For example, they may respond, 'I'm actually a nice person if you'd get to know me.'

Of course, there will be times when tweens lack the confidence to push back with truth or it doesn't feel like the right response. Standing alone or heading straight to a trusted adult might be wiser moves. Yet, even when they employ either of these strategies, I advise tweens to push back with the truth in their head and heart. That's the critical place to start and end, no matter what takes place in the middle. If kids believe that they matter in the depths of their souls, the words will eventually follow. Ultimately, I want them to stand up for their right to be treated with respect.

Chapter 4

BIG, BOLD EMOTIONS

Key Message: We want to raise emotionally healthy kids who have felt it all, who are unafraid to express it all and who are comfortable responding to it all.

In my survey, one in three tweens identified their number one challenge as handling big feelings of sadness, anger or nervousness. As I read their comments, I was surprised by how greatly disturbed tweens were by big feelings, which are so central to the growing-up experience. I would have preferred for them to be concerned about losing their lunchbox or learning their times tables! Some were quietly carrying enormous guilt about the impact their moods had on the family. Many knew that their general disagreeability, their unwillingness to participate in family activities and their disinterest in chores were affecting the closeness they had previously shared with parents or siblings. Some looked at older siblings and were perplexed by the thought of following in their footsteps.

Interestingly, my survey revealed that parents shared the same feelings. There was a direct correlation between parents who said their tween had trouble regulating emotions and those who said they fought a lot with them. Big emotions seemed to be getting in the way of what was most important. How could they not? When left unmanaged, emotions drive a wedge between people and leave them with unmet needs.

In the upcoming years your tween's moods are likely to intensify. You will notice a shift in what triggers their emotional outbursts. It's normal for them to go from being on their parents' team to their friends' team! Ryan, another young adult reflecting on his tween years, insightfully says, 'Most big outbursts I had before I was 13 were with friends at school. It was over cheating at handball, or something like that. I was really competitive with a boy at cricket, and sometimes I had an emotional tantrum over who was going to bat first. Once I was a teenager, all my anger was directed at my parents. I thought they were the source of everything unjust, and I was always arguing with them about being able to do what my friends were doing.'

In this chapter I am going to help you lay critical foundations that will help your child now and hold them in good stead in the years ahead. I want to be as practical as I can and pay particular attention to how strong emotion intersects with our tweens' capacity to feel able to handle life's challenges. I'm determined to help this generation understand that their emotional world is not an unsolvable problem or something to be afraid of. I wish for every child to feel capable of navigating their unique human experience well.

Container Building

I'd like you to imagine you and your tween are doing a craft project together. Grab the plywood, superglue, paddle-pop sticks, decorations and paint because over the next few years you and your child are going to sit side by side, each constructing your own containers for life. The purpose of this container is to create a designated safe space for you to express and care for your own needs, and, in turn, be loved and treasured by someone who is caring for theirs. Strong, well-built containers are super helpful in relationships. They help people construct an understanding of where they end and where someone else starts – and they give people the tools they need to negotiate mutually appropriate and safe relationships outside of the home. Containers also help us determine where our emotions should travel, and enable us to enjoy a life where emotions are not in control, but we are.

The idea of building containers together is ideal, because kids learn how to craft their containers by watching us craft our own. Although you have a head start on the project, I promise that you will be working just as hard as they are. While growing them, we must be prepared to grow ourselves. I love this statement from Jaqueline, who refers to her daughter as challenging. She shares, 'She really makes me grow and step up as a parent. I can only be grateful for that; except on some days I want to hide under the pillow!'

What's most important is that tweens know it's not their job to build your container. The key to raising well-adjusted humans is making sure they don't have to change their emotional state to accommodate ours. It's not a child's job to make an adult feel good – ever. When we talk about creating safe environments for children, we are not only talking about environments that are free of abuse, but also about environments where trusted adults are able to regulate their own nervous systems, so that when people come together, they can do so in a healthy way. If tweens notice that we aren't firing on all cylinders, try saying, 'You are exactly right, but you don't have to worry about me. I'm going to take good care of myself.'

While you won't rely on them, tweens will rely on you often. Container building requires skills that are found in the prefrontal cortex, a part of their brain that is still developing. Because of this, there will be times when tweens will feel frustrated and overwhelmed with the project. It is a big job for a tween, so let's not underestimate this! Each time you 'show them how', without shaming their lack of skill, you strengthen rather than damage their developing brain structure.

The Four Walls

In this section we are going to identify four key concepts, which I would like to propose are like walls, for any container: *acceptance, identification, healthy expression* and *responsibility*. My personal lived experience is that, to function well, each wall of the container must be as strong as the others. If one wall is missing or underdeveloped, it affects the stability of the whole structure. If one wall is seriously underdeveloped, we can't hold ourselves up in a healthy way.

Most of us tend to put more effort into building a particular wall of our container. For example, we might believe wholeheartedly in emotional responsibility but give little time to emotional acceptance or identification. Alternatively, we might get fixed on emotional acceptance at the expense of emotional responsibility. The benefit of having parents and grandparents parenting collaboratively is that there is potential for our strengths to help tweens build different walls of their container.

Container Wall 1: Acceptance

We want our tweens to know there are no bad or good emotions, only human ones that are triggered by our brain's response to perceived experiences. Each emotion, even the nonsensical ones, are real for tweens. Ideally, we want tweens to be able to accept their feelings, without shame or guilt. Such acceptance opens the door, instead of shutting it. It invites discussion, instead of dismissing it. It sees and hears without assigning labels such as naughty or bad. We can choose to accept emotions within our home, in the same way we accept anything else about ourselves that we cannot change – our age, our height, our freckles or our ears.

Accepting a child's emotions is as important as accepting who they are and how they see the world. There is no doubt that temperament plays a big role in how our kids express their emotions. Some children process feelings internally and others externally. Some are easier-going, and others feel more deeply. Of note, my survey identified that tween boys were struggling with emotional regulation even more than girls, despite the stereotypes we often assign to kids. We need to be particularly careful that boys are given equal opportunities to honestly express themselves and to be soft, tender and vulnerable.

Just like ours, tweens' brains seek the security of being heard and understood in the process of regulating, and that is why opposing strong emotion usually backfires. If your tween is unreasonably falling apart, it does not necessarily signal a problem, but rather that they are not yet integrating their emotions with logic. When a tween is really overwhelmed, I always like to swap my frustrated tone for a more accepting one.

I find myself going from 'I don't have time for this now' to 'Let's sit with that for a minute'. It gives them, and us, a chance to breathe!

Container Wall 2: Identification

Strong emotion can be particularly confusing for tweens, and there is evidence to suggest that tweens are still developing emotional differentiation, the precision with which people know and accurately label their emotions. Interestingly, research from Harvard and the University of Washington connected emotional differentiation in adolescence with good mental health.[1] Those who were able to identify different types of emotions were more able to use effective coping strategies and move through their feelings much easier.

The study asked participants aged 5 to 25 to look at a series of unpleasant images, such as a baby crying, and rate how much they felt five negative emotions – angry, disgusted, sad, scared and upset. Their scores were analysed to see how often they experienced a certain emotion independently from the other four emotions. They found that adolescents tend to experience many emotions simultaneously, but they differentiated them poorly.[2] Emotions are a melting pot that is complicated and confusing to navigate. Tweens can become flooded with mixed emotions and feel overwhelmed very quickly.

Assumptions, especially within the family, can really damage relationships. We must not assume how our kids feel, or how big a feeling is for a child, or whether they have the ability to move through it without support. It's always best to be curious. If you are looking for a step-by-step way to help tweens explore and identify feelings, include these questions: What are you feeling? Where do you feel it in your body? If the feeling could talk, what would it say? What might this feeling be trying to tell you? Where do you feel it in your body? I particularly want to highlight the last question; it's a question we don't often ask, but it's so helpful for our kids to understand that emotions usually come with physical sensations. The presence or even absence of these sensations is the language of our nervous system.

Emotional literacy cards are another way we can help tweens clearly label their dominant emotion, and in doing so activate the part of the brain that helps them problem solve. Some emotional literacy cards include low-, medium- and high-intensity words, which are excellent for more accurate self-awareness and communication. For example, the word 'happy' can be better depicted as 'elated', 'glad', 'mellow', 'cheerful' or 'satisfied'. Sometimes there's even a 'help' card in the mix, which can be used when tweens are having trouble identifying their emotion. Let's also not forget that when language is missing, art can be a beautiful substitute. I have often asked tweens to draw me a picture, add an expression to a stick man's face or simply choose a colour to depict how they feel.

And finally, when tweens are naming emotions, encourage them to say, '*I am noticing* I am feeling worried' rather than, '*I am* worried.' This small but deliberate use of the word 'noticing' allows them to distance themselves enough from the feeling to objectively consider their next options. It also allows them to reflect on other times they have noticed the same emotion. I also let them know that noticing a feeling signifies it must be important, and warrants that they pause before responding.

Container Wall 3: Healthy Expression

Although we can't control what emotions we feel, we do have a choice as to how we handle them. Our expression of emotion matters, and we don't want to give our kids any other impression. Following on from that idea, Maggie Dent suggests that only three rules matter in a home: please try not to hurt yourself, please try not to hurt others and please try not to hurt things in the world around us.³ I love the words 'please try' because parents are acutely aware that home is simply the place where tweens can let their guard down and fully express themselves.

While there are times when we suppress our painful emotions for our own survival, it's far better for emotions to move through our kids rather than festering inside them. Think of emotions like a river. If it doesn't continue to find a place to flow naturally, it bottlenecks, stagnates or floods. We need to pre-empt the need for emotional movement in our homes and educational spaces, and welcome any opportunity to use the functional aspects of big emotions in constructive ways. We want tweens to ask, 'What do I need right now? What tiny steps can I take to meet these needs?'

One of the most powerful ways children can move emotion is through play. Any type of play (art, craft, drama, dance, sport, adventure courses, building forts or playing on slides) is much more than a distraction. It pulls kids out of their heads and back into their bodies – which is a powerful position to work from. We can also help them move through strong emotion by being playful, cheeky, unexpected or funny in our response to them. A simple laugh at a tween's clearly inappropriate overreaction may be just what it takes to diffuse an explosion.

I love the idea of discussing emotional preferences because it enables tweens to choose how they best move through big emotions. Here are some questions for tweens to consider when communicating how they want to handle big feelings: Do you want me to check in on you or leave you alone? When you've had a hard day, what can I do to make it easier? When I need you to do something, do you want me to tell you or write it down? Do you want me to listen or help you problem solve?

Container Wall 4: Responsibility

As I reflect on our tweens, I don't feel that they have it easy. Many kids have been exposed to significant stressors. However, what they don't have is many opportunities to handle low-level stressors, which develops their capacity to cope with the larger ones. Paul Taylor is a neuroscientist, an exercise physiologist, a nutritionist, the founder of Mind Body Brain Performance Institute and a father of two.[4] He shared this important message with me in our interview: 'When we take away low-level stress and discomfort, we are robbing them of the development of an efficient stress response system. When our kids are exposed to a measurable amount of stress for a period that is long enough to provoke adaptation, but not long enough to smash people around, what happens is their nervous system becomes more adaptive, and not maladaptive.'

When our children are overwhelmed with emotion, we so easily give them the impression they are incapable of following through on their normal responsibilities. In many instances, we initiate the option to opt-out or we offer them too much choice in an attempt to make them happy. How often do we give them permission to take days off school, or to not tidy their room, put their shoes away, unpack the dishwasher or turn up to sports events or performances? My concern is that tweens may begin to associate low mood with opting out, rather than seeing it as an opportunity to exercise courage. We don't want our tweens to lose sense of what is important. The words of my local psychotherapist ring true to me: 'You can overdo tuning to your internal body responses.' In layman's language that means it is possible for tweens to be overly aware of how they feel, at the expense of being connected to the world beyond them.

Holding our kids accountable for their responsibilities is looking after the big picture for them when all they can see are their immediate needs. We can ensure our kids are faced with low-level stressors by setting healthy boundaries that take everyone in the family's needs into consideration.

To help your tween handle low-level stressors, say:

- ◢ 'There are some things you have to do, regardless of how you feel.'
- ◢ 'I know you have had a bad day, but you still need to pick up your shoes.'
- ◢ 'There are other people's feelings to consider too, and we still need to work together as a family.'
- ◢ 'You have to come down for dinner, even though you are in a bad mood.'
- ◢ 'I know you are feeling sad for your friend, but you can't be on the phone all night.'
- ◢ 'Let's take a break for 10 minutes, and then talk through this again. I don't want to leave things unresolved.'

While not the perfect fit for all children, we can't ignore that competitive team sports offer kids lots of low-level stressors, such as: coaches getting things wrong; having to show up regardless of how you feel; things being unfair; and sometimes missing out. Dance and performance arts are other areas that help build incredible emotional stamina and resilience in tweens. Short periods of intense exercise give tweens' bodies a chance to push beyond their comfort zone and then recover. When tweens drop out of sports, they also lose the opportunity to develop mental strength through exercise. Paul Taylor explained in my interview with him, 'When tweens push their bodies hard, the level of adrenaline is very similar to a panic attack, so the body is in a threat state. This gives them the opportunity to regulate their breathing and is the perfect training for anxiety. When our body is strained with exercise, it exhibits a lot of the same characteristics as when it is stressed or anxious.'

Survey responses from parents when asked, 'How would you best describe your tween's moods?':

⬣ Stable – 11.88%
⬣ See-sawing but manageable – 69.77%
⬣ Volatile – 18.35%

Of note, parents report that those tweens 8 to 10 years of age had significantly higher challenges in regulating emotions compared to those 11 to 12 years of age. It appears that with age, and time, a stronger container is built.

Bring on Happiness Triggers

We spend a lot of time helping kids navigate intense feelings, but we don't always focus on helping them maintain and build positive feelings. Simon Sinek, in his book *Leaders Eat Last*, talks about how we *feel* happiness by expanding on four primary chemicals – dopamine, oxytocin, serotonin and endorphins – that can drive the positive emotions we feel throughout the day.[5] We can think about happiness triggers like having 'snacks' throughout the day. They nourish our kids and keep them going.

I'm always on the lookout for environments that deliberately structure activities to support these chemicals. I especially appreciate environments that offer tweens the opportunity to boost more than one chemical at a time by using an 'accompaniment'. An accompaniment is anything that is added to a core experience that amplifies its benefits. Listening to music could be an accompaniment to study time or chores. I think of a parent's attentive presence (during a cupcake baking session), a positive group of friends (to play sport with), or a trip to the ice-cream shop (with a hug) as other examples of accompaniments.

Throughout this section, I also offer insights from Allison Davies, an incredible colleague with lived experience as an autistic person. She is a music therapist, and the creator of online programs to help people of all ages regulate emotions through therapeutic music-based experiences. If you are a part of the neurodivergent community, I'm sure her words will resonate with you. Every child's brain is astoundingly unique, regardless of the labels we do or don't put on their differences. The environments they gravitate towards (or the behaviours they choose) are often a direct attempt to boost the neurochemicals their brain does not make in normal amounts or is temporarily low in.

The Role of Dopamine

Dopamine is the good and bad habit former, which you might have heard spoken about a lot in relation to our technology use You get a little hit of dopamine when someone likes your post on social media, when you hear the 'ping' of a message received (someone wants me!) or when you complete a level on a game. It's just as evident in real life and is released when we complete a task, receive a compliment, eat nice food or enjoy something new. This hormone can keep us engaged and motivate us towards a distant goal, one step at a time.

The effects of dopamine hits are fleeting and short lived, so they won't provide our tweens with long-term happiness.

They will only last long enough for them to be able to check another social media post. There is also some evidence to suggest that the milder the hits of dopamine, the better for long-term overall happiness – as happiness is only felt based on our current experience of it. The more intense the hit of dopamine, the greater the next experience will need to be to produce the same feeling. That's why when we give our children gifts or fun experiences to lift their mood, the end result is usually a child who is just as, if not more, unhappy or disgruntled the next day.

The best way to use dopamine to our kids' advantage is to drip-feed it slowly, in micro-moments. If they are able to attune themselves to the smallest moments of happiness and catalogue them as significant, they will get a fuller benefit from them. Things like watching a sunset, building a cubbyhouse, going for a swim and drinking a milkshake can be amplified when they are wrapped in gratitude.

The Role of Oxytocin

Oxytocin is released in the brain during physical or social contact with others. It gives us the feeling of being calm, safe and loved, and it is the hormone behind deep trust and friendship. Because hugging plays a powerful role in the release of oxytocin, it doesn't hurt to hold on to our kids a little longer after a tough day. For some children hugging is too much, and this is something you need to move towards in baby steps. Allison Davies suggests, 'One way we can move towards this is to constantly respect their boundaries. If they don't want you to touch their hair, don't. We want them to get to a point where they feel safe and are okay with being close to others.'

Be on the lookout for how your tween prefers to experience closeness. Some families know their child's favourite thing is to sit side by side with them while they are drawing. Others know that patting their back, holding their hand, play wrestling, brushing their hair, reading, watching movies or playing video games with them is their preference. Don't forget that hugging pets can have a powerful impact on our kids' brain chemicals, as can positive social interactions outside the home. Remember that tweens may have a higher need for closeness when they feel stressed or unwell. The reassuring and calm voice of a loving parent also gives them an almighty dose of oxytocin, and they may seek it out after a fight with friends or siblings.

The Role of Serotonin

Serotonin is another social chemical, but it functions entirely differently than oxytocin. Interestingly, it is often called the 'mood stabiliser' and is essential for the proper functioning of your prefrontal cortex and for the regulation of emotions. It is also linked to learning and memory, and it is believed to affect sleep, appetite, bone growth and organ development. Because it plays such an important role in regulating body functions, it is no wonder that it is mostly found in the digestive system. Practical things like a healthy diet, exercise and exposure to sunlight play an important role in boosting serotonin levels. You can also get serotonin directly from tryptophan-rich foods and supplements, and some professionals suggest snacking for serotonin by eating protein and carbohydrates together to aid absorption of the chemical in the brain.[6,7]

Parents of neurodivergent kids are often challenged to accept that their child's brain and body functions differently. Allison Davies again explains an excellent point, saying in my interview with her, 'This is where we start to accommodate their inherent needs. We can let go of the idea that there is a right way of doing things. It's about being radically acceptant, and child-led.' For some families, not giving kids a bedtime or not forcing them to eat dinner is for their greatest good. For most families, the consistency of routine ensures that the production of this chemical is supported.

Serotonin is also heavily related to pride, loyalty and status. We feel the positive effects of serotonin when we get a sense of accomplishment or recognition for our actions. Receiving appreciation from others for a job well done or for finishing a race, or receiving a good mark on an exam, will all release serotonin. Ideally, we want our kids to be proud of who they are and not just proud of the achievements recognised within the formal schooling system, something we'll talk about more in Chapter 6, 'Talents, Interests and Abilities'.

Visualising a happy place or memory (or looking at photos of favourite people and places) can also boost serotonin. I personally have a go-to happy list, which is possibly something you could create with your tween. When I suggested this to a mum whose daughter was a volcano of emotion, she said, 'I think we might need to refer to that go-to happy list very, very often!' As an example, my current go-to list includes:

◢ Looking at an antique clock that sits on my kitchen windowsill, which my father gifted me during a difficult time. It reminds me of how much I am loved.
◢ Looking at green grass and our beautiful garden, especially when I know my husband has put time into maintaining it.
◢ Thinking about the special café my husband and I often visit on a Saturday morning. I can almost feel the sun on my back and taste the homemade jam!

The Role of Endorphins

Endorphins are the natural painkiller, and the reason that exercise is so helpful in response to stress. They are released in response to pain, and this predictability makes them very useful as a tool to manage wellbeing. They are the hormones that help us push our bodies beyond their comfort levels and persist when we might want to give up, so they are excellent for endurance. Interestingly, endorphins do their best work once the pain of the moment is over. They leave us with a high or a relaxing feeling.

My grandfather used to take a freezing shower in the morning, which confused me as a child. I now know that if he could withstand the 20 seconds of physical discomfort, it gave him a daily endorphin boost (and an immune boost). It's even been argued that the joyful feeling you get from deep belly laughs is caused by endorphins; the contraction of stomach muscles is enough 'pain' to release a few feel-good endorphins into your body.

A rush of endorphins is typically experienced after a specific event, such as eating a certain food, laughing, dancing, creating or listening to music, relaxing in hot tubs, trying aromatherapy, watching a dramatic TV show, exercising, facing a stressful situation or even experiencing something physically painful. Allison Davies offers this interesting thought: 'Some of the really silly, quirky or gross things kids do actually give them a boost of endorphins. Neurodivergent tweens may find humour in the most unusual of things.' It's important for us to recognise that tweens may experience a rush of endorphins after they engage in risky behaviour, such as lying, vaping, stealing, self-harming or getting into a fight, and that their emotional state may impact the risks they are prepared to take.

The responsibility to shape their moral compass during the tween years doesn't escape any of us, but it becomes even more critical as they grow and can more easily take risks without our knowledge. Paul Dillon, director and founder of Drugs and Alcohol Research and Training Australia (DARTA), who has been passionately keeping kids safe for over 30 years, explained in our interview, 'Although vaping in primary school is the exception rather than the rule, we have to realise that if there is accessibility, children tend to experiment – and therefore protection is needed.'

Although there is no research on children under 12 vaping, the Resilience Survey cross-section report of 27,000 students tells us that 4 per cent of boys and 3 per cent of girls in Year 7 have vaped, and 2 per cent of students surveyed have vaped often and always.[8] Dillon encourages parents to be proactive, saying, 'Primary school parents tend to think that this is an area they don't have to worry about yet. They tend not to have the conversation at all, but if you get the conversation started now, you have a better chance of things working out better in the future. It won't inoculate your child against any of these things, but it will instil healthy values. I encourage parents to take every opportunity to have those conversations.'

Please Don't Apologise

While some tweens are naturally more even-tempered than others, most find emotions confusing and at times overwhelming. Please remind yourself that your tween is born with a neuro-logical profile that is unique to them, and that their emotions are an expression of its response to the world. For some kids the daily demands of sitting still, staying quiet, producing their best work and being socially responsible citizens, are stretching. I am constantly confronted with teachers who are both apologetic and embarrassed by children who excitedly blurted out their thoughts, or laughed out of turn, or spoke to a friend next to them while I was presenting. 'Please *don't* apologise,' is always my response. I love kids the way they are, even when they don't fall in line with my agenda. If the truth be told, I think I have a special type of love for kids who can't conform.

Take particular care to temper expectations and extend patience when tweens are experiencing a lot of change. When dynamics within families, peer groups or other significant relationships shift, it adds a layer of uncertainty that brains don't like. That uncertainty is like dropping a rock in a glass of water that is already full. The spillage is normal, expected. What really concerns me is the shame that gets assigned to the spill. Most times, parents and teachers try to mop it up quickly and cover up the mess. Shame is like a blanket that covers our greatest treasures, eventually suffocating those things that are meant to be life-giving. If I could give you any advice in preparation for the teenage years, I'd say, 'Expect your tweens (and soon to be teens) to make some big mistakes, to act up at school or at home, or to erupt in unhelpful ways.' That doesn't make them a failure. It makes them humans who are learning to build their container for life.

Chapter 5
STURDY
SELF-ESTEEM

Key Message: As our tweens look into the souls of others, they often unexpectedly, and momentarily, glimpse their own soul.

In my 2020 survey I asked parents what challenges their tween was currently facing. Every single parent (yes, 100 per cent) told me that self-esteem and confidence was their most pressing concern. All noticed that their tween had begun to limit themselves in fear they would be laughed at, judged or criticised. From refusal to participate in dance class because they felt uncomfortable in their costume, to hesitancy walking into a party holding a gift because they believed everyone would be looking at them, tweens seem to be pulling back rather than pushing forward.

Parents included lengthy comments in the survey, sharing how insecurity was surfacing. While some parents mentioned that their tween had tended towards low self-esteem during childhood, most noted 'out of character' responses to small issues, which left them wondering what was wrong. Although hormones or changing social circles were commonly blamed for unusual outbursts, I got the feeling that parents were plucking ideas out of thin air in order to interpret their child's unusual behaviour.

Top three survey responses from parents when asked, 'What challenge is your tween currently facing?' Parents could select multiple answers:

▲ Self-esteem and confidence – 100%
▲ Friendship issues – 62.14%
▲ Trouble regulating their emotions – 59.69%

Low self-esteem may surface as any of the following thoughts and behaviours:

▲ believing others are better than them
▲ finding it difficult to express their thoughts or needs
▲ focusing on their weaknesses
▲ having trouble referring to their strengths
▲ searching for evidence of their weaknesses
▲ experiencing fear, self-doubt and worry
▲ having a negative outlook on life
▲ feeling an intense fear of failure, which stops them trying new things
▲ having trouble accepting positive feedback, saying no or setting boundaries
▲ exaggerating negative feedback
▲ putting other people's needs before their own.

Interestingly, research tells us that how our kids feel about themselves follows a clear trajectory, which gives my survey some context.[1] When our children are young, they tend towards high, over-the-top confidence that's a little inflated.[2] Younger kids usually believe that every picture they draw is award-winning. They are convinced that they can be a pilot and an Olympic medallist before lunch and then fly to the moon with the paper wings they just made. Does anyone else remember feeling embarrassed by a child wanting to sell their craft projects to family, friends and neighbours, without the slightest clue or care of its market value? Oh my gosh, I do!

However, in the tween years, they gain a broader under-standing of the world and start to receive more honest feedback from people around them. As you can imagine, it's hard for tweens to transition into a world where praise no longer meets them at every turn and adults expect more from them. Many tweens understandably crave the more freely given, uncondi-tional acceptance they once received as a young child. What complicates things even more is their growing capacity to compare themselves to others, which we are going to talk about in this chapter. They begin to feel pressure to keep up with the impossible standards set by culture, media, schooling systems and peers. It's a world where everyone wants to be a winner. Everyone wants to be the best. Everyone wants to be perfect.

As humans we often search for our self-worth in accomplish-ments, possessions and external praise, instead of turning within. My lived experience and advice for my own children is this: in the pursuit of knowing ourselves, willingness to really listen is what we must strive towards. A vision of who we are only becomes lit within us when we are attuned to the inner prompting, dreams, intuitive hints and nudges that enter our inner world. All of these things are a gentle reminder of what is already in us, and that the world itself is crying out for us to manifest the best of who we are. The essence of who we are is singing to us even when we are children. I have often said to my own kids, '*You* are what you are looking for.'

Getting Definitions Right

Let's start by talking about what we mean by self-esteem and self-worth, words we use loosely that could benefit from clarification. In my mind, there is a need to separate the concepts of self-esteem from self-worth in order to put our focus in the right place. The term 'self-esteem' is typically used to describe how you feel about yourself and is interrelated with a sense of security, identity development, a feeling of competence and belonging – and has also been linked to personality traits such as optimism and temperament.[3] Naturally, this is in a state of constant flux, and some have a higher baseline than others.

While no research would support the idea that low self-esteem is good, it does support the idea that investing in our tweens' self-worth may be a sturdier way to achieve such positive feelings about themselves. It's an inside-out approach that understands that self-worth is not based on your tween doing something great and subsequently feeling good about themselves, it's based on understanding that their inherent worth is immovable.

It could be suggested that by focusing kids on feeling good about themselves, we may be part of the problem. We must consider whether we are unknowingly setting them up for failure by encouraging them to feel positive about themselves. When our children feel low, do they perceive their emotions as defective or fully human? The danger lies in tweens reaching for an exclusively positive mentality that is armed against negatives, and thinking, *My world needs to revolve around how much I am admired*. Sadly, this can lead to kids belittling and controlling others so they are admired more, because their self-esteem has become reliant on that admiration. I want our kids to move as far as possible away from the idea that self-promotion is the key to their happiness.

Social Comparisons

Social comparison theory suggests that people come to know themselves by evaluating who they are in comparison to others, and suggests that we have an internal drive to reduce uncertainty and gain accurate self-evaluation.[4] It's an incredibly normal behaviour strategy. However, comparisons are fraught with complications for our tweens, who are basing their judgements on a very small sample size – perhaps their four friends! Tweens' limited cognitive abilities may lead them to compare their peers' social media lives, houses, outfits, grades, athletic abilities and freedoms in naive ways. They may begin to say things such as, 'Why does she get a big house and I don't?' or 'Why is their life so good and mine isn't?' Late bloomers in particular can struggle when they see their peers charging ahead of them. It can lead them to conclude that they aren't going to be able to keep up, which is not a conclusively accurate long-term picture. You might have heard your tween observe:

- ◢ 'I play the guitar better than my friend.'
- ◢ 'I can't run as fast as everyone else in my grade.'
- ◢ 'When I tell a joke everyone laughs, but when my friend tells one it's not as funny.'
- ◢ 'I am always the first to finish my maths tests.'

◢ 'I like speaking to new people but my next-door neighbour hates it.'

To ask our kids to not compare themselves to others is both unrealistic and unhelpful to their development. It is, however, *how* they compare themselves that will make the most difference. This is where I'd like to introduce three types of comparisons – upward, downward and lateral comparisons. It's highly probable that you will hear all three of these types of comparisons from your tween. Although each type has a place in our lives, you may see a particular strength in lateral social comparisons.

Upward Social Comparisons. Upward comparisons, where someone compares themselves to someone they perceive to be better than they are, often leads our kids to feeling inferior. However, they can also inspire tweens. Heidi offers a perfect example when she says, 'My 10-year-old has been feeling a bit defeated at school. He is not a sporty boy, and no matter how he tries he doesn't get trophies or medals, which upsets him. I try to cheer him on, but it doesn't work. He recently took the ACER scholarship exam, did so well and was invited for a scholarship interview. He is not excited because he thinks he won't get it. How can I teach him that what really matters is him trying and persevering, and not the medals and trophies?' When my own children were in a similar situation, I found myself asking, 'I wonder if there are any kids who wish they were invited to the scholarship interview?'

Downward Social Comparisons. Downward comparisons, where a person compares themselves to someone judged to be worse off than they are, can lead our kids to feel pity or to mock someone's position in life. Matrice, father of 10-year-old Lachie, gives us a great example when he says, 'Lachie is not great at maths, but I can hear his relief when he says, "At least I am not as bad at maths as Amy is!" I guess he has a point. Amy is in his learning support group. We've all thought like that about someone at some point!' I distinctly recall using downward social comparison when one of my sons was accepted into a state-level sports team. His friend wasn't chosen, despite investing in the same training as my son had, and I pointed out to my son, 'Seeing someone else's struggles can make us grateful for what we have in life – especially those things which come naturally to us.'

Lateral Social Comparisons. Lateral comparisons, where tweens are comparing themselves to someone that they consider to be their equal, lead them to a deeper appreciation of their own uniqueness. This type of appreciation recognises that we all share similar emotions in spite of different experiences. We want our tweens to base their comparisons on the firm fact that they are not less than or greater than someone else and that we should all have the same level of respect and power. I find myself often saying to my own children, 'Don't ever be deluded into thinking your friends don't have their own set of challenges. You can't compare your up season with someone's down season because everyone will get their moment to shine.' Both upward and downward social comparisons ideally lead us to lateral social comparisons.

We commonly think about belonging like a warm hug of acceptance – and it is. But I have also found that belonging can be just as dividing as it is welcoming. Belonging actually separates us. It fine-tunes us. Belonging clarifies who we are until we are certain of what we have to offer the world. It allows us to see, hear and acknowledge each other and invites us to do the same for ourselves. Each day that our children interact with others they learn about humankind, and in doing so they also learn about themselves.

As our tweens look into the souls of others, they often unexpectedly (and momentarily) glimpse their own soul – a characteristic that is very familiar or unfamiliar. These glimpses provide our children with a 'partial view' of themselves, which will take further exploration to discover in full. Over time those glimpses will turn into gazes. Only after tweens notice their differences in comparison to others can they stare directly at the spectacular uniqueness of themselves and the people around them.

Processing Feedback

The research paper 'How Do Students React When Their Performance is Worse or Better Than Expected?' illuminates the incredible amount of skill it takes to respond well to feedback. I personally found the report very insightful when it comes to understanding tweens. The research uses the ViolEx (short for violated expectations) theoretical model to shed light on how people react when they perform worse than or better than expected.[5,6,7] In this next section, I'd love to share some thoughts about these three response types: immunisation, assimilation and accommodation.

Response 1: Immunisation

Tweens might immunise themselves against feedback by devaluing it, ignoring it or doubting its validity or relevance. They basically reject it, so they aren't knocked down the ladder.[8] For example, after receiving a bad mark on a test that they didn't think they were going to fail, students might tell themselves that it was an unusually hard test. You may have heard tweens defend their poor performance in a running race by saying it was a one-off unexpected occurrence that doesn't truly reflect their athletic ability. I recently overheard a boy tell his mate that he got 10 out of 10 on a spelling test at his old school and that his current teacher didn't know how to mark properly. The words 'It wasn't my fault . . .' are a perfect example of immunisation.

Opting out is another way that tweens immunise themselves against failure. I imagine there are times when they have a gigantic, completely understandable internal 'huff' when they are confronted with feedback that is difficult to digest. The huff might say, 'If I can't be the best, I don't want to try at all!' or 'If I can't be like him, I don't want to be me!' or 'If I can't be seen as the prettiest, I am not going to like anything about my body!' I distinctly remember the internal huff surfacing in my own children during the tween years. I recall a conversation with my son, who said, 'I'm just going to walk the cross-country race today.' When I asked why, he said, 'I'm not good at it.' Truth was, he'd probably place in the top 10, but if he couldn't win, he didn't want to try at all.

Research tells us that when students are expecting negative feedback, they are more likely to try and immunise themselves against it. If they continue to receive lower than expected feedback, there comes a point when they lose their ability to protect themselves.[9] Once tweens become pre-guarded against negative feedback, they are no longer learning from the experience but shutting off from it.

I can't help but think about those who achieve things that take enormous amounts of grit and determination. These people are often very good at drowning out the feedback of others, even if they offer a sensible voice of reason. Their ability to cocoon themselves in their own echo chamber has benefits, especially in the short term. However, immunisation left unchecked can also hinder people, leaving them unable to see the bigger picture, to learn from failure or to accommodate the needs of others. It may eventually destroy the very thing it is trying to protect.

Response 2: Assimilation

Tweens may take an active role in adapting their expectations and behaviour to reduce the risk of future disconfirmation. Instead of feeling knocked down the ladder, they adopt a growth mindset that enables them to adapt. For example, after receiving a bad mark on a test that they didn't think they were going to fail, students might work harder for a better grade on the next test. When they don't make the basketball team, they might reflect on their performance rather than blame their coach. They begin to take out the token of truth, however small, within feedback and apply it to their lives. They move away from flat-out rejecting it to assessing it.

Assimilation is often a healthy response. When we approach life with a teachable heart and a mindset to learn, we are able to wisely adapt. However, tweens often don't find assimilating easy. Willingness to lower one's expectations becomes easier as children grow older. Typically, tweens' expectations are higher, so they are challenged to do an enormous amount of assimilation throughout the day, which can feel brutal on their self-esteem. Assimilating reminds me of hitting a roadblock, something that hinders one's normal line of sight. Tweens have to reroute in order to get to their destination, which takes a little extra brainpower. Their brains are rerouting all day, every day, multiple times a day – no wonder they are so exhausted after school.

90

Remember, when tweens receive feedback, they try to fit it into what they already deeply know about themselves. That makes the feedback they receive in the early years of life the reference point for processing feedback in the future – we are their lifeline for the core values they hold about themselves.[10] It's not a surprise that research clearly indicates that the emotional content of parental discourse is the greatest predictor of children's understanding of self, and it impacts the way they process future information.[11] As tweens seek to expand their view of themselves, it's their positive inner knowledge, often experienced first at home, that becomes powerful in helping them. We will unpack this when we talk about the blueprint on page 106. When our kids can say, 'I like that I had a go' or 'I know this feedback isn't about my worth as a person,' they are in a place to strengthen their positive knowledge.

Response 3: Accommodation

Tweens may change their concept of self, so it matches the unexpected feedback they experienced. For a few children, accommodation will be a useful response, but for most accommodation can lead them away from their authentic self. For example, after receiving a bad mark on a test that they didn't think they were going to fail, students might believe they will fail every test. They might say, 'It must be true, because my teacher or older brother said it.' They fixate on one experience or negative comment and define themselves with it.

Our tweens' self-esteem can't develop in a vacuum, and sheltering them from the world and its often harsh and unhelpful feedback isn't the answer. However, we must teach them that some feedback is more trustworthy than other feedback, and there are also some relationships that haven't earnt a seat at our decision-making table.

Dealing with the Mind Chatter

In Paul Taylor's presentation at the 'Happiness and Its Causes' conference in 2018, he shared a mindset strategy he uses with his own two children.[12] The strategy required them to create two inner characters, which are essentially a positive and a negative version of their inner self. It asked them to use their imagination in order to explore what each character would say (and do) if they were under pressure. I particularly love the visual and creative element of this strategy, and the fact that there are only two options – this makes it easy to communicate to young minds.

Here are some responses I have received from the tweens I have mentored using this strategy:

What does your negative character say when you feel like a failure?

- ◢ 'You aren't good enough.'
- ◢ 'You'll never fit in.'
- ◢ 'You are ugly.'
- ◢ 'No one likes you.'
- ◢ 'You like them better than they like you.'
- ◢ 'There is no point in trying.'

What does your positive character say when you feel like a failure?

- ◢ 'It's okay not to be the best at something.'
- ◢ 'I can get better at this.'
- ◢ 'I like you even if you aren't perfect.'
- ◢ 'What's one thing you can do to help this situation?'
- ◢ 'Let it go.'
- ◢ 'I don't need everyone's praise all the time.'

We often encourage children to tune in to their positive voice, to amplify it, and in doing so drown out their negative voice. I'd like to suggest that there is more power in showing tweens how to use their kind, compassionate voice to coach or mentor their inner critic. They should not be in competition with each other. I personally feel that an internal war is too much for me to handle! Questions such as, 'How would your kindest self reply to that?' or 'That's an understandable way of feeling – how can you compassionately respond to that feeling?' might help bring both characters towards each other. Self-compassion is the key every time.

This is also highlighted in my interview with Dr Mary Kaspar, clinical psychologist and author of the brilliant book *The Popular Girls: Helping your daughter with adolescent power struggles*. She explains how acceptance and commitment therapy (ACT) uses the analogy of a chess board to highlight the importance of accepting that we are not every thought that we have. She suggests imagining that the pieces on one side of the chess board represent positive thoughts and feelings (high self-esteem, happiness, achievement, confidence) and the opposing pieces represent negative thoughts you don't want (self-doubt, anxiety, worthlessness). It can sometimes feel like a battle between the two sides, with the positive pieces trying to advance and get rid of the negative pieces.

Let's apply this analogy to your tween. The positive pieces might say, 'I'm brilliant at soccer. I just kicked the winning goal.' The negative pieces might say, 'Amy just got named most valued player. I'm not good enough.' When kids get caught up in the battles between the different pieces, they can spend a lot of time and energy trying to boost their positive thoughts, and yet the negative ones still return. It's like a war waged within that they can only momentarily win at best. Dr Mary explains,

'A strong self-esteem is not about the positive pieces moving forward and the negative pieces staying still. The reality is that positive pieces attract negative pieces. The art is in stepping back and realising our mind is constantly chattering, often with a negative bias.'

There is a skill in being able to step back, observe and ensure our mind chatter comes with us, instead of us with it. We want our kids to see themselves as the whole chess board, absorbing the back and forth and describing their experience in a way that represents humanity, instead of being absorbed by and reacting to an internal struggle. Only then can they invest their energy into their values instead, and respond rather than react.

When my own kids' self-esteem wobbled, and I could see the negative mind chatter taking centre stage, my number one go-to strategy was to try to move in with more consistent or intense levels of reassurance, praise or encouragement, so they could see the magnificent person I could see. I didn't realise it at the time, but I was trying to advance the positive pieces of the chess board for them. I wanted to offer them a lens that magnified their strengths and minimised their fears, so they could catch a glimmer of their worth as a person.

For many years I was confused as to why it didn't work. What I failed to realise was that my affirmation could not replace the work my kids needed to now do for themselves. My pompoms didn't acknowledge that my feedback was only a small part of the feedback they were processing as they grew. Although I would never suggest that there isn't merit in providing a supportive and loving perspective, tweens must process others' feedback too, and eventually they must develop their own eyes of accept-ance by themselves, for themselves. Today I deliberately use less emotionally charged language when speaking to my two young adult sons. I say, 'When I look at you, I see a young man who is much stronger than he thinks he is, but that is just my perspective.' I might also offer the following thought-provoking question when a child is coming to terms with not being able to be the best at something: 'If you can't be the best, what can you be?'

Try Not To's

No one is going to feel good about themselves all the time – no one. I'd like to suggest that confidence is a fleeting goal. It will wax and wane based on what we are measuring ourselves against and why. I personally don't want to strive to be confident but to have courage. That way I'm not looking for something that I can't control. It takes courage to be who we are and allow failures not to define us but to educate us. It takes courage to let the outcome be our least motivating factor. It takes courage to keep moving, playing, having a go and interacting with the world, even when you are not the best or people do not recognise your effort or accomplishment.

Below are five recommended 'try not to's' that will help you give feedback to your tween in a way that supports the development of courage over confidence.

Try not to be the expert on them. The truth is that we can't tell a child how to be themselves, because we are not wired like them. They are uniquely connected to the world. It's important that our feedback doesn't give our kids the impression that we own the truth about them when we don't. I don't own the truth about anyone. Your child will not (and cannot) do things the way you would, because they are a different person. You can't give kids a bunch of tactics that work for you and expect the same tactics to work for them. I wholeheartedly agree with motivational speaker Marcus Buckingham when he says, 'We have a bias that is incredibly strong, and we don't even know it. All ratings reflect the rater, not the ratee. We have known this in psychometrics for years.'[13]

Try not to offer feedback unless specifically asked. If they directly ask for your feedback, offer it honestly. What happens if they don't ask for it? Try to remember that even the most well-intended feedback can be disempowering unless it is asked for, and that our expectations can become too much. When my kids were in primary school, I tried very hard to refrain from opening my mouth unless I had a very good reason to – such as when they just won their grand final at soccer, or if the situation requires a 'mumma bear' moment, which we will talk about on page 99. It would be totally inappropriate to not respond during either of these times! But when watching their sports games or reading their report cards, I wanted to get their feedback first.

Try not to praise outcome but effort. Make sure your feedback contains concrete examples and that your praise is correlated to their effort. You might say, 'Some days you will play soccer better than others. It's about giving your best effort on the day, and today I could see you gave it all you had.' Tweens need to be reminded that some days they will perform more impressively than others. When they perform well, they will receive lots of praise from people. However, there will be lots of days when they aren't shining as brightly, and it will be someone else's turn to take centre stage. Things people say when you are performing well can feel lovely, but they can't be the only thing we hang our self-esteem on. Next time your child is gloating over one of these compliments, enjoy the moment with them and then say,

'Gosh, if they lived with you and saw how much courage you use on your less glamorous days, they'd love you even more.'

Try not to dismiss average. One of the greatest things you can do for your child, right now, is to accept an average outcome or failure as an option for them. So often I hear well-meaning parents encourage their kids by saying things like, 'You are going to have a great day today!' What we aren't doing is allowing room for failure. We aren't allowing room for anything other than great. We must be careful not to place unrealistic demands on kids, even unintentionally, and leave them striving to keep pace with someone else or trying to appear to have a perfectly happy life. Allowing time for kids to sit with the disappointment of their reality is so important.

Try not to make success all about you. Dr Lisa Damour, a clinical psychologist who is recognised as a thought leader by the American Psychological Association, co-hosts an excellent podcast called *Ask Lisa: The Psychology of Parenting*. In series 2, episode 64, she talks about being careful that we don't make tweens' successes all about us by saying things like, 'You've made me so proud!' Instead, she suggests saying, 'I can imagine you feel very proud about getting an A on your exam. How did that make you feel?'[14] Too often we need to see them achieving for our sakes and not theirs. Dance groups and sporting fields are full of parents who want to live vicariously through their kids. Sometimes it pays to stop and ask yourself, 'Is this their dream or is it mine? Why is this so important to me?'

Try not to focus on uncontrollable outcomes. Self-esteem is best built when tweens focus on what they can control rather than what they can't control. If tweens feel stuck, we must remind them of what they can have power over, which is often effort rather than the outcome. Instead of saying, 'I'm sure you will get picked for the basketball team,' try saying, 'I know you'd like to get a place on the basketball team. What can you commit to doing to improve your skills, so you have the best chance?' I always start with helping kids appreciate the small things they can do. These are the seeds that have the potential to implant in their heart, and then reach up to the sunlight as they grow. In the right environment, where effort is appreciated, kids get a lot of sunshine and water, and weeds of self-doubt can be quickly attended to.

When They Mess Up

Among all the filters attached to self-esteem is self-compassion. It's a forerunner of the type of sturdy self-esteem that isn't knocked around by an immediate outcome. Research tells us that young people with higher levels of compassion demonstrate greater wellbeing, and, ideally, I'd love for all children to be okay with their flaws and acknowledge that everyone has them.[15] If we encourage them to treat others and themselves with kindness, self-esteem will more naturally follow.

If your child's friend posts something inappropriate on social media, such as a suggestive picture, an unwise comment about a teacher or a nasty snap at a classmate, we might see this as an opportune time to teach them right from wrong. It might be; however, please be mindful of the language you use. This is actually your chance to teach them how you would react (and think about them) if they made the same error in judgement. Try saying, 'People make mistakes, especially when they are growing up. That may not have been a very wise choice, but there is no problem that can't be solved with the help of trusted adults.'

When thinking about what our kids need most when they mess up, I'd like to refer to the life experience of Marina Passalaris, the chief executive officer of Beautiful Minds, an organisation that offers life-changing programs to help tweens and teens develop their purpose, potential and wellbeing. She offered me a beautiful example of how we can all be involved in a tween's journey based on her own childhood experience. In her place of birth, Zululand, the word 'ubuntu' is commonly used. It's a concept that means it takes a village to raise a child. Practically, in Zulu culture, this means that if a child was acting up, they would bring them to the centre of the tribe and talk to them about how incredible they were, and what they had to offer the world. It was the basic understanding that unity, affirmation and support were the way to nurture a child when they were unable to believe the best in themselves. It was an understanding of shared responsibility – I am because we are. I know so many of us try to replicate this idea within our communities. However, for it to be effective, teachers, sports coaches, mentors, aunties, uncles and grandparents must all be prepared to be a collective voice that sees your kid's potential, rather than their shortcomings.

Mumma Bear Moments

I'm sure there's been a time when an adult has said something unhelpful to your tween at a moment when they were already feeling low. Maybe they commented about their new bra or changing body. Maybe they offered them some advice about working harder or being more like their sibling – *eye roll*. Thanks for the extra parenting help – *not*! Regardless of whether their words were well-intended or not, didn't you just wish you could have put a sock in their mouth? When tweens' self-esteem is already low, they will have more trouble referring to their strengths, and they'll be more vulnerable to negatives. They are also more likely to accept evidence that confirms or supports their negative line of thinking and might more easily gravitate towards people or experiences that align with their negative self-perception.

It is very easy for adults to 'talk to' a tween's physical development without considering their cognitive or emotional maturity. In my interview with Dr Michael Carr-Gregg, one of Australia's highest-profile psychologists and author of 14 books, this was the first thing he highlighted. His words mirrored those of so many parents I have spoken to when he said, 'One of my clients is 13 years old and 6 feet tall. You look at him and you would immediately think he was 19 years old. There are massive expectations that he will behave four years older than he actually is.'

I shared a similar experience to this young tween, except, instead of being tall, I was unmistakably small for my age. On the outside, I looked like a small child, but on the inside, I was a deeper thinker and socially intuitive. This became more of an issue when I was nearing my teen years and my external appearance didn't reflect my emotional, social or cognitive development. Everywhere I went, people commented on how short I was and talked to me like I was a small child. This repeated focus on my physical appearance had the potential to become a big hang-up for me, especially as I got older and people constantly thought my younger sister was older than me.

Interestingly, my mother, who is usually a quiet and reserved person, stepped up with a ferociousness that I have rarely seen from her and reframed the story people often told me about myself. Whenever someone would make a comment about my height, she would directly and bluntly correct them. She didn't dismiss or sidestep the topic. Her tone was confident, quick and sharp. It often involved responses such as, 'Once she opens her mouth you will know exactly how old she is.' Basically, she made these adults keenly aware that their opinion wasn't helpful, accurate or welcome.

I distinctly remember her taking on our GP when he suggested my height needed addressing. I had visited the doctor with the flu, yet he hijacked the entire consult to inform my mother that she had a window of opportunity to give me steroid injections to enhance my growth. My mother fiercely protected my self-concept and told him that it was the most ridiculous idea she had ever heard. She went on to tell him that there was nothing wrong with my height, and – in more pressing news – I was healthy. She clearly let him know that he was the one with the problem – not me.

Later, in the car, she reframed every word that the doctor had said. She firmly communicated that she felt this doctor was misguided. Although growth hormones were becoming a more common intervention at the time, mum didn't feel they were necessary in my case. Instead, she provided me with examples of the commendable women in our family who were small in stature, and then moved on to heroic figures who were equally as important. It was quite the history lesson! She told me I should not let anyone question my worth based on my appearance. I think the reason I remember this so clearly, and the reason it impacted me so greatly, was because she so fervently believed in it. I certainly wasn't going to argue with her!

I call this a mumma bear moment, which ferociously uses the art of reframing to help push back against unhelpful feedback.

When we reframe unhelpful labels that teachers, coaches, family members or peers assign to our kids, we line them up with what we know about them that others don't. We help them see around the corner, where their appearance won't be the only focus. But please note that this type of reframing must come from an authentic, enthusiastic space within us and it should not be a token gesture. Put some muscle behind your words – tweens need us to see them when others don't.

Chapter 6

TALENTS, INTERESTS AND ABILITIES

Key Message: While not impossible to overcome, inferiority is a steep mountain to climb. It is imperative that kids come out of the tween years with a sense that 'they can'.

One afternoon, while walking around the streets near my house, I noticed a young boy riding his bike down a hill. After picking up a bit too much speed, the inevitable happened – he flew over the top of the handlebars and tumbled to the ground, screaming. I assumed he had broken a bone or two, so I ran as fast as I could towards him, yelling reassuringly, 'I'm coming!' Thankfully I discovered he was more shaken than damaged. Within no time at all, the boy was safe in his parents' arms, and the world was right again.

Fast-forward a few months. I was on another afternoon walk and accidentally stumbled across a group of feisty magpies. I am not particularly fond of birds, and magpies and I have a particularly tense relationship – so I panicked. I screamed a pathetic, mumsy scream and hid behind a tree, shaking.

'Hey, are you okay?' asked a boy, who seemingly appeared out of nowhere.

'I'm okay. I'm just really scared of magpies!' I responded honestly.

Our eyes locked. It was the same boy who had fallen off his bike months earlier. Without any further discussion, he yelled (and waved) to a group of his friends. 'It's *her*,' he thundered. 'Come on, boys! Let's get her out of here!'

Within the blink of an eye, I was surrounded by boys on bikes and skateboards, all of them reassuring me that they had the situation under control. They each grabbed sticks (anti-magpie weapons) and gave me the largest of their pickings.

Taking charge, my now best friend explained the plan to me, 'Put your stick above your head and just keep walking. We will look after the rest. We do this all the time, so don't worry, we won't get scared.' They formed an entourage around me and escorted me all the way to my front door.

'Boys, I don't know what I would have done without you today,' I explained genuinely. 'I am so grateful you were there to rescue me. You were level-headed and worked together like professionals.' They beamed back at me. They felt their impact. Never have I seen a bunch of boys so proud of themselves. No A+ on an exam would have given them the same feeling of competency.

Please Pick Me

According to Erik Erikson's 8 stages of psychosocial development, there is a window of time between the ages of 6 and 11 when our children either develop a sense of industry or inferiority.[1] This is the time when they either believe that they can make their own outcomes in life or not. Inferiority happens when tweens do not see themselves as competent or capable, and that's going to be an obstacle for them as they grow. This is perhaps why Erikson believed that industry was an essential developmental milestone, rather than an optional extra. While not impossible to overcome, inferiority is a steep mountain to climb. It's imperative that kids come out of the tween years with a sense that 'they can'.

Between the ages of 9 and 12 most kids are looking for opportunities to develop new skills. It's an age where their brains like to be busy, and that is why it is not uncommon for tweens to have multiple projects or interests on the go.[2] Simple things such as riding their bike to school, making their own lunch, being the family DJ, washing their clothes, finishing a crossword or puzzle, baking a cake, learning to rollerskate or rescuing damsels in distress like me all give them an exhilarating feeling of accomplishment. Please remember that competency is not only developed within the four walls of a classroom, which we are going to talk about throughout this chapter. Learning happens everywhere, and some of the most impactive learning happens after school is over.

Competency is something tweens wear like a badge, and the more public that badge is, the more attractive it is to them. Ask a Year 5 class if someone would be willing to do a job, and everyone's hand enthusiastically shoots up! Tweens all assure you they are willing and able to be of assistance. 'Pick me! I can do it' are the words they are trying to communicate. I see the drive to show competence in almost every tween I meet, because mastery of a skill is one way of developing self-esteem. It's critical we understand how important being useful is to them.

This cute story highlights the way tweens love to naturally stretch themselves. A young girl I spoke to was heading to a sleepover with a group of her friends. It was her second sleepover that month, and she was so excited. The last time the gang had been together, they stayed up late into the night phoning takeaway restaurants, thanking the employees for the incredible work they were doing for the community. This made me giggle. Apparently, they didn't want to prank call people (because that wasn't nice), but they did want to pick up the phone and make calls like a grown-up.

I'd like to step back and talk about the innate talents, interests and abilities that are unique to every child, which are not always highlighted in formal learning or in our homes. Because competency is so closely linked to self-esteem, we need to get to the heart of how to best support it in all children, not just a select few with obvious or easily identifiable talents. These powerful words from Jeanette describe what happens when her children connect with an area of strength and have an opportunity to express it to benefit others. She says, 'Elliana had a bit of low self-esteem last year. She didn't feel her friends valued her or that she mattered. Something clicked this year. She is 12 now and a completely different child. It happened quite quickly after she participated in the school musical and was selected as a class captain. The social responsibility, and the sense she was needed, changed her. I found myself saying, "Is that my daughter?"'

The Blueprint

My uncle Tony was 28 when I was 10. He was the youngest of four and stood out because he had a limp, a paralysed right hand and epilepsy as a result of him falling ill with meningitis as a child. Although my uncle had many physical limitations, he excelled at drawing. His pencil sketches, drawn using one hand, were exceptional. I admired his work every week when I visited my grandmother, whom he lived with. Even as a child I somehow understood that a little interest and extra attention from me made his day.

Where most people called me Michelle, Uncle Tony called me Shelley. Over time Shelley turned into Jelly. Although I never understood why he called me Jelly, I went along with it as it always seemed to bring a smile to his face. As a child, I never thought to ask why. But on Christmas Eve of 2021, Uncle Tony randomly sent me this text, which cleared things up: 'Jelly hope you have a Merry Christmas 2021 and a Happy New Years 2022 and let me say the reason why I named you that because you were as soft and gentle as you are now – Give all our regards to everyone, we'll have to catch up soon. Guess Who!!!!' Oh, my heart!

Even 38 years later, my uncle continued to both recognise and elevate the very essence of who I was. He was appreciating what Howard Gardner's theory of multiple intelligences calls being 'people smart'.[3] It takes eyes of discernment to do this, and Uncle Tony certainly had that in abundance. As a side note, endearing nicknames can greatly affirm your kids, especially if the names resonate with them. Equally, they can tear tweens down, as so many have sadly experienced.

I want to emphasise that inside your tween is a baseline temperament, an intelligence quotient (IQ) and a set of talents and abilities that makes them incomparable to anyone else. I am going to refer to this as their 'blueprint', a term used in the work of Kyle Riley from ph360, a research-based lifestyle program that works beside families and schools to help them lean in to the genetic road map inside of children.[4] Researchers argue that 50 per cent of behaviour stems from genetics.[5] Some researchers are now discussing the nature of nurture, arguing that what we think is caused by the environment is actually biased by our parents' biology too, which puts more emphasis on the genetic influence in our children's lives.[6] That combination of genetic makes them a one-off masterpiece, not a mass-produced product.

Viewing a child's blueprint is a bit like viewing a house plan. You can make renovations and plan for upgrades, but it's best to work with the existing architecture. The more we honour the original structure, the more authentic the end result. When it comes to tweens' blueprints, there are no mistakes, failures or errors of design. Each of our children has a magnificent structure inside of them that deserves to find expression in the world. Of course, our children get a choice in whether they lean in to that blueprint or not, and they have a choice in how they express and explore themselves in the world. Some spend years working against their strengths. Some parents spend years frustrated by their child's innate disposition. I believe honouring it is a deeply important starting point, and we need to teach them to do that also.

Kyle Riley's work resonates strongly with me because throughout my tween (and teen) years I always felt I was exploring a blueprint that was already inside of me. I can now see that every decision I made with confidence and clarity passed through this blueprint. Choosing to reject other feedback and honour my blueprint has, at times, been intensely challenging. The world around us has so many attractive but ultimately hollow ideas about who we should become, and it has an equal number of critics about who we are. The more we can help our kids find and honour their slipstream, which accommodates not only their talents but also their pace of development, the less resistance they will have to work against. When a child's sense of industry is developed around their strengths, their life has a special type of flow.

Autonomous Learning

Marcus Buckingham, who we met in the previous chapter, works at the ADP Research Institute and is the author of numerous books, including *Love and Work*. He works extensively in the business sector but has a passion to see children understand their blueprint.[7] His words, which are directed at managers, ring equally true for us as parents and educators. One of his most powerful lines is, 'I am not trying to fix you. I am trying to see you.' If our school system was run according to this motto, it would be life-changing for so many kids. It is psychologically damaging for kids to feel they have to adjust to be who we want them to be. Buckingham suggests that the greatest discovery our kids can make is identifying what strengthens and weakens them, not just what they are good at. He defines a strength as something that makes us feel energised, satisfied, complete and authentic after we complete it. Always try and keep your child involved in something that energises them – their soul needs it.

Autonomous learning, made famous by the Montessori method, is based on the idea that children have the capacity not only to choose what they learn but also to evaluate and monitor the learning process. It puts the child centre stage, as the engine of their dreams. Gavin McCormack is Montessori Australia's Ambassador, a TEDx speaker, a bestselling author and one of *The Educator*'s most influential educators for 2022. He offers some thought-provoking ideas about education. I encourage you to expose yourself to his work, which champions what I believe to be the heart behind good education. Although the Montessori method isn't the right fit for all children's formal education, I feel that every child would benefit from aspects of its learning method. Although I'm sure that my own parents had never heard of autonomous learning, it is the philosophy they intuitively used to direct my after-school hours. If you'll indulge me, I'd like to share three tips that correlate to memories from my tween years and connect them to the benefits of autonomous learning.

Tip 1: Protect a Sense of Play

When I was about 10, I knitted myself a cool vest with supersized knitting needles and fluffy mohair wool with glitter threads in it. It was basically two squares of fabric joined together on either side, with just enough room for my small arms to slip through. I proudly took it to school to show my friends. Everyone loved it, and so in response I announced I was starting a vest-knitting business. For about $1, each of my friends could have their very own sparkly vest. They began to save their tuckshop money, and within days I had a stream of orders coming in.

One vest took me a few days to knit, and I had no hope of delivering on all the orders. I didn't have the slightest idea what to do next, so I went home and confessed to my parents that I was in over my head. If this had been my child, I am sure I would have given them some type of lecture about delivering on promises, but I don't recall an ounce of scolding from my parents. My personal takeaway at the time was that I had been brilliant and inventive. I vividly remember both of my parents commending me for having such a wonderful idea, which I now find amusing. They purchased more wool and an extra pair of knitting needles for my mum, who helped me knit the vests!

Looking back, my parents wisely used the power of play to teach me critical lessons about myself. They allowed me to believe I was running my own business when I was actually 'playing' or 'pretending' to do so. They purposefully kept the overall vibe very positive, taught me what they could from the experience and let a lot slide. Next time your child has a grand idea, protect the playful, creative side of them. Protect their curious energy. Take any expectation of performance out of it. Without play, our tweens only have pressure, as we often see on sports fields every weekend.

Tip 2: Resource Them in Bite Sizes

My next business idea, only a year after the knitted vests, went a little better. The details as to how it came into being are a bit sketchy, but basically Dad and I asked the local baker if we could buy a larger order of lamingtons at a reduced price. The baker agreed. Come Saturday afternoon, we picked up my 'lamington stock' in Dad's air-conditioned car so they didn't melt. Dad drove down our quiet street while I ran door to door asking, 'Would you like to buy my lamingtons?' I'm sure the neighbours thought that I had made them.

A few dozen lamingtons soon turned into 10 dozen, then 20 dozen, and eventually we were ordering 50 to 70 dozen lamingtons and selling most before sundown on a Saturday. My little sister became my first employee. She would knock on doors down the left side of the street, and I would take the right side. To this day, I can't believe the patience of my father, driving 2 kilometres an hour down the road with a car full of lamingtons, ensuring the air-conditioning was on full blast so they didn't melt. It reminds me of the endurance it takes to transport children to their endless extracurricular commitments, particularly sports and dance. They seem to take up so much time, as Simone explains, 'Can we have an extra day just to drive the kids to sport? It literally takes up half of my life!'

I am sure my parents knew, from the start, that I had no hope of sustaining such an enterprise. What I really appreciated was that they didn't pressure me to build an empire or make a long-term commitment. Each week Dad would ask me how many lamingtons I wanted to order, so it was up to me to set the pace. I certainly didn't feel like a failure when about three months into the venture I got weary of the idea and began to order fewer lamingtons. The opportunity to explore is something that not all children have access to, but I deeply wish they did. When an adult, particularly a parent, invests time and money into a tween, they plant seeds that can grow with them.

Tip 3: Don't Fear Obsessive Interests

In the first year of high school, I became obsessed with drawing. I'd ask my parents to buy me how-to drawing books. I constantly wanted to visit grown-up art shops to look at the glorious array of supplies on offer. I drew religiously every day in my studio – the lounge room. I particularly liked drawing flowers and landscapes. I found a niche, a passion, something to fill every waking hour of my day. Once I discovered chalk pastels, then oil paints (which came boxed in a set of 10 colours in teeny tiny tubes), I was well on my way to becoming an artist.

One day, while driving to visit family friends, I noticed a sign outside someone's house, which said 'Art Gallery'. It must have been a house converted into a business, where local artists could display their work. My eyes were opened to what was possible, so I announced that I was going to turn my bedroom into an art gallery. And I did. Every centimetre of every wall had my drawings stuck on them. Day by day I would continue to draw until I was happy with the variety of artworks on show. I remember standing on my dressing table, using it like a ladder, in order to pin my most precious pictures near the top architrave.

I was in business. Finally, I put a sign out the front of our house, which said 'Art Gallery Open'. No one came, but I didn't care. I loved the process.

Our culture doesn't like kids to be obsessive about things that don't have a clear end goal or purpose. When our tweens get obsessed with off-the-beaten-track hobbies or ideas, they can come off a little quirky. Parents worry when their kids can't shut up about Pokémon cards, magic tricks, rocks, certain types of clothing or the latest computer game. My youngest son was obsessed with all sorts of things! At one point he spent hours and hours trawling through the internet to find designer shoes. He asked me to purchase them, without any real understanding of the value of money or other priorities. Christmas and birthday gift lists were full of requests for shoes way beyond my pay grade. It's very hard to teach tweens the value of money, which requires complex thinking and life experience to fully grasp. Today he is 21, and, no, my son isn't a shoe designer, but he still has an entrepreneurial mindset. Always remember – same, but different. One thing leads to another.

Intentional Environments

Research very clearly tells us that the environments kids are exposed to during the tween years have a critical impact on their development. I'd like to share the words of Dr Lisa Mundy, whose work I have leaned on heavily in my research for this book. These words are so central to this book's message that I will share them again on page 196, 'Mental Health and the Path Less Travelled'. In my interview with her, she says, 'In my mind, the final message should be around creating the right environments for children to thrive – then we only need to intervene for those that really need it.'

Messages like this from Tina, mother of 9-year-old Sienna, break my heart because there is so much more we could do to prioritise wellbeing in our education environments. Tina writes, 'My daughter is struggling with school but doesn't get enough assistance because she is not considered intellectually disabled. She has dyslexia, dyscalculia and short-term memory issues. How do we help a child with their self-esteem when they are lagging so behind and tutoring is not helping? How do we get a child through school when there are so many struggles?'

Similarly, Sarah, mother of 10-year-old Charlotte, shares this heartfelt truth with me: 'My biggest challenge is helping them have the confidence in themselves even when they aren't good at school. Charlotte is being tested for autism and dyslexia. She still gets belittled by older teachers who tend to see it as not trying. I get letters sent home that say Charlotte can't do this and this, but we are doing everything we can. How do you support a child's self-esteem when they are getting so many messages about not measuring up?'

My father also struggled with severe dyslexia and didn't learn to read until he was about 30. Those were the days when poor academic results were mistaken for children being naughty, bad or dunces. Needless to say, his self-esteem wasn't strong when he left school before the age of 13. Soon after, he recalls watching someone cut hair in the storefront of a local hairdressing salon, and having an 'ah-ha' moment where he thought, 'I could do that!' Once he could see himself succeeding at something, and got positive feedback from his then-employer, nothing could stop him. It wasn't long before he was highly successful, working at a high-end salon in Oxford Street, where movie stars, singers, belly dancers and businesspeople would visit. Things only turned around when he found an area of competency.

If you have a tween who doesn't fit the schooling mould, please hear me when I say magnificence is in them. Those who have learning difficulties have a future as strong and true as that of an A-grade student. I desperately want our traditional systems to recognise that neurodivergent tweens are a gift that our world desperately needs. The education system is outdated and overloaded; it is broken, not them.

One of the challenges is finding soul-enriching environments where tweens feel empowered to take risks and grow. These environments, whether educational or recreational, are distinctly marked by adults who support a growth mindset and provide helpful feedback. Look for environments that bring out the best in your child. If they are drowning in limiting and unhelpful feedback, stop and question if they are in the best place. Things like making grades public, ability grouping, not providing opportunities to ask questions or to review work, and overlooking non-academic talents can be particularly damaging for some children. Homeschooling or alternative schooling are options for parents to consider and can work well for some tweens. An article published in the *Canadian Journal of Public Health* describes the problem of amalgamating broad age groups when making recommendations, saying, 'the tween years represent a "sensitive period" in which youth have the best chance of reaching their full potential when they are exposed to stimulating environments, learning experiences, and social interactions that promote and strengthen their capabilities.'[8]

To Quit or Not to Quit?

Survey responses from parents when asked, 'Does your tween participate in any extracurricular activities?':

▲ Yes, more than one type of activity – 55.68%

▲ Yes, one activity – 29.33%

▲ No, not at the moment – 14.99%

I am always reminded about the quickly changing nature of tweens when I buy a birthday gift for my 11-year-old nephew each year. When I asked, 'Is he still into anime characters?' his mum answered, 'Oh, no, that was last week!' We both laughed. It's pretty common for a tween to want to quit something they were super excited about the week before. They might be bored, tired, scared, lonely or uninterested. The reason why they want to quit has a big impact on how we should respond to them.

I'd like to share a story about a parent who spoke to me about their highly academically intelligent son, who was struggling with anxiety and a lack of friends at school. His confidence was low – the chips were down. He was increasingly refusing to participate in his weekly dance class, which was something he had previously loved. His parents were reluctant to allow him to give up something he was so good at, yet they were equally tuned in to how he was feeling. They were questioning how much they should decide what was best for him, and how much they should allow him to take the lead.

During our conversation, I shared the thoughts of Dr Lisa Damour, which are expanded upon in her excellent book *Untangled*.[9] She suggests that robust self-esteem is like a lake that has a range of titrators. When there is only one stream flowing into the lake, it can too easily dry up. While academic learning is one stream that flows into the self-esteem lake, it should never be the only stream. If we see our children's extracurricular interests as having equal importance to their academic learning, we have a better chance of keeping their self-esteem lake full.

As I spoke to this concerned parent, we decided to make sure their tween had choice. His parents offered him a range of extra-curricular options with the requirement that he choose one. He reluctantly decided to stick with dance. A year later, his parents told me how grateful they were that they chose this approach, as dance had remained an integral part of his life. It had also kept their son exercising and provided him with another set of friends when he needed them the most.

On occasion, your tween might jump into something that is too much of a stretch for them or isn't a great fit for their innate skills. You might relate to this story that a dad shared with me: 'My daughter signed up for soccer, but it's been a disaster. She's not great at it and she hates it. She offered me $20 if I'd let her quit. I told her that I had paid for it and so she had to finish the season. But $20 was every cent she owned! Am I doing the right thing?' One of my all-time favourite movie lines is from *Chariots of Fire* – 'We can't put in what God left out.'

Although it's not helpful to rescue a tween if there is a lesson to be learnt, sometimes the lesson has already been learnt, or perhaps they were not ready for the lesson in the first place. Samantha, mother of 11-year-old Joel, says, 'Whether he finishes the season or not, the money is gone. If he really hates it, is there much point in pushing? What is the chance he will like it or improve, or is it just a case of leaving him to feel inadequate?'

Compassionate Kids

The global world that our tweens live in provides ample opportunity for them to interact with adult-sized issues. In their lifetime they have likely experienced a global pandemic, natural disasters that have wiped out communities, senseless school shootings, war and threats of war. I consider our tweens to be large-hearted kids, willing to contribute in meaningful ways when we lead the way. Some kids have a greater innate tendency for compassion, leadership and justice. I love to hear of tweens contributing at school, visiting family or older people who are sick, or raising money for charitable causes they feel strongly about. To close this chapter, I'd like to share this precious story emailed from a member of my online community. It is incredibly empowering for our kids to find ways to make a difference within their sphere of influence:

My daughter has watched the injustice and despair of the Ukraine war and she often spoke of it disappointingly. She is 9 years old. A new girl at her school is from Ukraine, and my daughter could empathise with her about the enormous stress that she would be under – the whole complex situation of having been over there and now being here. I was so proud of her because while others sat with their well-established friend group, my daughter saw a need. She went over to this girl, while others didn't. Even the language barrier wasn't a hurdle for them – they used iPads to translate at times. There's a lot lost in translation between them, but I think it's those unspoken words between them that speak volumes. The compassion and resilience these two [Year 4 kids] showed was amazing. Maybe, just maybe, we can raise a generation that can change the world. Meeting this young girl has allowed my daughter to see the reality of the situation in the flesh. It's a little mind blowing to think that this encounter might ever have happened. I am particularly proud because life isn't easy for my daughter. Her abilities go under the radar and recognition for her ability is often rare. She's resilient about this, although it doesn't go unnoticed. This recognition is worth more than any academic award in my opinion. All tweens are exposed to so much more than we were as kids, and while they are adaptable and have the capacity to think and behave beyond their age, the world is not an easy place for them (mentally) or for us as parents. I hope she can, one day, put her traits to good use to help others.

When our spirit touches the world around us, something special is always felt. I want our kids to experience this! I just love how Ed Mylett, inspiring entrepreneur and author of *The Power of One More: The ultimate guide to happiness and success*, emphasises that contributions matter. He refers to kindness as the ticket into the stadium, not the ultimate destination. Once we are in the stadium, it's our responsibility to get on the field and give it our best.[10] That's a life motto I want for your kids and mine.

Chapter 7

SEX AND OTHER TRICKY TOPICS

Key Message: Anyone can offer kids information. Only you can offer them your values.

Sex wasn't a subject freely spoken about when we were growing up. Those who were lucky share stories about their parents handing them an educational book and instructing, 'Come to me if you have any questions.' Some remember an awkward discussion that left them more confused than informed. A rare few of us experienced a father–son or mother–daughter weekend away, where the information was downloaded in a single memorable event. Very few recall their parents speaking openly, honestly and often about sex – which meant we were left to handle sexual feelings and experiences alone, as best we could. Looking back, it would have been nice to have someone safe to lean on.

Research tells us that over 50 per cent of our teenagers think the sexual health education they received from their parents was inadequate.[1,2] As a parent of a tween, this is worth taking note of. You don't want to be in the position where you are offering too little too late or where you find that your child is searching for answers in places that are unsafe. The ideal scenario is when natural curiosity is channelled through safe people and places. You want to establish yourself as your tween's trusted, go-to person – someone who is knowledgeable, dependable, predictable and an absolute vault – and you want to do it now.

In order to truly be useful, we need to acknowledge that tweens' sexuality is developing as puberty emerges. This simple starting point can be hard to accept. I remember the day my son and I were travelling in the car on the way home from school. We were listening to an interview with a famous trombonist, who said, 'The trombone is a great instrument but no one who plays the trombone gets laid. It's always the guitarists who get the girls.' I turned my head to see my 12-year-old son quietly chuckling, and then suddenly I realised that he played the guitar. I thought, *Okay, stop that clock!*

Louann Brizendine is the author of *The Female Brain* and *The Male Brain* and the founder of the University of California San Francisco Women's Mood and Hormone Clinic.[3,4] I'd like to highlight her work on sexual hormones and early adolescent behaviour because this is the stuff that dramatically shifts kids' worlds. We know that between the ages of 9 and 15 testosterone levels skyrocket in our boys, increasing by about 250 times. The area in the male brain allocated to sexual pursuit is 2.5 times larger than that of the female brain.[5] Tween boys are likely to not only experience wet dreams but also start to think about sex, have sexual fantasies, talk about sex with their mates and look at butts and breasts obsessively. I've sat with too many boys who haven't been properly educated or supported and as a result have felt overwhelmed, or even traumatised, by the thought that they may be turning into a pervert.

Girls are very different. They have a fluctuation of sexual hormones, but not an absence of them. That's important to note. Interestingly, Brizendine shares that the purpose of a hormone is to change behaviour.[6] She explains that three or four days before ovulation, a girl's sex hormones skyrocket, and that's something we don't often talk to tween girls about. They might start flirting, dress differently and desire to be sexually active more so than at other times. However, very soon those same hormones begin to plummet.[7] It's no wonder that our girls also wonder what is wrong with them!

As a wellbeing educator who visits schools, I am always surprised at the number of kids who choose to speak to me, a total stranger, as opposed to their parents. Recently, a precious 10-year-old came to me after a sexual health presentation to ask me a private question. I responded by saying, 'If it's an important one, I'd love for you to ask your mum.' That's always my first response when I can see a tween wanting to explore something meaningful. She responded with words that I am sure would have broken her mother's heart: 'I can't talk to Mum, because she might think that I am rude.'

My question is, How can you be the parent your kids want to talk to, about anything? We can believe we are approachable, but it means nothing until our kids believe it too. They have to experience it. Approachability starts with us, not them. If we want open conversations, we have to be prepared to initiate them. Even from the most loving families, few kids get a clear message that says, 'As you start to get older, your hormones might cause you to have some sexual feelings that make you feel warm, tingly, excited or more interested in sex and relationships. That's completely normal and it's happening to everyone else in your grade, too.'

The Significance of Our Voice

While writing this chapter, my husband and I reflected on our children's tween years and some of the more shocking questions they asked. They were usually seeking clarification about something they had heard at school or on the news, but my husband recalls feeling challenged to know how to answer their questions (for example, what a sex shop is) when he hadn't even fully explained sex to them. I guess this is why I resonated with the words of Tony, the father of a 10-year-old boy, when he explained, 'He asked me what rape was yesterday. Rape! I don't know how well I answered him. Sometimes I think, *what is sexual language to a kid anyway*? I didn't have a clue at his age.'

The highly sexualised world tweens live in offers a depressing, morally challenging minefield that puts them at the front and centre of issues like pornography, sexting and consent at strikingly young ages. It demands that we better educate them about biological changes, body safety, self-acceptance, dating responsibilities and healthy relationships. I loved this honest statement from Ruth, the mother of two tweens, who said, 'One of the challenges of being a twenty-first century parent is maintaining optimism among all the toxicity; by that, I mean the internet, including social media and all the stuff they can stumble on.'

Of the multitude of voices speaking to your kids, your voice is the most influential. I'm convinced that, without trusted adults in the mix, there is a colossal gap between the sexual information tweens are exposed to and the values they need to ensure that their sexual development remains healthy and safe. We are seeing more and more sexual harassment, peer-initiated abuse and experimentation during the tween years. There is no doubt that early exposure to adult content is causing children's sexual development to progress in problematic, rather than healthy,

TWEENS

ways. Unfortunately, Aunty Google and Cousin YouTube make it easy for our tweens to find unhelpful answers.

Scroll through social media and you will see tweens who know more about sex, talk more about sex and look way sexier than we ever did at their age. As one mum put it, 'She is 11, has reached puberty and thinks she is 16.' While I regularly hear such stories from parents who are perplexed at their daughter's drive to look and act sexy, I also hear from teachers about increasing reports of tweens in Years 4 to 6 moaning, twerking and humping while dancing or roleplaying. Amanda, mother of an 11-year-old, says, 'Looking at what her friends are doing online . . . OMG. The photos they have taken of themselves, it's like they are 16 or 17, and they don't understand the gravity of what they are putting out there. My daughter told me her friend wouldn't wear her normal swimmers because they aren't a G-string . . . they are 11!'

The Information Update

**Survey responses from parents when asked,
'Have you spoken to your tween about puberty?':**

- ◢ Yes, we talk freely and openly – 40.44%
- ◢ Yes, I have made a start – 41.09%
- ◢ Yes, but it didn't go well – 2.58%
- ◢ No, not as yet – 15.89%

We have been providing messages about body parts and sexuality all of our kids' lives. However, there comes a time when they are physically, cognitively and emotionally ready for what I call an 'information update'. I use this term because we are building on conversations already begun in childhood, and extending into topics such as cyber safety, gender diversity, homosexuality and, importantly, protective behaviours that have a different context than when they were younger. Many of these are knotted and tangled issues, even for adults, so there is no greater place where we need to mould our language to meet our children where they are at.

If we are able to provide this update early enough, we can capitalise on the benefits of concrete thinking, a concept we discussed in Chapter 2, 'Speaking Tween'. During this cognitive stage tweens will more likely absorb information and be open to your guidance. It's the perfect time to stamp your values all over the technical information you offer them. Don't be fooled into thinking that if your tween is 'embarrassed', they are too young to discuss sexuality. It's more likely that they have progressed to formal thinking, which will make them more inclined to be self-conscious, embarrassed and override your moral judgement with their own.

When communicating with tweens about anything, especially tricky topics, it is very important to acknowledge factors such as maturity, IQ, temperament, birth order, mental health and learning disabilities that might impact comprehension.

Although you need to tailor content to cater for your child, remember too that they live in a world that doesn't always cater for their uniqueness. They will most likely hear about sex and puberty at school and in the media, which necessitates your involvement. In my survey I noticed parents of girls spoke to them much earlier and more frequently about puberty. I think our sons are often at a disadvantage because they don't have a 'monthly moment' to discuss their body changes.

Tips to Help You Get Started

Below I'd like to offer you 10 quick tips to help you kickstart open conversations with your tween about puberty and sex. These tips will be particularly helpful for parents whose tweens are flat-out refusing to talk about the changes they are experiencing. I hear about so many young ones who put their hands over their ears five minutes into a conversation or who start screaming 'lah lah lah' over the top of their parent's voice, even though they are about 15 minutes away from their first period! This can be stressful for parents who want to prepare their kids well.

We know that children learn best when they feel safe, which means when their individual needs are taken into consideration. The premise behind all of these strategies is to offer tweens more control and choice over what, when, where and how they learn, and in doing so create the safest environment possible for them. I have also tried to offer a few novel approaches, which are great for getting kids' attention. Remember, discussions are about what they need to know, so our job is to carefully journey beside them, not in front of or behind them.

Lower the bar. If you can simply have an 'okay' conversation about puberty, celebrate, because you can build from there. Aim to eventually have conversations that are 'good' and then 'very good', but don't put this pressure on yourself from the beginning. If things get off to a rocky start, remember that the more conversations you have, the easier they will become – guaranteed. Try saying to your tween, 'I totally understand if it feels weird talking about this. It's normal to feel awkward talking about something so private, especially if it's the first conversation about it.'

Create a list. Try creating a list of puberty-related topics (with a few fun ones thrown in for good measure) and ask your tween to choose the topic they want to talk about. This gives them power to choose their entry point. Usually, kids might like to start with the least sensitive information (like hygiene and using deodorant) and slowly build up to more weighty topics. Try saying to your tween, 'Together we could make a list of the grown-up topics you might like to learn about this year. What if you were to choose a topic each week, or whenever you want to talk about them?'

Temperature check. I am a big believer in listening to and respecting kids' personal feelings and boundaries when it comes to conversations. Pushing past their comfort levels sends them all the wrong messages. When their eyes start glazing over, stop talking. You have time. Once they ask a question, check their response and only offer more information if they need it. Keep 'temperature checking'. You are testing and measuring their willingness to engage. Try saying to your tween, 'Does that make sense? Do you have any questions?'

Plan mini-conversations. Prepare a list of two-minute mini-conversations that you can offer when the time feels right. If you have a short list of go-to topics in your mind, you will be able to incidentally cover more ground. If even these short conversations are too much, ask your tween how you can make it easier for them. Try saying to them, 'How can I make this easier for you? What if we talked for five minutes now, and then five minutes tomorrow? That way, it's not too much all at once.'

Give longer chats definition. If you are planning a longer chat, let them know how long it might take. I know this might sound weird, but they need to know you are going to shut up at some stage or they might opt-out too early. I also recommend spending less than an hour talking, before their interest and attention span wanes. Try saying to your tween, 'I want to have a grown-up conversation with you – just you and me. It might take half an hour. Do you want to talk in your room or go for a walk?'

Use quality resources. Using educational resources (books, videos, websites) can be another way to make the experience more comfortable and structured, but please read or watch the whole resource first and make sure it aligns with your values and your child's needs. Resources should be an extension of you, rather than a replacement of you. One of my great joys was producing the books *A Guy's Guide to Puberty* and *A Girl's Guide to Puberty* and the online video series *Talking about Puberty* to help parents with these initial discussions. Lots of families ask me if they should read the book with their children or give it to them to read alone. I suggest that you ask them. Some children may want to dip in to the content before being confronted with a conversation about it, as it might make for a more predictable introduction. If you have a reluctant talker, you might like to put a book about puberty or sex within a stack of other unrelated books for them; not surprisingly, most times, the book about puberty or sex ends up in their bedroom first. Try saying to your tween, 'I've read this book, and I thought you might like to read it too. Do you want to read it with me or by yourself to start with?'

Be creative. There is no one way to talk to children about puberty, so be creative. A shared journal or the use of text messaging can be a non-confrontational way to talk to a tween.

If you use a journal, make sure you have a strict turnaround time of 24 hours with your response. Try saying to your tween, 'I know this stuff isn't always easy to talk about, so you can always text me, or even use this journal. If you'd like, we can use it to write back and forth about growing-up stuff.'

Introduce the experts. Now is the perfect time to let tweens know about trusted professionals and sources of information that you turn to when you have a question. They should be aware of the GPs, gynaecologists, expert educators and other mentors they can go to if they have a question that they don't want to ask you. When it comes to Google, it's not ideal for our kids to get the impression that's where we go to for answers. If you do mention Google, please be sure to talk about quality websites and warn your kid about the extensive amount of inappropriate content and misinformation available online. Try saying to your tween, 'If I don't know, I will find out. I can check with experts like doctors and gynaecologists, who know a lot about puberty, but I won't just google it randomly.'

Take the pressure off. Right up front, take the pressure off tweens to understand everything in one sitting. It's a lot for their brains to absorb, and some kids need to take it in in tiny chunks. I always like to tell the tweens I speak to in schools that they won't be getting an exam at the end of my presentation, and it's meant to be enjoyed. After hearing about how babies are made, the top two questions kids ask me are, 'How long do you have to leave the penis in there for?' and 'Do I have to do that?' They want reassurance that their body will be safe and protected. I always reassure tweens that anything to do with sex is for when they are much, much older and that it should always be their choice. They never have to have sex if they don't want to, but it's a decision they can make later in life – which relieves many of them! Try saying to your tween, 'It's okay if you don't understand all of this at once. Even if you just understand 10 per cent of it, we can keep talking as you think of questions.'

Answer questions thoughtfully. If our kids do ask questions, don't sidestep them. You might delay them, but don't ignore them. The more dedicated we are to giving them a thoughtful response, the more they will continue to draw on us as their safe person. If a question arises at an inappropriate time, such as in the middle of grocery shopping or just before you are heading out of the house, plan a time when you can give them your full attention. Always think, What is behind a question? A vulnerable heart. A thought process we can't assume. A curious mind, that normally won't rest until it is satisfied. Try saying to your tween, 'That's a great question. Shall we spend some time talking about it tonight? At 7 pm in your room?'

Heads up! These are some common questions tweens ask me:

- ◢ Do you need to leave the penis in a vagina until the sperm reaches the egg?
- ◢ If the baby is in a mum's stomach, where does the food go?
- ◢ How do disabilities happen?
- ◢ How are twins made?
- ◢ What if the condom gets stuck?
- ◢ Why does the baby cry when it comes out?
- ◢ What if actors who had sex got pregnant?
- ◢ What if two sperm reached the egg at the same time?

Gender Diversity

In my interviews with parents, I quickly realised the topic on the forefront of their minds was how to talk to kids about gender identity and dysphoria, and sexuality. I want to make a clear distinction between these two things. When we talk about gender identity, we are talking about who a person is and how they want to be identified. When we talk about sexuality, we are talking about who a person is romantically or sexually attracted to. Big topics for little people!

Many parents I spoke to had questions about the age at which a child truly knows their gender identity or sexual attraction. Dr Victoria Rawlings, LGBTQIA+ specialist and expert guest on ABC's *Parental as Anything* podcast, hosted by Maggie Dent, suggests that there is a big difference between being a girl wishing she were a boy and saying, 'I *am* a boy.'[8] When children are insistently, persistently and consistently telling their parents that they are a boy, a girl or any combination in between, that's the time when parents need to really lean in.[9] Rather than it being about an age-appropriate time, keep coming back to the words 'insistently, persistently and consistently' as your guide.

The overarching message in research is that children fair better when they have their parents' support.[10] Of the parents

TWEENS

I spoke to whose children were questioning their gender identity or sexual orientation, at the very heart of all their concern was the thought that their child would not feel loved and accepted for being different. This comforted me. Parents said, 'I worry that they will feel they weren't loved. I don't want to squash them later and find out I was the one wrong,' or 'I don't want to be that voice in her head that didn't accept her for who she was.'

Because sexuality and gender identity are fluid (especially during the tween years) and interwoven with social development, some experts recommend that young people don't start anything permanent until they are older. Social changes (such as changing their name, their haircut or how they dress) and even hormone blockers are reversible, but surgery isn't. We need to tread slowly and carefully, following the most up-to-date expert health advice, which was echoed in the sentiments I heard from many parents wanting the absolute best for their kids.

I feel a huge amount of compassion for kids who don't feel at home in their bodies. The idea of transitioning might seem simple to a tween, but it's complicated, ongoing and wrought with social challenges. Discrimination against LGBTQIA+ individuals in educational institutions is well reported in the literature and has a significant impact on a child's education and wellbeing.[11] Australian national research has shown that trans and gender diverse (TGD) young people are twice as likely to engage in help-seeking behaviours and activism than their cisgender, same-sex-attracted peers.[12] It's a massive journey for anyone, at any time.[13] As a society, we must continue to move away from intolerance of difference and causing shame about people's journeys.

We are talking about gender in a much different way than we did a decade ago. Ellie, who is 12 years old, explains, 'I feel like there are people who are really girls and those who are really boys. I think I am a little more girl, but I'm not completely girl. I am to the left of zero.' Left of zero is something that would have never rolled off my tongue as a child, even though I identify more with the traditional boy stereotype. Our tweens are living in a world where gender doesn't have the confines and limits it once did. There are so many versions of being a boy or a girl, and gender stereotypes are increasingly being smashed. One could argue that perhaps the terms 'man' and 'woman', or 'boy' and 'girl', don't tell the world enough about who any of us are. Perhaps we have the opportunity to be more expressive these days and are finding broader ways of describing ourselves.

Mark McCrindle, social analyst and co-author of *Generation Alpha*, also shares, 'This generation will grow up as the most culturally diverse population that has ever lived, with inclusion, equality and respect as central themes of conversation. There are no longer clear splits across genders, cultures or religious viewpoints, and our kids will debate us fiercely if we create them. They are sensitive to the needs and rights of all people. The good news is that they have a righteous sense of fairness. What unites them is an understanding that all people should be treated equally no matter what they look like.'[14] That's a positive, and I often think our young ones can teach us a lot about inclusion.

Dating and Crushes

I recently overheard a Year 5 teacher mentoring a small group of students through their relationship issues. It honestly sounded like she was talking to 16-year-olds, as a few of them were 'dating' or deciding who they should go out with. She advised them that if their partners were pressuring them to kiss or touch their private parts, they didn't really love them. I couldn't help thinking, *How old are these kids . . . 11? Do they really understand the gravity of the things they are talking about?*

It is developmentally normal for our kids to be playing the 'who do you like?' game when they are about 10 years old. That's why playgrounds are littered with curiosity, the exchange of ridiculously inaccurate information and many cute and uneventful crushes. This exploration in itself needn't alarm us, because romantic partnerships at 11 might mean you exchange a note; intimacy at this age is not always characterised by physical closeness. Harry, a gorgeous 10-year-old, told me that he could tell if someone was a good friend or not by their ability to keep his secrets – mainly, who he had a crush on. That was the sum total of what he wanted in a friend.

There is pressure on our kids to refer to crushes as 'dating'. Over the years I have been emailed by many parents whose tweens have asked if they are allowed to make their crush official. The fact that they are asking is wonderful! Give them a few more years and they may not be checking in with you first. When 'I like you' feelings first surface, we have a great opportunity to normalise, accept and direct our tweens. Sexual curiosity does not always develop at the same rate as responsibility, common sense, wisdom, self-awareness or communication skills. That's why they need us as big people to protect them from damage.

Here are four questions to help you discuss romantic feelings with your tween:

What do you like about them? If our kids like someone we want them to have good taste. Now is a great time for them to begin to identify the qualities they find attractive.

Do they like you? It's so important that our kids are accurately reading other people's cues. Their ability to do this may lead to appropriate or inappropriate behaviour.

What does 'dating' mean to you? How our tweens define intimacy in a romantic relationship is really important. We want to help them understand what is age-appropriate intimacy, and the rights and responsibilities that come with increased intimacy.

What are your body boundaries? While we want to send a clear message that sexual feelings are not wrong, our tweens need to be clear about age-appropriate body boundaries. We also want our children to be the boss of their own body and to remember body safety.

I am reminded of a cute conversation I had with a 9-year-old boy who wanted to 'date' a girl in his class. I asked, 'Where are you going to take her? The bubblers? The tuckshop?' We both had a good laugh before we talked about the validity of his feelings, and the gap between them and his current capacity to deliver. Helping kids learn how to channel romantic feelings is challenging, and sometimes crushes on rock stars and celebrities do provide a safe outlet! When romantic feelings surface, they want to 'land' somewhere (anywhere). Kids might think they are directly linked to a specific person in their world, but they are still developing the maturity to know where and how to channel those feelings, and they need our help.

This is a really practical example of a parent establishing what intimacy in a tween relationship should look like. Based on my discussions with mum Suzzanne, the rule in her home was that boyfriends were allowed but sleepovers with them were

TWEENS

not. Suzanne explains, 'Tamsin is 11 and was at her boyfriend Jack's house. I was picking her up at 9 pm. Because she has all these friends who are allowed to sleep at their boyfriend's house, it is putting pressure on me. She asks, "Can I stay at Jack's?" Nice try; no, that isn't going to happen. "But why do you think that something is going to happen?" she asks me. It's almost like she is a bit innocent right now, and she isn't looking at it with the right eyes. Her innocence is awesome, but it could get her into trouble.'

Same-sex Attraction

Sexual experimentation is not limited to heterosexual attraction, which sounds obvious but it's something you need to be mindful of in your conversations with tweens. I have seen a lot of parents who are blindsided by this or who haven't considered discussing it with their tween. I want to offer this statement from one mum I interviewed: 'My 12-year-old niece tells me that she only wants to be introduced as a pronoun because she is nonbinary and bisexual. My gay son responded, "You can be bi but there is no sexual when you are 12."' I love this!

When kids are going through puberty, sexual feelings are amplified, so it's normal for tweens to be attracted to a range of people. When those hormones are pumping, it can be difficult for tweens to tell the difference between admiration and attraction. It can be misconstrued as romantic love. They might have a crush on a rock star or their sports coach, and it's got nothing to do with the other person's gender but rather something they admire about the person. Charmaine explains, 'My daughter wrote a song for a girl she apparently romantically "liked", but really she felt left out and wanted to be a part of the group.

It was all about being more popular. She felt that no one cared about her so she created drama to get attention. It's been a mess, but I've needed to guide her through this as she is absolutely clueless about what she is portraying.'

Same-sex attraction in primary school can feel foreign for parents and professionals to deal with. Sexual experimentation between tween girls seems to be the more common concern within the schools I visit, probably because their development typically begins earlier than in tween boys. While speaking with a deputy principal from a local primary school, I learnt that her biggest concern was the girls in the Year 6 cohort. She says, 'I don't even think they know what they are experimenting with, and how to make sense of that. The concept of friendship gets messed up with romantic partners, and then they say, I am doing it because I am gay. I must admit I see far more experimentation between tween girls than boys.'

Body Safety as They Grow

Considering sleepovers with friends, body safety is something we must be more mindful of. Adults are not the only potential perpetrators of abuse, and, in fact, research tells us that one in four child sexual abuse cases in Australia involve a child abusing another.[15] Lots of parents ask me when they should stop talking to a child when they are naked. Here's one way to think about it: if you wouldn't be okay with your child going to a friend's house and talking to someone while naked, it might be best to do the same at home. This might even extend to things like allowing children to shower together or to walk into the bathroom while someone is on the toilet. Remember, as we talked about in Chapter 2, 'Speaking Tween', tweens aren't always able to take one piece of information and apply it to another situation. I've seen many parents horrified to learn that their tween showered with their friend, only to have them reply, 'But I shower with my little sister.' Sadly, I see tweens in considerable danger when they visit homes while maintaining the same trusting attitude they have in their own home.

And if you need an extra nudge, this message is the most recent of the hundreds I have received over the years. It reads,

Hi Michelle, I am after some advice regarding my almost-8-year-old daughter please. Recently we found some explicit sexual drawings and writing she and a friend of hers (a girl one year older) had done. They said they had done them at school after a kid at school had told them about it, but they don't know who. The pictures and writing described detailed oral sex activities between the two of them. I know my daughter has not been exposed to this kind of thing at home! I was so shocked when I first found them, I instantly told her they were not acceptable and asked where had she got these ideas from?! I have since found more pictures of the same kind. I am trying to talk to her about the pictures and what she understands about her drawings, but she completely shuts down and starts crying, covering her ears, getting agitated, not talking and has even said she doesn't want to be here, because she is a bad kid. I've told her she isn't in trouble, that it's ok to be curious and I'm here for her to talk to. Initially, when she reacted like that, my mind went into overdrive and I was thinking the worst, that someone had done something to her. When I asked her this, she did talk to me and said that no one has done anything to her. Do I leave it now and try dropping growing-up topics into future conversations with her? I just don't know what to do, she's only 8.

We need to get really good at talking to kids about tricky topics and explaining why some behaviour is unacceptable or dangerous. If you have a topic that you don't feel equipped to talk about, educate yourself. I recommend Dr Robyn Silverman's valuable podcast *How to Talk to Kids about Anything*. It offers parents the actual language they need to effectively open difficult conversations.[16]

Talking about Consent

The Me Too movement shed a spotlight on systemic abuse and gender imbalances in a culture-shifting way. The word 'consent' has been elevated and is now firmly embedded in formal education. Very few would argue against the idea that kids should be taught that those who are of the legal age of consent must gain wholehearted agreement before every sexual encounter without using coercion, pressure, manipulation, force, drugs or alcohol, and that there is never a time sex should be taken from someone against their will. However, I think it's crucial that kids understand that consent is a legal term, there for everyone's protection. It does not guarantee fulfilling sexual experiences, and there is so much more to healthy relationships.

Education starts in primary school. Not only do we want to transfer the values that underpin healthy relationships, but we also want to give kids the language and clear permission to be the boss of their body. We can also teach tweens about consent in a multifaceted way by helping them to say 'no' in non-sexual relationships. As they reach high school, consent is spoken about in more depth, particularly in relation to responsibilities, parties, drugs and alcohol.

When it comes to educating within our homes, I always suggest working backwards – start with the end goal in mind. What do you hope for your child's future romantic relationships? I hope that my children experience sex as an expression of proven love, trust and emotional intimacy. I talk to them about sex being safest in the context of commitment, when you know someone and have an opportunity to talk through shared desires and needs.

In the breakout box you'll find comments from parents of tweens who shared what they wanted for their kids' future romantic relationships. You'll notice a theme – mutual respect.

Parents' answers when asked, 'What do you want for your child's future romantic relationships?':

◢ I want my son to understand his worth. To know that he deserves to be treated with love and respect within his relationship. To understand he is part of the relationship, not responsible for the whole relationship.

◢ I want my daughter to love herself first, and not to need someone else to complete her. I hope she takes time to explore life and discover who she is. I want her to be safe, loved and listened to, respected and intellectually challenged.

◢ I hope my girls have partners who they can talk to without feeling judged. Someone they can 100 per cent be themselves around.

◢ I hope they never find themselves in a space where they have to diminish themselves in order to hold onto someone they love. I hope they have the ability to walk away if someone is trying to control them. And finally, I hope they find a lasting, authentic, life-sustaining love.

▲ I want my son not to expect to have all of his needs fulfilled within a romantic relationship – to normalise being emotionally intimate with platonic friends, as well as platonic affection like hugging. So many men don't have, and maybe don't know how to cultivate, emotionally intimate friendships and that results in social isolation.

▲ As the mother of sensitive and romance-loving sons, I want them to be safe to be themselves in their romantic relationships, to not feel like they have to fit society's expectations of what it means to be a man, and to not be in danger of being walked all over just because they are 'nice' guys.

Below are some of the key messages that form the basis of consent. These are the messages I share in presentations, books and *You! Who?*, my online show for tweens. It's the stuff I wish I was taught at their age!

Know your mind. The relationship our tweens have with themselves is an important starting point. We want to teach our kids to both ask and honestly answer the question, 'What do I *really* want?' So often tweens feel pressured into saying yes when they aren't sure, or when they want to say no. Most often they aren't faced with high-stake scenarios but smaller decisions such as whether to loan someone their new glitter pens, go to a sleepover, gossip about a friend or share their lunch.

Choose an appropriate delivery. I teach kids to say 'no' using either a 'soft' or 'hard' no, depending on the situation. A soft no is more like a hint or a PDP sandwich, which we spoke about on page 56. A hard no is very firm and sounds more like the type of no that would be delivered by a police officer. If tweens feel they need to 'arrest a friend' in order to get their point across, they need to be prepared to use a hard no. When it comes to their body, a hard no is *always* the right option, and our kids need to be clearly taught this.

Being nice is not the goal. It's critical that we teach our tweens that 'nice' is not the best starting point for a relationship – honesty is. Watch out for kids buying in to the idea that 'caring' means carrying someone else's happiness. This can, one day, easily transfer to them making sexual choices to please someone else at their own expense. Also of note – twisting someone's arm until they change their mind is *not* consent.

Listen to your intuition. When your tween is faced with a strong negative emotion, it may be a sign that they are operating outside of their boundaries. Please teach them to recognise this! It is too easy to dismiss, minimise, excuse or justify those feelings. Also remember that intuition is a safeguard against danger and can surface before our conscious thoughts kick in. I want to encourage all kids to channel their internal nudges into actions, or at least be curious about them. My husband and I tried to reaffirm our kids' instincts by saying, 'If you ever feel uncomfortable, anytime, anyplace, for any reason, listen to that feeling. We will always pick you up.'

Receive a 'no' well. Teach your tween to ask their friends, 'Is that okay with you?' or any number of variations such as,

'How does that sound?', 'Is that what you would like to play?', 'Is that what you were thinking?' or 'What are your thoughts?' They need to be comfortable both giving and receiving 'no', which only comes with practice. Many times, kids don't ask because they don't want to hear the answer!

Read others' body language. Consent is all about giving an enthusiastic 'yes'. Enthusiasm is best depicted in body language, which takes maturity for kids to read accurately. While they are developing this skill, we can help them identify enthusiasm by asking, 'Does someone's face light up? Do they move towards you? Are they nodding?' I always encourage tweens to be 'noticers' – notice their environment, how they feel and how others feel.

Own your body. We need to teach tweens that they have the right to say 'no' to anyone they don't want near their body. They also have the right to say 'no' to being alone with someone who gives them yucky feelings, even if it is someone whom they know very well, such as a family member. Additionally, they don't even have to give someone a hug or kiss as a 'hello' or a 'goodbye' if they don't want to. I recommend they politely offer a loving fist bump instead. This is another way we can reinforce that it is never okay to pressure someone to do something they are uncomfortable with or to use a person's body in any way when we don't have permission to do so.

Lastly, when we think or talk about consent, please be careful about the typical narrative – that our boys are pushing for sexual activity while our girls are feeling pressured to give it. This narrative can lead our kids to all sorts of assumptions and expectations of each other, and I feel it is becoming outdated.

While movies, music and social media drip-feed these stereo-types and other really destructive messages about relationships, it doesn't represent all of our kids and breeds unhelpful mistrust. It can also leave them feeling trapped in someone else's story, tentative about communicating their truth.

Chapter 8

THE CHAPTER YOU NEED TO READ

Key Message: I know what I am doing is working today, but it can all change tomorrow.

For most tweens, technology equals fun. They simply want to show up at the coolest event in this year's social calendar. That event might be held on any number of social or gaming platforms, including TikTok, YouTube, iMessage, Minecraft, Discord, Roblox, Fortnite and Call of Duty. The invitation is open 24 hours a day, 7 days a week, 365 days a year. You might have heard that everyone is going – they are. Social media has become the thing that our kids anchor their lives around. Newsfeeds promise to turn everyday kids into international stars, or at least local school celebrities, with dance moves, challenges and comedy skits becoming the sure ticket to a better life.

According to the Pew Research Center, based in America, 80 per cent of 12-year-olds have two social media accounts.[1] Until the age of 10, children are more likely to own a tablet device, yet between the ages of 9 and 10 smartphone ownership more than doubles from 23 per cent to 50 per cent. By age 15, almost all children own their own smartphones.[2] Until kids get their own phones, parents usually find theirs constantly hijacked. 'They come looking for your thumb to unlock your phone!' one mum told me. Another mum said, 'They make me eyeball my phone before I have even woken up!'

With today's extensive cyber safety programs being rolled out through schools and public campaigns, I am confident that parents are aware of the risks. We know that tweens are asking to enter a world that has 18+ content, and, despite our best intentions, it is impossible for us to completely filter the internet. We know that social media platforms are not designed with our kids' wellbeing in mind and that even grown adults struggle with the addictive nature of the internet. We know this generation of kids are forming identities in response to content they see online, which is far from helpful. We know a lot, but that doesn't make management any easier. In the words of Dr Michael Carr-Gregg, 'We have not found an effective way to manage the risks.'

I have called this 'The Chapter You Need to Read' because technology is a central part of our world, like it or not. Although there are some wonderful, creative, social connections and skill-building experiences online, I can hear a genuine weariness in parents' voices as they constantly confront the tension that technology brings into their homes. It's the bane of their existence. I receive many messages like this: 'A huge concern of mine is social media. Already I see videos from her friends back and forth on Messenger discussing weight and looks. She is 8. Her friends often call and text and she's not online as much. The messages get very angry if there is no response.' And I also receive an equal number of messages about gaming, such as, 'How can working parents be more involved with their tween's life? I don't understand their computer games and it worries me that they could be doing anything and I may miss signs that they are out of their depth.' Overall, I get the sense that parents are increasingly becoming deeply concerned about how technology is impacting kids, and so they should be. Unfortunately, tech companies occupy a particular worldview that doesn't represent our kids' best interests but their own bottom line.

'That phone has taken over their life,' Suellen explained. 'They don't want to participate in normal things, and we can't seem to reach them in the same way we used to. In hindsight, I wish I had never said yes to it.' You might also appreciate this honest feedback from Kim – I do. She says, 'My kids have a Fortnite playtime limit of only two hours once a week on a Saturday. I thought that these boundaries would create safe play, but I was never prepared for how addictive the game was. They release new characters (skins) to buy every day, which they market really cleverly as something that you need, so the kids are always begging to check the game. There are new challenges every day to help you level up faster, which, if you have the season battle pass, you need to do to earn all the free items. It's all they talk about, and I was never prepared for the game to take over their minds the way that it has.'

While writing this chapter, I found expert opinions varied greatly, and research specifically relating to tweens was available but limited. I have made a very strong mental note of Kids Helpline's findings. According to their 2020 report, children aged 5 to 12 accessed information about being safe online more than any other topic. In this age group, 23,418 children used the website to seek out their own solutions for staying safe online. This topic was followed by fights with friends, bullying, feeling lonely and everybody makes mistakes.[3]

That Inevitable Moment

There seems to come an inevitable moment where tweens plead with parents for their own smartphone and social media or gaming account. You might recognise that the tone of their request is desperate, like their life depends on it. If your tween is asking for their own smartphone, or their own social media or gaming account, you can no longer dodge, dismiss or sidestep the topic. You must be decisive in what you want, or you will find yourself following rather than leading. I love this letter from a tween because it sums up the intensity of this moment perfectly.

Dear Mum
I am sorry that I cracked it about getting a phone but here are some reasons why I should get a phone:
I can text and call you when I am out with my friends.
If I get lost I can contact you.
I have enough money, so it would not impact you.
I can contact you when I go to the shops with my friends.
Phones help me figure out where I am.

If I had a phone I would pay for the phone plan.

All phone costs are on me.

I am 12, therefore I am responsible enough to have a phone.

I would not waste my money on an expensive phone, just a cheap one.

I can listen to music on it when I go for walks and jogs.

I can take it with me to places instead of a big iPad.

I can look mature holding a phone.

These are all my reasons and again, I am sorry for cracking it and yelling – it was rude.

Think about it please xoxoxo

Sienna

It's during these moments, parents send me messages like this:

Hi Michelle,

I'm wondering if you could point me towards any blogs or podcasts you may have done that talk about how to manage your daughter's right to privacy while they're still only young? My (almost) 11-year-old only has two ways to communicate with friends and that's via Messenger Kids, and she's now discovered Skype on the laptop we bought her for school. While I'm not worried about the content of their conversations, it's the secrecy of these things and her constantly locking herself away in her room to chat online that bothers me – so when I check to see how much is going on, she feels I'm invading her privacy and have no trust in her. I'm looking for an article to help with that balance at all if you've got any suggestions?

Thank you in advance,

Amanda

Questions Parents Ask

In this section I want to draw on cyber safety experts, and share some of my personal observations, to answer some of the most common questions parents ask me. I am not going to sit on the fence with any of these answers, but there are a few places where I felt it was important to offer two contradictory perspectives because each of them had merit for some situations. I have also included a bullet point summary at the end of the chapter, for those who want to refer back to my main points at a later date.

What's the Magic Number?

When is the right age to give a child a social media account or their own phone? There is no easy answer, and so much of it depends on your unique child. Experts suggest delaying for as long as possible, usually until they are in high school. Yet, in saying this, many children have their own social media accounts or phones earlier than this, and these decisions are often couched in genuine complexities. An example of this is shared custody arrangements, where technology can be useful to keep in touch, but more difficult to manage when mutual values are not shared. The Apple Watch SE has given some families the opportunity to send texts and make calls (and look cool) without their tween needing their own phone, eliminating the ability to mindlessly scroll through social media feeds, which I think is great!

To gain clarity about the law in regard to children's social media use, I turned to Susan McLean, a cyber safety expert with a longstanding commitment to child safety. She points parents to the terms and conditions of each platform, most of which expressly state users have to be at least 13. In my interview with her, she explained, 'Platforms cannot legally collect personal information of children under 13 years old. That's the issue from a legal perspective. In Australia, it's not a crime but more of a breach of contract.' The eSafety Commissioner adds, 'Generally, the 13-year-old age requirement is not necessarily because the site is unsafe for children to use but to comply with a US law.'[4]

Susan McLean passionately goes on to explain that we are sending kids the wrong message when we allow them to lie about their age to use these sites. There is such power in communities (and, at the very least, parents of kids in the same friendship group) having consistent boundaries. I regularly meet groups of mums who make pacts to keep their kids off social media until high school and to not allow tech at playdates and sleepovers, as they recognise the power in agreement.

Where Do I Start?

Right now, you hold all the cards. Remember that. It is easy to be pressured into saying 'yes' too quickly or without adequate restrictions, boundaries and supervision in place. Argue with yourself, and debate with your partner. Glean from the advice and education cyber safety experts offer. Once you have settled on your own thoughts, transfer your expectations into an agreement with your tween. Even if you are not a charts-and-checklists type of parent, when it comes to social media a written contract really is essential. Nothing should be left unsaid. Children don't do well with unclear or inconsistent messages, so it is important that everyone is on the same page. Contracts force everyone to communicate their assumptions and express their ideas, and their disappointments, upfront. The eSafety Commissioner offers a guide to creating a family tech agreement, one of the many options available through a quick Google search.[5]

Keep the contract in a visible place. This will be a good reminder for both you and your tween that it's important.

During the busyness of life there will be times when it will be more difficult to follow through with your expectations. That is normal, especially given all the responsibilities today's families juggle. This comment from Allison sums up how many parents feel: 'My issue is feeling time pressured between children, responsibilities at home, partners and work. I want to do it all but know it's impossible. I know I need to be more attentive to their tech habits, but it's hard to fit it in.' If you are nodding in agreement, keep this thought in your heart – if you put in the groundwork upfront, I promise it will save you time and energy in the long run.

I encourage parents to let their tweens know that the agreement isn't a rigid representation of your authority as a parent. Parents should be free to parent over and above the bounds of the agreement, understanding that it is impossible to write down every scenario that might take place. Please give yourself permission to lead as necessary. It is okay to change your mind. If you are paying the bill, you still have a lot more say than you realise.

It is not just *when* you give privileges, but *how*. In my interview with Leonie Smith, a family counsellor who helps families deal with issues around digital device use, she advised that parents teach 'side by side' before giving tweens more autonomy with realistic boundaries. This is the approach I took with my youngest son. I literally shared an Instagram account with him for about a year, before I felt he was ready for more autonomy. I'm glad I didn't miss the window of opportunity where he was willing to work cooperatively with me on this.

How Much Privacy Should They Have?

Unapologetically, none. I want you to insist that your tween is completely transparent when it comes to their time online. You might think, *Don't kids deserve privacy?* My response, the internet is a public place, not a private one. By giving them privacy, we are reinforcing the faulty belief that their social media account is their private space. It's not. However, in the back of most parents' minds is the nagging, unsettling reality that tweens can (and do) set up fake profiles, so we flinch. We hesitate. You might have just breathed in and said to yourself, 'Is that even possible? Do I have the right to ask them that?' Yes, you do, because their safety is your responsibility. And even if they make different choices, you still have a responsibility to point north.

The good news is that these days excellent safety software allows you to more easily follow through on your request for transparency; a quick google will provide you with a variety of options. If you choose to access all their private messages, please don't jump on every swear word they say or every error they make. You will see some things you don't like! Remember that they talk to their friends all day long without you watching over their shoulder, so don't get overly or unnecessarily involved. This is where asking for privacy backfires.

Once tweens have social media accounts, please know that they absolutely cannot do this without you, as their brains are not developed enough to be able to navigate the complexities of the online world. My best tip is to check their account settings regularly and help them curate their newsfeed so it remains empowering. If you allow them to follow people outside of their friendship group, try to make sure their newsfeed is diverse, because the algorithm is so good at feeding them more and more of the same. The trick is to help tweens unfollow accounts that pull them into the comparison trap and leave them feeling crap about themselves. I also recommend googling your tween's name occasionally. You might be surprised by what you find.

Is There Ever a Time to Take Tech Away?

Parents always ask me if there is ever a time to take technology away from a child. Based on my 25 years working with young people, my strong but unpopular response is, 'Damn straight, yes!' Many cyber safety and parenting experts will disagree with me, insisting that taking technology away drives poor behaviour underground. If this strategy is overused, unfairly used or used as a veiled threat, I agree. But most kids I have worked with who are in over their heads have been relieved when their parents stepped in, took the reins and held them accountable. There are moments in tweens' lives when they need us to draw very clear lines in the sand. In my opinion, it is totally okay to remove tech access for a period of time if it is linked to a specific inappropriate action. Technology is a privilege that comes with responsibility; it's not a right. However, there are some complexities associated with consistently communicating this message to tweens.

This is an example that a Year 6 teacher recently shared with me that highlights this point perfectly. Almost the entire grade got involved in a group chat. Students went from sharing photos of their afternoon adventures to using vulgar language and posting themselves giving each other the finger. As things progressed, the whole chat became a competition as to who knew the greatest swear words. Motherf****** c*** and the like were sprayed in the comments. Tweens weren't having a discussion but were just trying to outdo each other's foul mouths. Although the incident happened outside of school hours, teachers spent copious amounts of time contacting families with the evidence and dealing with fallout. Because iPads were still needed to support class learning, the school decided to 'talk' to the students collectively but left individual families to follow through with their child (and the ongoing management of iPad time) as they saw fit. The incident occurred again, not long after, proving the difficulties associated with managing technology usage. In my opionion, some space from technology would have helped the tweens understand the gravity of their actions, and also would've offered parents the time they needed to re-establish expectations.

How Much is Too Much?

One sure sign that tech is not helpful is when it comes between you and your relationship with your tween. When kids are distracted, the speed and quality of communication will undoubtably deteriorate. In my survey, most parents who reported challenges with excessive technology use also felt their relationship with their child was distant. This is the obvious conclusion – excessive technology use and disconnected relationships go hand in hand. If we want to connect with our kids, we need to enjoy device-free time with them. If their head (or ours) is constantly 6 inches from a screen, our relationship with them will struggle.

Supporting this is research from Macquarie University led by Associate Professor Wayne Warburton, who looked at case studies such as a primary school student displaying game-related aggression. His work shows that although anyone can develop a gaming disorder, those most vulnerable to developing internet gaming disorder (IGD) not only struggled with their impulses but also felt unsupported or disconnected from their families and disempowered in their outside environment.[6] Again, when kids' basic needs are met, including feeling they are good at things and being in control, they are less at risk. We need to carve out time to ensure these needs are met in healthy ways.

We must also realise that how they use their time will literally shape their future strengths and deficits. Our tweens will use and lose different neurons to the ones we lost at their age because they are participating in different activities. This means that what they do online matters. Mark McCrindle offers this truth, 'While technology affects us all, the impacts are greater when experienced in our formative years. Our research consistently shows that the age at which we're exposed to a new technology determines how embedded it will be in our psyche and lifestyle.'[7] What our kids are exposed to shapes the way they see the world. I often think about the potentially harmful lens that violent games are imposing on our kids' sense of safety.

The Outsideologist Project's 2021 survey of 1028 children aged 5 to 12 outlines that 89 per cent of kids choose to play inside.[8] That's a big number. Tweens can 'play' almost everything they can in real life on a device – they can have pets, build imaginary worlds and talk to friends – but replacing real-life play with online play has some implications, which Dr Amrit Kumar Jha outlines in the paper 'Understanding Alpha Generation'. Dr Kumar Jha believes that changes in brain plasticity, cognition, sleep disturbances and obesity will constitute future problematic trends in this generation of kids.[9] Research is also clear that the longer young people are online, the more likely they are to engage in risky behaviour. More time on social media, especially for girls, is strongly associated with compromised mental health, self-harm behaviours, low life satisfaction and low self-esteem.[10,11]

What If My Child is Addicted?

There may be times when technology isn't the right fit for a child. Removing it from the routine is not a disciplinary action, but common sense. The research article 'Internet Gaming Disorder: Evidence for a Risk and Resilience Approach' indicates that, for most, gaming will remain a harmless and enjoyable pastime, but for a small minority it could be a trigger for serious problems. Please know that for many kids gaming provides both a sense of connection and competence, both of which have a positive impact on them.[12] However, for 2.8 per cent of our kids gaming at pathological levels is leading to school refusal, stealing parents' credit cards, threats of self-harm and aggression towards family.[13] We know that a child's poor executive functioning (self-control) in tandem with unmet needs in off-screen everyday life (social exclusion) are the factors that most strongly predict problematic gaming use. Other significant predictors include a child's impulsivity, self-esteem, control over their current external environment and parent–child attachment quality.[14] Some tweens who already have problems with transitions due to conditions such as ADHD report particularly struggling with technology consumption.[15] It's plain and simple to me – what is too much for one child, may not be for another.

We have to be conscious of the dopamine flood that is impacting this generation and the consequences of overexposure to digital environments. It is widely reported that screens have the potential to leave our kids constantly aroused and to impact the reward–punishment sensitivity balance.[16,17] Results from a set of independent studies, mostly conducted in East Asia, on young males with internet gaming disorders led to the conclusion that the functional alterations they experienced were similar to those observed in substance abuse, with the studies likening it to drug addiction.[18] That's a scary thought for parents!

Having watched students in schools for decades, there is no doubt in my mind that this generation struggles to linger on tasks and spend time pondering ideas. However, the impact of technology can be far more serious for some, and, as a result, the term 'problematic internet use' has recently been included in the *Diagnostic and Statistical Manual of Mental Disorders* (*DSM*). If it's a problematic behaviour, it's always best to address it with the safety of expert support. Leonie Smith said to me,

'When nothing works, parents need to seek help. I am hearing about children who are threatening suicide if they don't have their iPad with them all the time. Parents are naturally terrified. I am also hearing about children refusing to go to school because they want to play games online.'

Should My Tween Use Tech to Calm Down?

When I see tweens continually reach for a screen to 'calm down' or 'feel better', I am witnessing the avoidance of big, strong emotions. Technology becomes underage valium. While valium has its place and can be helpful when accurately prescribed, it can also cause massive deprivation of emotional growth when it's misused. When technology is used as their dominant emotional regulation strategy, it narrows a kid's world. When we tell a child they can't play online games tonight, and it is followed by a meltdown of catastrophic proportions, the question I ask myself is this: Is the meltdown because they desperately want to have fun on that game, or socialise with friends, or is there a bigger picture? Are they missing the 'downtime' that they need to regulate their emotions each day? I wonder if we are witnessing a generation of children who don't have coping mechanisms to regulate themselves without technology.[19,20]

I'd like to raise an interesting thought offered by Allison Davies, who I introduced in Chapter 4, 'Big, Bold Emotions'. I felt it was important to offer this alternative perspective, which again highlights the unique way each person interacts with technology. In my interview with her, she said, 'For some children, the dopamine flood that comes from technology tops them up to the level they need.' We went on to talk about the shame, guilt or confusion that many families feel about a child's extended or obsessive technology use. We also discussed the lack of specific research on how technology impacts neuro-divergent kids. I conclude that for some children technology plays a bigger role in their lives than it does for others and that some neurodivergent children will actively gravitate towards dopamine-boosting activities facilitated by technology because their baseline for this essential hormone can be lower than that of their neurotypical peers.

Should Technology be Allowed in Their Bedroom?

From a psychological point of view, putting a screen in your tween's bedroom doesn't have any benefits. From a child safety point of view, it is disastrous. There's a massive gap between parents' perception of the risk and the express messages of law enforcement. In my interview with her, Susan McLean said, 'According to the Internet Watch Foundation, research conducted looking at over 2000 cases of online live streaming abuse committed against children found that 98 per cent of those victims were under the age of 13. In every single case the abuse occurred when the child was in a bedroom or bathroom when no adult appeared present.'

Let's also help our tweens establish tech-free night-time routines that protect their sleep. Research tells us that screen time within one hour of going to bed drops melatonin levels to daytime levels, disturbing their circadian rhythm and sleep quality.[21,22] While blue light glasses or screen covers can help this, they won't restrict the late-night drama and emergency texts that often come from your tween's peers. This some-times interrupts their sleep quality more than anything else! Remember, we need to lead the way with this – if the rule is there are no phones in rooms, that includes yours (unless there are reasonable circumstances, such as when you are on call for work or have a young-adult child that is out late).

Survey responses from tweens when asked, 'What do you want adults/parents to know about technology?':

- ◢ We like them
- ◢ It is normal for us to like to use them
- ◢ That I want a phone to talk to people when I am struggling
- ◢ You can't pause online games
- ◢ We're not addicted
- ◢ We are not hiding something if we don't want them going through our phones
- ◢ We need more screen time
- ◢ Technology is not always what is affecting us.

What About Parties and Sleepovers?

Once tweens begin to come to playdates, parties and sleepovers with devices, there is a new dynamic to manage. Alex, the father of two tween girls, explains, 'When their friends come to play, I don't have much of a choice but to give them more time on the iPad because their friends don't know how to play and that is what they expect when they come over.' I can hear a similar concern from mum Amanda: 'I'm looking for some advice as to what to do when my 13-year-old daughter invites friends over and all they want to do is sit on their devices, even though we have a pool, a pool table, a Wii, a dog and a bird. I want to constantly nag them about doing something together other than being on the device, but then I wonder if her friends won't want to come over if I'm the only mother who is nagging about it?'

Oh, this is a hard one! All parents will have a different management style when hosting sleepovers and playdates. My suggestion is to get good at communicating your boundaries – that way your tweens' friends won't define them for you. You can go as far as creating event invitations that paint a picture of what the experience will (and won't) be like. One family I spoke to shared that they sent out birthday invitations that announced a tech-free party, and some kids didn't turn up. That's the reality with boundaries – not everyone will like them.

Keep in mind that each one of your child's friends is adjusting to your rules and vibe, and they will be highly attuned to the differences between your home and theirs. If you are more lenient, they will be eyes wide open to what you allow them to do that is different to their home. If you are stricter, they will take a moment to understand how to enjoy themselves without their usual freedoms. The use of technology is the biggest difference between homes and it causes parents the most concern – understandably.

If you do choose to have tech-free or limited-tech playdates and sleepovers, make sure kids know they can always come to you to contact their parents anytime. Separation anxiety is real, and technology is the link to parents and emotional regulation for some kids. While tech-free social time can be wonderful, it can also cause some kids a lot of stress. It's all about being mindful of this and preparing some different activity options if things start to go pear-shaped.

If you allow tech within your home, please be mindful of the responsibility you have – it's massive. Bullying, harassment, nudes and other poor choices are so much easier for kids to make when they are in a group. Things happen at sleepovers that wouldn't ever happen in another context. The classification ratings on games and the potential for exposure to inappropriate content are all yours to manage. If something goes wrong, it is on your shoulders.

Discussions about Online Safety

The following is a perfect example of how tweens take risks online. A Year 6 class used OneNote as a tool for class learning. A boy added a folder in OneNote called 'Personal, Not for Teachers to View', with all his tween-ish, mildly inappropriate stuff saved in it. Taken at face value, it's somewhat cute, but what happens when the stakes are higher? What happens when tweens bring that same naivety to interactions with ill-intending peers or unsafe people? What happens when they get caught in a rabbit warren of filth or darkness? Sadly, this is too often the reality.

Recently I was contacted by a parent whose daughter's best friend attempted the blackout challenge, which encourages users to hold their breath until they pass out. She tragically died. The first thing the police did was trawl through her phone and social media history. Again, I am reminded that at 12 most kids do not understand the finality of death or do not realise that hard times don't last forever. It sickens me to the pit of my stomach to hear stories like this and to hear how tween suicide, self-harm and other risky behaviours are continually linked to technology.

As we discussed in Chapter 2, 'Speaking Tween', tweens are incapable of assessing the risks because they haven't developed formal thinking that allows them to comprehend abstract concepts. Understanding that unsafe people exist is one thing, but it's an entirely different thing to comprehend that someone you haven't met can really harm you. Most weeks I meet tweens (especially boys) who brag about being able to 'break' the school safety software. They convince their friends that they outsmarted a paedophile because they gave them a fake name and address. They might even believe that if they send pictures of their private parts, the harassment will stop or they will get the public recognition they desire.

I'd like to suggest four conversations to have with your tween, all of which will support their online safety.

Define online friendship. Discuss what constitutes an online friend as opposed to a friend in real life. Because tweens are literal, you have to clearly define what an online friend is, and don't assume that they understand who should or shouldn't fall into that category. Does their aunty or uncle? Does their aunty and uncle's friends? Does a friend of a friend? Who tweens add as a friend and follow will impact their newsfeeds. Again, because of tweens' concrete cognition, we have to keep drawing a separation between real life and the online world. These are some critical questions for tweens to answer to help them see if the friendship is secure or if the effort required for that social media streak is worth it.

Out of all the people you have an online relationship with:

◢ 'Which of them would contact you if they hadn't heard from you in a few days?'
◢ 'Which of them would wait for you while you're in the tuckshop line at school?'
◢ 'Who would try to visit you if you were in hospital?'
◢ 'Who notices when you're absent from school or when you don't seem yourself?'
◢ 'Would liking their social media post matter if a huge change happened in your life or family right now?'

Fear can be helpful. Another concept that we need to help kids understand is the role of healthy fear, which tries to warn them of danger. When they are riding their bike down a hill and it starts to pick up speed, healthy fear tries to step in, telling them to brake so they don't fall. It's their body's way of telling them that it is time to modify their actions, to be cautious or to retreat and find help. We want tweens to feel a sense of healthy fear when using technology, knowing it can hurt them if used unwisely. Fear and excitement can feel similar, so it is easy for tweens to confuse them. I could tell endless stories of tweens who confused the two feelings and made train-wreck decisions that were completely uncalculated. Know that if things hit the fan, there is always a recovery plan and a path to restoration. Your relationship with your child is the most important thing to protect. Please also remember that when your tween leaves the house, they may be exposed to things they wouldn't be exposed to at home. That's reality. You may be able to minimise this, but I guarantee that you won't be able to eliminate it, which makes your relationship with them the only thing you can 100 per cent rely on.

Scary, rude or nasty. I break internet dangers into three simple areas – things that are *scary*, *rude* or *nasty*. These words are kid-speak for harmful online behaviours such as image-based abuse, insult tagging, cyber-ostracism, negative bystander behaviours, catfishing and impersonation, grooming and unwanted contact, sexting, extortion and blackmailing, scamming, stalking, problematic gaming and exposure to pornography. What's important is that we lift the shame that tweens might feel when stumbling on these things, and that our kids know exactly how to respond when they do.

The safety net. Although we must filter the internet for tweens, that filter isn't 100 per cent effective, and that is why educa-tion and how-to plans come into play. I talk to tweens about the internet being like the sea, which has a lot of sharks in it, and safety software being like the net that stands between those sharks and swimmers or surfers. Occasionally, the net gets broken or doesn't do its job. Sometimes sharks are strong enough to bite through it.

Some platforms or games have their own safety net. Some have a more effective safety net than others. The software we add to computers only strengthens this safety net. At the time of writing this book, TikTok is of great concern to me, because it is almost impossible to filter. Leigh, mother and social media agent, says, 'OMG, I couldn't agree more. My 10-year-old daughter has friends who are on TikTok. I spent one day on it to check it out and there is no way she is getting on that platform. And I own a digital agency, I work in social media, I understand the platforms. This is one of the worst and I despair about all the children using this. And I can't believe parents actually let their young children on it.'

Nothing Can Replace You

After offering a Year 6 cohort of 70 students the opportunity to come and speak to me if they were experiencing anything unsafe online, approximately 25 kids lined up. Each child was prepared to skip a portion of their lunch break to speak privately with me. Out of those 25 students, 8 were facing significant harm online that required parental or police notification. The others needed reassurance and a guiding hand as they tried to apply my presentation to their lives.

Was this a particularly 'bad' school or cohort of kids? Absolutely not. These kids were like every other group of students, except they had the chance to ask for help without shame or harsh punishment. They were surrounded by open-hearted adults whom they felt safe with. I have always reassured parents, 'If the average age of pornography exposure is 11, we must be on the front foot. It's not if they see it, but what they do when they see it that will make all the difference.'[23] When children can come forward during times of uncertainty or trouble, they have a safe place to land and learn. Bring that on!

Many children bury themselves in shame when they experience challenges or make mistakes online. They may be concerned about getting into *big* trouble, being accused of doing something wrong or not being fully understood by the adults in their world. I want our kids to know that no matter how they arrived at an unsafe place, there are always safe people to turn to for help. The most precious thing about this age group is that they often willingly hand themselves in for questioning once they find a safe space, even when they know they have done the wrong thing.

When it comes to technology, parents have a lot more influence but far less control than they realise, and that's why I suggest we lean in to communication as our highest priority.

In closing, I loved this statement from Joey, mother of two tweens and one teen: 'I know what I am doing is working today, but it can all change tomorrow,' she explains. Technology is a moving target. Prepare yourself to move with it.

Bullet Point Takeaways

The following are practical bullet points for easy digestion, all endorsed by cyber safety educators who are passionate about protecting our kids' wellbeing in this tech-saturated age.

◢ If your tween is asking for their own smartphone, social media or gaming account, you can no longer dodge, dismiss or sidestep the topic. You must be decisive in what you want, or you will find yourself following rather than leading.

- Delay access for as long as possible. Once devices become portable, risk increases.

- Technology should be owned by you. It should never be a gift. This simple shift in power ensures you are the captain of the ship from the very onset.

- Anything to do with tech is a privilege, not a right, and it comes with responsibility.

- Establish a contract with your tween. Digital contracts or agreements are all about managing expectations and making sure everyone is on the same page. Always reserve the right to have the final say or change your mind.

- Once you set a boundary, your challenge is holding that boundary. Nothing will challenge that more than technology.

- If you aren't ready to talk to your child about pornography and paedophiles, you aren't ready for them to be online. Preventive education and a clear 'what to do' plan are essential.

- You can reduce the risk, but it is impossible to get rid of it altogether. You know your child and if they are ready for that responsibility.

- The internet must be filtered. Parental controls are essential.

◢ Regular open communication is essential. Any parental control that you put on a device is a guardrail only. If tweens (or, more likely, teens) want to get around them, they will – or they will use the device of a friend who isn't burdened with the same restrictions. Being a digital parent is all about realising this and not relying too heavily on safety software as the absolute answer.

◢ The health of social media newsfeeds needs to be consistently assessed. Try to help tweens evaluate their newsfeeds and encourage them to unfollow, block or delete accounts that are not playing a positive role in their lives. It's important that our tweens regularly consider who holds their attention and time. Ask them, 'How is it helpful? How does it make you feel?'

◢ For most, tech-free night-time and sleep routines promote better sleep habits.

◢ Try and encourage positive tech time by building it around their interests and dreams. Remember too, if your tween has been interested in cooking since they were 13 and posts about their efforts on social media, it becomes a track record for employees to look at.

◢ Be honest about your own tech habits and what you are modelling for your tween. Come on, parents – do you sleep with your phone in your room? Do you have uninterrupted family time without it? Do you feel addicted to technology?

Chapter 9
BUILDING BODY CONFIDENCE

Key Message: If it's important to them, it has to be important to us.

Caron watched as her healthy 11-year-old daughter examined her body in the mirror. 'Look at my stomach,' she insisted. 'I think it's bloated. I'm putting on weight.' Caron paused as she decided how to answer. She contemplated offering to swap bodies but, in the end, opted for, 'You are skin and bone. You look like you need to eat a burger!' Later that night, she wondered if she had said the right thing and why on earth she needed to talk to an 11-year-old about her weight anyway?

Most parents accept that their kids will, at some point, become preoccupied with their appearance. However, today's parents find that from an early age children are using words like 'fat' or 'ugly', and the extreme pressure they are putting on themselves to conform to body ideals is very confronting. Rosa says, 'My 8-year-old is already telling me what is cool to wear and what is not . . .' and Melinda, mum to two tweens, shares,

'It's not that I didn't feel the same feelings of insecurity, but I was older. That is why it's alarming, because at my son's and daughter's age, I don't remember having any hang-ups about having a wobbly tummy. It was probably more in the teenage years.'

These are some concerning, but important, statistics that give us insights into the depth of the problem surfacing in this generation of kids. According to the Australian Institute of Family Studies, children are expressing dissatisfaction with their bodies as early as 8 to 9 years old and the majority of 10- to 11-year-olds are trying to control their weight.[1] By the time our kids are adolescents, 83 per cent of boys and 86 per cent of girls will experience dissatisfaction with the size, shape or function of one or more parts of their body.[2] Anecdotally, I hear about girls desperately wanting braces, so they can have the perfect smile, or begging their parents for fake nails or eyelash extensions at 11 years old. I am also hearing about boys weighing themselves daily and insisting on 'bulking up' to increase their muscle size.

To further expand this discussion, I'd like to also introduce you to the term 'body uneasiness' which I feel accurately describes many tweens' (and teens') experiences.[3] This is a more comprehensive term that extends into the emotional, psychological, cognitive and behavioural components associated with a lack of body confidence. It encompasses things like social avoidance, compulsive checking and self-monitoring in the mirror, along with other associated emotions such as anxiety, worry, mistrust, embarrassment and detachment from peers.

Stay close to your tween's experience and their evolving relationship with their body. They are currently subscribing meaning to the way their body looks and functions. Unlike our adult worlds, appearance is often the most important thing on tweens' radars. Comparatively, they have far more time and energy to devote to it, so it can become all-consuming. But if it's important to them, it must be important to us. The words of Janet, mother of a 14-year-old girl, encapsulated this beautifully when she said, 'My daughter has grown over the past couple of years in lockdown to 5 feet 9 inches, and she has some stretch marks. She doesn't like her height. Appearance is such a focus, and I am prepared to support her while this is a constant part of her life. I hope it becomes less of a focus in the future, but for now I will be where she is.' By offering compassionate, sensible guardrails and accurate education, we do so much to guide their journey.

Understanding Gender Differences

Before we get started, I want to talk about the similar, yet noticeably different, experiences between boys' and girls' developing body confidence, which I feel are critical we understand. According to research from the *Journal of Eating Disorders*, which predicts symptom trajectories, a girl's body dissatisfaction increases significantly between primary school and high school, while it remains relatively stable in the transition from high school to early young adulthood.[4] In boys, an opposite pattern exists. Males experience an increase in body dissatisfaction later, particularly in their transition out of school, but most younger adolescent boys report no significant change.[5] Research also highlights that boys' social acceptance is far less dependent on body ideals during the tween years. The desire to be masculine might surface in play and in discussions about who is stronger, who could knock down who or who could take who on, but the peak of body dissatisfaction is often still ahead of them.[6]

Earlier puberty changes in girls seem to influence the timing of body dissatisfaction. Given this, I am particularly concerned that our girls are confronted with endless talk about their appearance at a very young age, when their cognitive maturity often struggles to support it. Stories like this one from Cathy are particularly worrying but not uncommon as we see girls fight against the natural growth of their bodies. She writes, 'For some time now my 10-year-old daughter has appeared somewhat uptight about moving from a size 6 uniform to a kid's size 8. Eventually, she spilled to me, telling me she couldn't possibly move up a size as her peers made a point of checking the labels of each other's uniforms to ensure they stayed in the "suitable range"! My daughter has been a size 6 since Year 1.'

The fact that girls grow away from social body ideals, while boys grow towards them, is also a reality we must be mindful of. I am reminded of this when I overhear students talking about the growth of new body hair. Boys parade their under-arms like a trophy, while girls hide new hair growth in shame and beg their parents to allow them to shave it. Boys anticipate getting bigger, while girls seem to be particularly fearful of being bigger or taller, and a combination of both is a disturbing mix for them. Combined with menstruation, a more naturally fluctuating BMI and greater fluid retention, our girls have a lot to cope with.

This is not to say tween boys don't experience body confidence challenges. In my interviews, it wasn't unusual for parents of boys to tell me that their son won't be seen in his swimmers because he has a 'roll' on his tummy. Body-defining nicknames such as bag-of-bones, chubster, whale or jumbo are often an acceptable part of boy banter, but they can cut our boys deeply. Kerry, mother of an 11-year-old, explains, 'I think body image in boys is underreported. My son is a very slim boy, and he was called fat once, and we noticed a change in his eating. We had to keep an eye on him.'

This leads me to also note that those who do not identify with their gender of birth are far more likely to struggle with body dissatisfaction and uneasiness and are at much higher risk of associated poor mental health.[7] Given that kids struggle most when they feel 'out of sync' with peers, this makes perfect sense. It's no wonder that a key message in the *Embrace Kids* film and book, championed by Taryn Brumfitt from the Body Image Movement, is the inclusion and self-acceptance of all children.[8]

Balanced Conversations

How can I convince her she is beautiful? How do I help him realise that the strand of hair growing on his toe is not the end of the world? How can I reassure her that these pimples won't be there forever? If you are a parent asking these questions, please know there is no easy way to skip the learning our kids must do to develop a healthy relationship with their body. If there was any way to 'convince them', I promise I'd let you know! I think we must accept that consistently beaming body confidence is not realistic, especially given their developmental stage and the intense changes they are experiencing. I'd like to refer you back to some of the thoughts we explored in Chapter 1, 'Almost a Teenager', and Chapter 5, 'Sturdy Self-esteem', as they underpin this chapter so beautifully.

Body confidence is characterised by personal acceptance and appreciation for how your body looks (including your shape, size, weight and gender identity) and the way it functions. It doesn't mean you like everything about yourself, but it does rely on you having more positive thoughts, feelings, attitudes and beliefs than negative ones. It's the general 'I like me' vibe, which we can model in our own lives and unpack in our daily conversations with tweens. Ideally, we would like our kids to grow in their love and appreciation of their bodies, and to avoid a lifetime of self-loathing.

Below, I'd like to offer you five balanced conversations to support your tween's developing understanding of their body. These conversations hold critical messages that have the potential to carry them through the years ahead. From my experience, body uneasiness may surface in the tween years but tends to increase in complexity as our kids grow, so these foundations will become critical for them to return to.

Conversation 1: Your Health Matters

I've been quite inspired by Craig Harper, a leading voice in the health and performance industry and the host of *The You Project*, which is a roaringly successful podcast that I love and listen to regularly.[9,10] Craig was a self-proclaimed fat kid (his words, not mine) who now uses his story to inspire people towards better health. I have noticed that he uses the word 'fat' compassionately, deliberately and with accuracy. In my interview with him, he explains, 'We like to pretend that it is not a bad thing to be fat. We know 100 per cent that there is a correlation between weight, obesity and disease. Being fat is a biological state.'

His words hit a raw nerve in our politically correct world, but he makes a challenging point. Among the important message of self-acceptance, I don't want us to shy away from the reality that there is a correlation between weight, fitness, body function and disease, and that it is our responsibility to love and nurture our bodies. I really want our kids to get this message! I too could sit and drink ice-cream sodas all day, but that wouldn't be a healthy choice.[11] I have said to my own kids, 'We can't live like we are on holidays all the time. Eventually, our health would deteriorate with the quality of our diet.'

A more important message than 'junk food makes you fat' is 'junk food isn't good for your health.' Always bring it back to health. An equally important message is that healthy people come in all shapes and sizes, which can vary greatly from person to person. Books with diverse illustrations, such as *Love Your Body* by Jessica Sanders, are a perfect, concrete starting point to help tweens understand all bodies are good bodies and that there is no ideal body shape that makes someone superior.[12] There are, however, superior ways of looking after one's body.

Conversation 2: Your Body, Your Business

Because tweens are in the process of finding their own mind, they are highly impressionable.

If someone calls your tween 'fat' in the playground (or any number of variations, such as 'gross', 'weird', 'ugly', 'smelly', 'disgusting'), it's not easy for them to subscribe accurate meaning to that. What does the word 'fat' mean to them? Fatter than who? Are they fat enough to have no friends? Are they fat enough to look ugly? Are they fat enough to be spoken to poorly or publicly humiliated?

Not all inappropriate comments are mean-spirited or designed to erode body confidence – but many are. In time, and with experience, I hope our tweens can clearly discern motive and recognise when someone is being unintentionally inappropriate or deliberately degrading. I like to remind tweens that if they are assigning too much worth to other people liking their appearance, they are looking to find their identity in something that can be taken away from them very easily. In the words of Dr Lisa Damour, 'When our kids hinge their self-esteem on something as flimsy as their appearance, they become fragile.'[13]

During my conversations with tweens, I emphasise that only a few people are qualified to comment on their body – a health professional and the few adults they deem to be trustworthy in their life. No one else gets a seat at this table! If peers try to use body shaming tactics, it can help tweens maintain perspective to push back either in real time, in their own minds or in a debrief with an adult after the event. No one should define beauty for them – no movies, no advertising and not even their friends or romantic partners.

When I speak with tweens, I emphasise the importance of pushing back against someone's right to comment about your weight, rather than pushing back against the validity of the comment itself. The critical point is that they get to decide how to look after their body, not their peers. They can also love their body even if others don't. Here are some empowering statements to help your tween push back:

- ◢ 'You look after your body. I'll look after mine.'
- ◢ 'My body is none of your business.'
- ◢ 'What do you mean by that?'
- ◢ 'That's rude!'

Conversation 3: You are More than a Body

Without thinking, we often talk to a child about how they look before we speak to them about anything else, giving them the impression that their body is the most important thing about them. Our tweens listen to the judgements we make, and they'll learn to say, 'If I am perfect enough, I might protect myself from the discomfort of judgement'. Let's commit to talking about who a child is and always refer to body function over appearance. The less we frivolously comment on how other people look, the better. This includes our comments about their peers, family friends, people online or strangers. Here are some empowering statements your tween can use:

- 'My body is working hard for me.'
- 'My beauty shines through my clothes.'
- 'I pay more attention to what the mirror can't see.'
- 'My body is the least interesting thing about me.'

As our tweens look around to find what appears beautiful to them, I hope they ultimately gravitate to internal qualities such as strength and joy. I hope they find beauty in you and every word you speak, no matter how many wrinkles are on your face or how wide your thighs are! One of the most beautiful things my boys say to me is, 'I don't know why you bother putting make-up on. You look just as good without it.' What they are seeing is not picture-perfect beauty, but who I am as a person. That means the world to me as a woman, and as a mother.

I hope tweens also experience beauty in all sorts of places. Alex Noble was paralysed from the legs down after injuring his spinal cord while training with the under-17 NSW Rugby Sevens selection squad. His powerful story was fittingly featured in the *Embrace Kids* film and showcases the mindset of a young man who embraced his body in the toughest of circumstances. He says, 'You only have one life, so you don't want to get stuck in a loop of feeling sorry for yourself about something that you don't have control over.'[14] Powerful stuff that has the potential to model body confidence for our kids.

Conversation 4: Appreciate What is Yours

Amanda Stokes is an educator and author who does a brilliant job of working with mothers and daughters to start conversations around self-acceptance, responsibility and kindness, and she encourages us all to 'appreciate what is ours'. She champions the empowering truth that one person's beauty does not overshadow another's and that true confidence is walking into a room without comparing yourself to anyone else. I want each tween to believe that they are stunning humans, yet no more or less stunning than anyone else. I'd ideally like them to believe they are valuable not compared to others but because of who they are.

The biggest lie that the beauty industry offers is that there isn't enough beauty to go around and that someone is going to miss out. That makes beauty scarce, expensive and for the elite. The result is that our tweens live with a deficit mentality, believing that there is only room at the top for a few. Then, in a few short years' time, they will be offered the magic bullet – botox, injections and surgery. Here are some disempowering statements sadly too often adopted by tweens:

- ◢ 'There are only a few people who are pretty.'
- ◢ 'I will never be pretty enough.'
- ◢ 'I won't get attention if I am not thin and beautiful.'
- ◢ 'There is only one "right" body size and shape.'
- ◢ 'I will never be happy if I don't look like someone else.'

Of all the grave concerns around technology, I am most worried about it encouraging our kids to aspire to be someone they are not rather than to invest in who they are. Their social media feeds are full of fads and filters that promote perfection. As we talked about in Chapter 8, 'The Chapter You Need to Read', the more time our tweens spend on social media, the greater the link to body dissatisfaction. Not surprisingly, an academic review of 67 studies examining the links between problematic internet use and body image concerns in adolescents supported the association between internet usage – particularly appearance-focused social media – and heightened body image and eating concerns.[15]

In speaking with our teenage girls, I know they are exhausted by unrealistic heroines – beautiful, bad-ass, independent and able to fall in love and save the planet all in an hour. Their souls are weary of newsfeeds that offer a life they are unable to actualise. The adults our tweens truly admire are those who are transparent and who have the courage to use their darkest moments and weakest areas to shine a light for others. This generation wants to talk about the courage it takes to live authentically. They are looking for people who relate to the fears that tempt them to change, limit or hide parts of themselves to please other people, to conform or to fit in.

Conversation 5: Feelings are Not Facts

When tweens allow body dissatisfaction to dominate, they stand in front of a hurdle that I want them to grow bigger than. They hold on to a limiting belief that might stop them from engaging in the life in front of them if they tune into their feelings too much – limiting, unhelpful beliefs that have hindered people for centuries and that stand between us and our potential.

To explore limiting beliefs with your tween, ask them to answer this question, filling in the blanks: If I was _____, then I would _____.

Limiting beliefs might sound like any of these statements:

- ◢ 'If I was thinner, then I would have more friends.'
- ◢ 'If I could run faster, then I would be more popular.'
- ◢ 'If I don't have muscles, then I won't get a girlfriend.'
- ◢ 'If I am not pretty, then I can't be happy.'
- ◢ 'If my tummy wasn't wobbly, then I wouldn't be embarrassed when swimming.'
- ◢ 'If I can't be beautiful, then I need to be acceptable or talented to compensate.'
- ◢ 'If I can't be attractive, then I need to work hard to be likeable in other ways.'

When a limiting belief has become unconquerable, tweens are usually stuck in a worry loop. Their worst fears play on repeat in their mind, over and over, despite our best efforts to help them move into a more positive headspace. It's important to know that tweens' worry loops are all emotion, and tweens don't have the capacity to interject with logic. In these times stress isn't extinguished but gets attached to situations way longer than it needs to. Highly effective individuals do get stressed, but they are able to switch it off very quickly. Just like finding the electricity switch, I ask stressed tweens, 'Can you find the off switch?'

I salute all the tweens and teens who are pushing back against unrealistic body ideals that surface in gross amounts of pressure, insecurity and unnecessary drama. I like to speak particularly to girls about the importance of stepping up and deliberately creating a positive body culture in their friendship groups. One conversation I had with 11-year-old Alex was priceless! She decided that there was way too much drama associated with what she and her friends were wearing to parties. It was exhausting her, so she decided to add these words to the bottom of her birthday invite – 'BYO: Kindness and your most comfortable clothes (even if they are super daggy or have holes in them).' You nailed it, Alex – go girl!

Changing Relationship with Food

I asked a family friend how her 12-year-old son was travelling, and she said, 'He's grown a bit wider. Last time we went to a restaurant he ordered a rump steak for breakfast! The time before, he ordered two main meals and then he started picking at my food! He's eating like a horse. The funniest thing is that I heard him tell his mate that if he were skinnier, he'd absolutely have abs!' Lesa, mother of a tween girl, also shares, 'OMG! Two days before she gets her periods, the mood is suffocating. I'm sure she eats a whole jar of peanut butter. It's serious comfort eating. I'm not game to stop her, because she will rip my head off!'

During puberty tweens' bodies not only look but also feel different. Many tweens (and their parents) distinctly notice both an increased appetite and weight gain, both of which can be uncomfortable, but they are normal and prepare their body for growth.[16] Just to complicate things a little more, it's typically a time when unhelpful lifestyle factors kick in, like dropping out of sport and spending more time online. Tweens rarely correlate food with fuelling their body, gaining weight or adding nutritional value, which doesn't help them make healthy, good choices. Most kids can eat a whole pack of chips or biscuits without thinking about what they are ingesting or how it will make their body feel afterwards.

This next section is going to give you some thoughts that will be particularly helpful if your tween's relationship with food is changing. The reality is that when it comes to diet, exercise and lifestyle, parents are ultimately the role models and decision-makers. There is no way to sidestep this fact. If we are eating an unhealthy diet, so are our kids. This is very challenging for busy parents who may have decided that eating well is just too hard or not their highest priority. For those who know their health needs an overhaul, here are four insights that I hope will be helpful.

Tweens need structure. What we want to try to avoid within our homes is a diet culture that drives eating disorders. While it's safe to make moderate changes in diet and exercise, irregular, extreme or unsustainable eating patterns are a recipe for disaster for our kids. I get really sad hearing about tweens who want to go on the latest green, clean health kick they have seen on TikTok. A move away from diet culture is a move towards intuitive eating, where we listen to our body's internal wisdom rather than depriving ourselves or demonising certain foods. I want our kids to get the message that their body speaks to them by sending signals to indicate what it needs. This acknowledges that our appetite is an inbuilt system that helps manage the amount of energy that goes into our bodies. Each kid's operating system is different, so we need to make room for that. However, intuitive eating falls down when we are decision-fatigued or when our willpower is depleted. Most kids will need structure around eating because they aren't able to control impulses or make intuitive links. That is why three meals a day, with healthy snacks between meals, is still a great fallback position for families. If your tween is asking to go on a diet, first ask them why and then try saying, 'There are a lot of reasons why diets don't work, so let's talk about that word first. I can definitely help you with healthy eating.'

Tweens need to enjoy food. Be intentional about your choice of language around food, especially if you have come from a home where unhealthy eating habits have dominated. Try to avoid demonising food or describing it as 'good' or 'bad'. Some families prefer to use the words 'sometimes food' and 'always food', while other families don't want to assign any restrictions in an attempt to keep food consumption shame-free. The moment we demonise food, it's even more attractive. Eating 90 per cent for the body and 10 per cent for the soul is a beautiful benchmark that Dr Jodi Richardson, co-author of the excellent book *Anxious Kids*, offers us on her podcast, *Well, Hello Anxiety*.[17,18] My personal benchmark is much closer to 70 per cent for the body and 30 per cent for the soul!

Tweens need us to comment less. Research also tells us that the less we comment on kids' eating habits, the better. The Mental Health Foundation's report on body image in the UK found that 29 per cent of young people (21 per cent of boys and 37 per cent of girls) agreed that things their family said have caused them to worry about their body image.[19] One study of adolescent girls found that over half of them had experienced weight-based teasing from family members, particularly girls who weighed more, and these experiences were related to higher levels of body dissatisfaction and unhealthy eating behaviour.[20] Try to catch yourself before using unhelpful words such as, 'Should you really be eating that?' or 'Do you need another plate of food?' Please also consider the tweens years as a particular period of time when we need to filter how we talk about our own bodies. The fact that tweens amplify and mimic us is great motivation to monitor the way we talk about our own appearance.

Tweens need us to crowd out takeaway options. If your family currently has some unhealthy eating habits, try the 'crowding' concept, which creates meal plans based on all the foods that we want to add to our diet, which by default crowds out less healthy choices. In other words – more vegetables and less takeaway, more balanced main meals and fewer snacks. Don't forget there are many food companies that offer families home-delivered healthy menus, ingredients or pre-made meals to help. If your child is always craving takeaway food or sugary snacks, try increasing their protein intake as it stabilises blood sugar. We went through heaps of protein powder and cooked plenty of chicken in our house!

Positive Association with Movement

In Madonna King's superbly articulated book *Ten-ager* she shares the research of Dr Gavin Sandercock, a professor at the University of Essex and its Centre for Sports and Exercise Science, to point to the conclusion that our tweens are missing out on the health benefits of being fit, strong and flexible.[21] This research shows that today's children are overall weaker compared to the tests conducted 16 years ago. Their raw strength (measured with a pinch grip) was down 10 to 15 per cent, and their ability to exercise in a way that takes effort was down by 45 per cent. One exercise, which required tweens to swing on monkey bars, was a complete failure as too many children were unable to complete it. They simply didn't have the strength to grip the bar or hold their weight, so the test became too dangerous to complete. Sixteen years ago, every child was able to complete the same test.

This research fascinated me! Today, the average dropout age for team sports is 12 for girls and 14 for boys.[22] Girls are 20 per cent less likely to participate in sports than boys, a worrying statistic when the link between exercise, academic performance and overall happiness is significant.[23] Time that might have once been spent visiting parks and climbing trees is often being replaced by screens and sedentary indoor activities. Understandably, these options are both convenient and easily accessible in our modern world.

I've talked a lot about movement in this book, so I won't labour the point here. To cut to the chase, it is of paramount importance that kids maintain a positive association with movement. It's this positive association that becomes a memory map for our kids to return to. Ideally, it's best if they choose what type of movement they enjoy. Sometimes kids need to move away from competitive sports to activities that are more fun and social. If they can do it with a friend, it's much easier because tweens like to travel in packs. Anything novel such as skipping, surfing, walking the dog, gymnastics, trampolining, martial arts, playing with pets, horseriding, scootering or playing with Nerf guns can help to add to their movement count.

Survey responses from 10- to 12-year-olds when asked, 'Why do you want to drop out of sport?':

- ◢ It's not fun anymore
- ◢ I'm not with my friends anymore because it's graded
- ◢ Uninterested.

When It's Not Enough

Body image issues and eating disorders are highly unique. Mum Leora expounds, 'When my daughter started putting on weight at about 12, it fundamentally changed who she was. No matter how many times we told her she was beautiful, nothing helped. She spiralled downhill quickly, and it was frightening.' My time working with teenagers at Youth Excel's psychology clinic taught me how important early intervention and prevention is. Once established, destructive thought and behaviour patterns can be persistent and difficult for young people to overcome. At the pointy end, we see long-lasting issues like eating disorders, depression, social anxiety and low self-esteem.

There is often a quickly moving line between low-level body dissatisfaction and fixed and destructive thoughts that impact mental health. You can't argue with a child who is fixated on food being the problem. You have to lovingly guide them through it. Research tells us that the majority of young people struggling with their body image also struggle with solving other problems in life.[24] I encourage you to see body image issues in context with their overall mental health. There are multiple drivers of body dissatisfaction, not just one. Even though the impact of screens is undeniable, so are their peer group's body ideals, their role models, our relationship with food and lifestyle, and their underlying mental health. Over the years I have watched how these elements can all interact at critical turning points in kids' lives, sometimes creating a crisis that is far more pervasive than people realise.

If their tween is struggling, many parents visit dietitians and specialists who focus on diet. While this has its place, one of the most underrated intervention strategies is mentorship by a personal trainer who can help them explore the function of their body – its strength, its limits and its intelligence. Tanya says, 'My girls (12 and 14) are also loving CrossFit. Youngest wasn't as sporty and competitive as older sis, then she gave it a go. She's transformed her body and seen herself improve in strength and fitness. Subsequently, she's not intimidated to participate in school sports now and has seen her judo improve.' As far as preventative strategies go, this one is my favourite.

If the tips in this chapter don't feel 'enough', please seek professional advice sooner than later. The Butterfly Foundation is an excellent starting place for supporting tweens showing signs of eating disorders or body image issues and offers a national helpline, chat or email service for parents, and referrals to professionals.[25] Other excellent organisations include endED's House of Hope and Eating Disorders Families Australia, which both offer group support for siblings and parents of those who are struggling. I'd like to close with these fitting words from the

Butterfly Foundation's website, which I think are particularly important: 'There is in fact no evidence that eating disorders can be caused by particular parenting styles. There is strong evidence that eating disorders have a genetic basis and people who have family members with an eating disorder may be at higher risk of developing an eating disorder themselves. However, although a person's genetics may predispose them to developing an eating disorder this is certainly not the fault of their family. Genetics play a role in many illnesses; both mental and physical.'[26]

Chapter 10

MENTAL HEALTH AND THE PATH LESS TRAVELLED

Key Message: Poor mental health is not an automatic doorway to self-discovery, compassion and purpose, but it can be.

My life's work has been about helping kids move forward in the face of adversity. Over the past 25 years, I have supported thousands of tweens and teens struggling with poor mental health in my role as a mentor, and then as the founder of Youth Excel, a charity that offered a variety of services including a multidisciplinary clinic where psychologists, counsellors, social workers and mentors worked together side by side. Youth Excel was a beautiful hub of hope for hundreds of families each week. From the caring intake process, right through to the well-thought-out decor, I wanted people to feel they were in safe hands. Today my greatest joy is getting messages from former clients who are now all grown up, often with a baby in tow!

To begin this chapter, I'd like to again refer to the work of Dr Lisa Damour, who challenges us to clarify what it means to be mentally healthy. She explains that one of the things we can do right now to support our kids is to get really, really clear about what mental health is and isn't. The definition that has emerged strongly over the last 10 years is that you know your kids are mentally healthy if they 'feel good'. But this has never been the way psychology has defined mental health. She goes on to explain, 'A way to better define it, which helps reassure and then direct us, is to remember that mental health is having the right feeling at the right time (a feeling that makes sense in its context) and managing that feeling in a way that brings relief and does less harm – as opposed to managing it in a way that deepens it or does more harm.'[1] I find this such an empowering message.

This definition opens the door for all of us to be mentally healthy, because it places more emphasis on how we interact with who we are. Although there is no doubt that some people struggle with their mental health more than others, I desperately want our kids to learn to love and look after themselves, no matter their neurological profile, or life experiences. I don't want them to buy into the idea that there is a happy bubble saved for a chosen few.

Firm Facts You Can Rely On

While not nice for any family to experience, poor mental health can draw out something very special in the adults that surround a child. I have seen parents, carers, grandparents and extended family fiercely commit to championing a child's unique journey. Their expression of love becomes deliberately refashioned, having been stripped of preconceived ideas and unhelpful expectations. I wish I could bottle this radical acceptance and give it to every child. Wouldn't it be incredible if all kids could get the message, 'Your struggles are not a disappointment – they only amplify my love for you.' Of course, that isn't everyone's experience. Some parents tell me that tension drove them away from their kid's side, and their capacity to give collapsed. Other parents felt they needed to hide their child's struggles from extended family for fear of being judged, which created distance between them and those whose support they needed. Again, very difficult stuff. My compassion extends to parents because it can be just as tough for you.

Whenever we feel unstable, it helps to have something immovable to hold on to. That's why in this section I'd like to condense what I know about tweens' mental health into five firm facts. They have the potential to become powerful filters for discussions and decisions about mental health in homes. I hope they can offer you both comfort and guidance as you make decisions. However, I want to add a word of caution. It's very important we don't police how any human, including our children, experiences mental health. These messages are not designed to be toxic positive statements that we project on our kids. While terms like 'superpower' and 'differences are our gift' carry a comforting ring for parents, they seldom reflect tweens' true experiences.

Firm Fact 1. I want you to deeply know that regardless of your tween's struggles they were not born for suffering. The greatest suffering will happen when our kids identify themselves as wrong, flawed or less than others. We want them to predominantly identify themselves as human, loved, accepted and a part of a familiar tribe.

Firm Fact 2. Mental health lives on a continuum that is constantly moving. Children who may struggle in one season of life can go on to experience rich and fulfilling futures. Too often we think children are set in stone when they are not. I have supported many kids who were crippled with poor mental health in their teen years but who went on to flourish later in life.

Firm Fact 3. Each of our children are highly individual, and their happiness baseline is greatly impacted by genetics. I want you to remember that what 'thriving' looks like for one child may be quite different to what it looks like for another. This makes comparisons between siblings and friends, or even people in the media, unhelpful. At the heart of what we want to communicate to this generation is that there is no shame in being who they are, and that some tweens will naturally need to invest more time in self-care than others.

Firm Fact 4. It's not your fault. While poor mental health is often generational, it's not a curse that we deliberately pass down to our kids. Most parents are very hard on themselves when their kids are struggling. They feel like they are failing when the reality is they are absolute champions. Instead of asking yourself to be perfect, aim to ease more suffering than you cause. If you can stay in that headspace, it will allow you to be a helpful part of their journey.

Firm Fact 5. Instead of focusing your efforts on changing your child's experience, focus on fostering courage. Courage is what it takes to be human in every season of life. Courage is the ability to be terrified while we keep walking. It's this willingness to move forward that is so important to nurture in tweens. Learning to love and look after ourselves is courageous work, and tweens who struggle with mental illness have to be brave in order to face puberty and the way it interacts with their brain.

Let's Talk about Biology

Puberty is a challenging time for most kids, so we can expect periods of poor mental health. Research also indicates that during the tween years we see the most rapid rise in psychological illness. Specifically, there is a rapid escalation of anxiety, depression and problematic behaviour from ages 10 to 13, and suicide has spiked to be in the top five leading causes of death in this age group.[2,3]

I'd like to draw attention to the biological component of poor mental health, and the work of Dr Lisa Mundy, who I introduced in Chapter 1, 'Almost a Teenager'. One of her areas of focus has been why poor mental health typically emerges in this age group. She explains, 'For a long time we didn't have a handle on why poor mental health was emerging in this age group. There previously wasn't any data in this age range to look at it. The CAT study gave us an opportunity to study mid-childhood to better understand these issues.'

The Child to Adult Transition (CAT) study set out to shed more light on tweens' emerging mental health challenges by measuring saliva samples of 1200 kids aged 8 to 14 and tracking them against depression and anxiety indicators. Interestingly, the study revealed that 8- to 9-year-olds with higher levels of hormones called adrenal androgens (which typically rise in children around ages 8 and 9) correlated with emerging poor mental health, including emotional and behavioural problems. They were also intriguingly linked to greater levels of body dissatisfaction.[4]

The study also found that treating mental health problems early was critical not only to tweens' wellbeing but also to their learning – which is interwoven in their feeling of competence and their self-esteem. Higher levels of emotional problems in primary school had a direct learning loss, and those students were more than two times as likely to disengage from school. In many cases, tweens with higher levels of emotional problems were about one year behind their peers in NAPLAN by the time they got to Year 7.[5,6]

The really important message is that we need to build the emotional and social skills of children in mid-primary school and intervene for those struggling, with the wisdom and help of professionals, before problems are established. When symptoms are first emerging, that is when intervention is likely to be most effective. The right environments can often be enough to strengthen tweens. Dr Lisa Mundy made a critical point in relation to this, when she said to me, 'In my mind, the final message should be around creating the right environments for children to thrive – then we only need to intervene for those that really need it.'

For some tweens, medical intervention is absolutely necessary, but it's not the quick or easy fix many perceive it to be. Diagnosis can be complex, and a crystal-clear picture is difficult to gain among the changes associated with puberty. The side effects of medications can also be really difficult for kids to live with. However, these words from Siobhan, the mother of 12-year-old Ellie, may offer some hope to those who desperately need answers. She explains, 'We had a really tough two or three years with anxiety, which showed up as school refusal. We did everything we could – changed schools and then COVID happened. Once she started on medication, she blossomed. Without the overwhelming weight of anxiety, it allowed my child to move into who she was. That is one of those times when "I knew" and I am really pleased that we kept searching and pushing through with what she needed.'

Perfectionism as a Risk Factor

Tom Nehmy, author of *Apples for the Mind* and founder of the Healthy Minds Program, based on his four-year research program at Flinders University, reveals perfectionism as a broad risk factor for psychological distress.[7] I wanted to briefly touch on this topic because I often see perfectionist tendencies celebrated in late primary school. We wrap them up in a bow and call them 'caring about their work' or 'trying hard'. Unfortunately, we often celebrate these tendencies, which can do great damage to our tween's wellbeing. Tom suggests that the antidote to perfectionism is to teach kids to be less concerned about making mistakes and more focused on self-compassion for their shortcomings. When tweens view difficulties as an opportunity to learn, and apply balanced, helpful and realistic thinking, problems become less insurmountable.[8]

The Impact of Trauma

Trauma can come in all shapes and sizes. In scientific and clinical practice, what trauma is and how it impacts us is finally being redefined, giving people everywhere validation and access to needed information about how our brains and bodies function. We all, in some way, have experienced things that rattled our sense of self and safety. I don't think anyone gets out of it, no matter how picture perfect their social media feed is. From bullying at school, to bitter family separations, unexpected accidents or abuse, the dark and disappointing side of life tends to reach us all at some stage.

To help me explore this important topic, I'd like to share part of my story that is heavier going. You may wish to go to the next section in this chapter, 'My Greatest Takeaways', on page 201, if you feel it won't be helpful or if you are sensitive to discussions about sexual abuse. For those who continue to read, I hope it adds value and perspective.

My tween years were some of the most difficult and lonely I have ever experienced, and perhaps that is why I am so passionate about connection with kids at this stage of life. On the outside, you would have described me as a happy, thriving and talented child who was surrounded by a loving family. On the inside, life didn't feel quite that simple.

Like so many others, I experienced an incident of sexual abuse at about 8 years old that became pivotal in how I saw the world. It was during the Christmas holidays. The perpetrator was a senior man who lived locally. In retrospect, it was a pretty horrific experience, but I'm not sure you have the ability to gauge that as a child, so you look to others to help make sense of the senseless.

Sadly, the events following the incident became messy and complicated for me. I will choose to spare you the details, except to say that the news of the incident never reached my parents' ears as I believed it had. Despite me having told numerous adults, this man retained his position as a trustworthy part of our local community. We waved to him each morning on the way to school. I spent extended time alone at his house, and he and my father would regularly see each other and have a chat.

Because my assumption was that my parents were aware of this incident, so much that followed didn't make sense to me.

My heart knew that my parents loved me, but my head couldn't reconcile the inconsistency between that love and my perceived neglect. I wondered why no one spoke to me further about the incident, why no one stopped me from returning to his house and why the hell he wasn't held accountable when I couldn't even get away with not doing my homework or making my bed in the morning.

Like all traumatic events, the incident is only a small part of the suffering. It was the story we wove, to make sense of the senseless, that carried long-lasting weight. In the absence of a safe place to process pain, we fill in the gaps with some pretty awful stories about ourselves and others. This statement by Gabor Maté, a world-renowned expert on trauma and mental health challenges, rings true to me: 'Children don't get traumatised because they get hurt, they get traumatised because they're alone with the hurt.'[9] His book *Hold On to Your Kids*, co-authored with Dr Gordon Neufeld, is a recommended read for any parent wanting to stay connected to their kids through challenging times.[10]

For me, the only conclusion I could come up with was that the adults in my world couldn't or wouldn't acknowledge my experience and they were perhaps not the all-knowing, capable people I had believed them to be. In my eyes, they were incompetent – at best – and I was angry and overwhelmed. This obviously affected so much in my life, including my behaviour. I'm quite saddened to think of the choices I made during this time, which were just as ugly as the story I was telling myself. During my angriest moments, I was the 10-year-old who was wagging school, lying, smoking cigarettes and stealing. It certainly didn't set me up well for adolescence.

A lifetime of work goes into rewriting childhood stories. Mine is a lot more balanced and life-giving these days, but

I have also come to appreciate that the original story was there to protect and provide my brain with certainty and safety. Brené Brown, in her book *Rising Strong*, refers to the work of Robert Burton, a neurologist and novelist, who gives us further insight when he says, 'Stories are patterns. The brain recognises the beginning, middle and end of a story and rewards us for clearing up the ambiguity. Unfortunately, we don't need them to be accurate, just certain.'[11] That's incredibly important to note – certainty over accuracy. Karen Young, who I introduced in the chapter 'Almost a Teenager', explains it like this by saying, 'The feelings are real, but the story often isn't.' I love this distinction.

Children often make meaning with mistruths, half-truths or the only truth they have access to or the ability to understand at the time. You will notice that all tweens quickly move towards some harsh, black-and-white, overly simplistic stories when they are unsure. They might use extreme words such as 'you hate me' when 'I don't feel understood' would be more helpful. Remember, imagination has a talent for unhelpfully filling in the gaps, so the more gapless our conversations are, the better. If you are going through any type of traumatic event as a family, make the story age-appropriately crystal clear with love at its centre. It's the secret stories that go unchecked that are most likely to drive our tweens to unhealthy places.

Our kids' lives are a narrative unfolding and evolving over time. Their life's work will be to bring meaning to experiences and to continue to stitch together that meaning until it unites with present circumstances and future goals. Eventually, they will thread together a tapestry that makes sense to them. The beautiful thing about tweens is that they are fluid, mouldable and open. Their developing brains makes intervention effective, and thankfully every action we take imprints on them.

The good news is that trauma does not have to be permanently hardwired.

As an adult who has had a lifetime of reflection, I can see that life's challenges have the potential to be a springboard for our kids to connect with their voice and find meaning beyond themselves. Over time, I believe it is possible for them to write a story that is so deep, personal and profound that it shapes their offering to the world. This kind of story takes time to write. It can't be rushed. It needs space to grow with them. It's this story that qualifies people to help each other in their difficult moments. Although trauma is never good, it is how we adapt to it that can bring good into the world.

My Greatest Takeaways

Below I've listed 7 takeaways that I'd like to highlight:

Watch for small changes. In my survey, tweens themselves sent a clear message that their parents were 'missing stuff', which you can read about more in Chapter 16, 'Five Messages from Your Tween'. I found this message so interesting given my personal life experience. The rapid pace of our kids' development, and their expanding experience of the world, makes this a highly vulnerable time. While no loving parent would want to be absent during a time of need, it's easy to dismiss kids' small bids for attention. We don't always correlate subtle changes in behaviour with significant struggles, but they can be linked.

Stay curious about your tween. When tweens reach a tipping point and they behave poorly, parents all have a biased fallback position. What is yours? You might say things like, 'Oh, it's just hormones' or 'She's friends with the wrong crowd.' Both usually come from an assumptive rather than a curious place. While these statements may carry some truth, please be open-minded enough to realise that in blaming one thing we are more likely to miss the bigger picture. Also, realise that your tween's language and self-awareness may not be developed enough to give you quick answers or insights when you probe. If your gut tells you there is more to the story, it might take multiple conversations to get to the bottom of things.

Respond to extreme language. When tweens are unsure how to articulate big feelings, they may opt for broad statements such as 'I'm suicidal,' 'I want to kill myself,' 'I'm depressed' or 'I hate myself.' Parents often understandably wonder if their tween really 'means' or 'believes' those statements, or if they even comprehend the significance of them. We might be tempted to avoid further discussion so as not to exacerbate their already big emotions. I'd like to encourage you to lean in rather than away. In many instances, an appointment with a mental health professional may be the best safe, neutral space for them to unpack their feelings, gain support and, for some, find more helpful language to express their thoughts.

Don't beat yourself up. My parents only discovered what had happened when I was about 30 years old, when a counsellor suggested I bring some of my questions directly to them. It was a bit of a shock for all of us to say the least! I have worked with many, many families who have been confronted by a similar situation and wondered, *How could I have not known they were looking at pornography every night? How could I have not realised they didn't want to go to school because they were being physically assaulted? How could I have not seen the signs of sexual abuse?*

There isn't always a clear answer, which in itself is difficult to accept. What I have come to understand is that we often don't see what we aren't looking for, and what matters more than how you missed it, is what you do about it once you know.

Keep educating your kids. In my day, sexual abuse wasn't talked about, and protective behaviours weren't a part of education priorities. I can't remember there being a school counsellor or designated safe place to turn to when I was a child, but I feel this would have made a huge difference in my life. If you are a wellbeing teacher or a counsellor working in schools, your presence is so needed. Giving tweens the language and a pathway to talk about trauma is lifesaving. One confronting, but memorable, email I received last year shows the power of education. It was from a grateful mother whose daughter had returned home after my cyber safety presentation to explain an incident of sexual abuse. 'Mum, pornography has happened to me,' is how the conversation started. I was once again reminded that the right words, spoken in the right way, give children the confidence to communicate with trusted adults. Their limited vocabulary grows with every conversation they have. Our words open the door to theirs.

Look beyond the trauma. When tweens coast, we coast with them. When they don't, we take a detour to the path less travelled. Poor mental health can be a lonely road for families, but the hidden blessing is that we get a chance to learn, grow and discover things that the crowds may not. It's in the backstreets that we see the world for the way it really is, rather than the way we want it to be. I don't for one moment say this lightly or suggest that any of these discoveries are made without intense work and dedication. Poor mental health is not an automatic doorway to self-discovery, compassion and purpose, but it can be.

Stay resolutely defiant. When I meet a tween who is struggling, I experience compassion and defiance in equal measures. Compassion for the overwhelming pain they are experiencing and defiance against the idea that that discomfort will rob them of an ounce of their potential. Every child deserves a trusted adult who is defiant on their behalf. When I ask young people about their darkest days and what made the *most* difference, the answer is usually the same – adults who were willing to step up and speak up.[12] Most adults know of at least one person who needs to feel noticed, heard, protected and safe. How we respond to those people could make all the difference.

Tweens and Self-harm

Self-harm is a deeply disturbing but increasingly common phenomenon, which I expand on extensively in my book *Self-harm: Why teens do it and what parents can do to help*.[13] I know so many parents of tweens find themselves baffled by this behaviour, commonly asking these two questions: 'Why on earth would my child want to self-harm?' and 'Where are they getting this from?'

Research indicates the onset of puberty as a time when young people often experiment with self-harm. Interestingly, a survey showed that the onset of self-harm was related to pubertal phase rather than a particular age.[14] The association between self-harm and puberty has been associated with a particular neurodevelopmental vulnerability during this time, which comes with increased risk of emotional instability. It has been suggested that the onset of self-harm is often later in boys than in girls because of the later onset of puberty.[15]

Also worth noting is that research places puberty in perspective with other elements that affect a young person's susceptibility to self-harm.[16] It explores the impact of genetic and biological factors, psychiatric disorders, personality factors (such as impulsivity, perfectionism and low optimism), exposure to suicide or self-harm in others, the availability of self-harm opportunities, and negative life events or social problems. While self-harm is not a mental illness, research clearly makes the connection. Puberty is also a time when parents are often sitting on the edge of assessment and diagnosis. It's tough.

If you find your tween self-harming or unable to regulate emotions despite your support and education, I hope you find these two contributions from parents comforting. Both highlight the importance of accessing the right support, not only for the tween, but also for parents or guardians who are on the journey with their child.

Tasmin writes me this: 'I would like to reach out as the mum of a 9-year-old who self-harms and has been doing so for many years. We are on an amazing journey with our human. While it is never easy to see or hear, I have had some amazing help and have grown so much as a parent. These instances have become less and less frequent, and we are blessed he is starting to learn his triggers and that harm is about a feeling and no matter how big it is, it goes away. I am certain we will face more challenges in the teen years, but I live in hope that we are helping him build a foundation that will help him through those years.'

Sarah offers this: 'Our Matilda is 12 years old. The first time she self-harmed, she was in the bathroom when she was supposed to be in bed. When I came in, my head and heart were exploding. On the outside I was trying to be calm saying, "Hey, mate. What's going on?" I put my arm around her, slowly took the scissors and gave her a hug. She said, "The pain in my arm takes away from the pain in my head." As far as I know she is not harming anymore. She is still struggling. Lots of things are going on – my partner and I got divorced, her school friends left to go to high school. This year she is definitely struggling socially. She is drifting from one group to another. My advice is to reach out for help, for you and your child – to the school or health care professionals. Reach out because that's what I've found to be the most stabilising for me so I can support her. My dear friend spends time with her too. That's so helpful for me as a single mum who works part time. She really needs that one-on-one connection. It definitely takes a tribe.'

While You are Waiting

I'd like to open this section by sharing these wise words from Bindi, mum of 9-year-old Alex. She says, 'I found that when my daughter was struggling, she would say, "I don't want to see anyone else. I just want you, and your help." I had to admit to her that I wasn't an expert on the brain or some of the challenges she was having. Someone who works with these kinds of things every day was the right person to offer her support.' Knowing when to get professional support can be really difficult for parents and tweens, and being actively involved in the process is essential.

Our private and public health systems are currently under-funded and understaffed, and those in rural and remote areas have limited options and very long waitlists. If you are currently waiting for an appointment with a mental health professional, a temporary 'while you wait' plan is essential to get you through. Be reassured that the little things you implement can make the world of difference. They set a solid base for a medical professional to build on. Just like a house, any additional support will be more effective if the foundation is sturdy.

Here are some other practical things you may like to consider:

- ◢ Lower your expectations and prioritise only what is most important without any guilt. While it might include a financial cost, it may be necessary to review everyone's schedules to make time for this season in your lives.

- ◢ If possible, try and recruit the support of extended family and friends. They may be able to offer respite in the form of sleepovers or outings. One day's break, every fortnight, can make the world of difference for everyone! But please brief them thoroughly first, so they are able to offer the sensitivity required. I believe we are at our strongest when mental health professionals, community programs and trusted adults work together. We can all, in any small way, create impactive environments where kids feel encompassed by safety and our love.

- ◢ Deliberately and regularly plan small things to look forward to – and try to engage your tween in the planning process. This can really help get them through each day, week or school term.

- ◢ Routines are powerful, so don't be tempted to drop them, even if they are met with more resistance. Preset mealtimes, bedtimes and wake-up routines all take the pressure off tweens having to make quality decisions themselves. They also provide an anchor of predictability in their unstable world.

▲ Encourage them to learn a new skill or explore an interest outside of the home. The additional benefit of this is that they may find mentors – lighthouses for their lives. Mentors may be able to say with ease what you might be unable to. Also, recognise that what makes mentors special is that tweens choose them because they believe they can add value to their world.

▲ When tweens are struggling, the temptation is to reduce their responsibility. However, it is critical that they feel needed and noticed within our homes. Consider building a small garden they can look after, or giving them a manageable, fun responsibility such as making snacks for school lunchboxes each week.

▲ Monitor online time carefully, knowing they are in a vulnerable place and may be easily enticed into risky behaviour.

▲ Play is therapy in and of itself. Create space for uninterrupted, agenda-less, non-adult-directed time. Fishing, surfing, painting, reading, knitting or tinkering on cars, among many other things, enables kids to reconnect with their souls. I recall Maggie Dent saying that she once got a pile of soil delivered to her backyard for her boys to 'play' with, which I thought was an interesting, out-of-the-box idea that I'm not sure how well I would have coped with. Imagine the things that tween boys could do with a whole pile of soil!

◢ Consider adding a pet to your family if you don't have one. Pets are loving, consistent company for kids and they are a responsibility that emphasises, 'You add value.'

◢ Create a coping kit that tweens can only access after a tough day. A coping kit might be a simple box full of things that distract them and soothe their soul. I recently built a coping kit with a tween girl, and it was filled with colouring-in books, sensory toys, journals, fluffy socks and the names of helpful adults who love her. The best thing about coping kits is that they can be tailor-made by the child, for the child.

◢ If you are having trouble getting your tween to agree to an appointment with a mental health professional, refer to this free blog post on my website for suggestions: 'How to Talk to a Teen about Counselling: Ideas that could make all the difference'. [17] This is my most popular blog post, so know there are many other families who find connecting their tween with professional support tricky.

Please don't forget the power of a good local GP, counsellor or social worker, because psychologists are not your only option; and if you are concerned about your child's behaviour or safety, don't hesitate to use the free services on offer including national helplines and your local hospital. That's why we pay taxes!

Tough Seasons

Of parents surveyed, the four most common concerns raised about mental health were:

- ◢ Intergenerational transmission of mental health
- ◢ Anxiety around specific events, especially starting in high school
- ◢ Risk-taking such as self-harm associated with poor mental health
- ◢ The impact of COVID-19.

The world our kids have been living in has been bumpy to say the least. They have experienced a global pandemic of historic proportions and have been challenged to adjust and recreate ways of coping. Some have faced other layers of complexity, such as family separation, economic hardship and natural disasters that have sent their parents into a zone of emotional despair or instability and brought considerable changes into a tween's world.

I'd like to share these words from Marina Passalaris, who we met in Chapter 5, 'Sturdy Self-esteem': 'We are starting to notice children coming to our programs and being in tears about their dad losing their job or saying we are in the middle of World War III. They overhear parts of the conversation and interpret it through their limited life experiences and skills. I think they are much more worried than the teenagers because they are less self-centred, and our little ones do not have the same language.'[18] To me, this again highlights the need to consider development and to make sure we offer tweens mental health messages and recommendations that take into consideration their development and that relate directly to their needs.

Australia's national Kids Helpline has become a critical part of our mental health system and a safe go-to place for so many tweens.[19] It was many children's first point of contact with the mental health system after the Black Summer, one of the worst bushfire seasons in Australia's history, and during the uncertainty of the COVID-19 global pandemic. According to Kids Helpline's 2020 report, there was one response every 90 seconds, with 17 per cent of calls coming from kids aged 5 to 12.[20] First-time callers were up approximately 38 per cent. The top four concerns of those aged between 5 and 12 were emotional wellbeing (31 per cent), family relationship issues (28 per cent), mental health concerns (15 per cent) and friendship or peer relationships (14 per cent). Notably, there was a 52 per cent increase in website use, with 21 per cent coming from kids aged 5 to 12.

According to Headspace, it's our tween girls who have statistically suffered the most during COVID-19 lockdowns.[21] Penny, mother of 11-year-old Alex, explains her family's experience with COVID-19, saying, 'We had huge anxiety and no way to discharge it. All the usual avenues that we used were not accessible.' Sandy, mother of 10-year-old Sam, also shares, 'COVID-19 was a thief of joy. All the usual highlights of the tween age were halted – no birthday parties, no school holiday sleepovers, no visiting family friends, no trips to indoor venues, less independence to catch up for a swim, or a ride to buy hot chips at the local shops, or to join a spontaneous front-yard cricket game with neighbourhood friends. What was common before became rare. I think it significantly impacted their feeling of connectedness to all but their own household.'

In my work in schools, teachers are constantly talking about post-COVID-19 friendship challenges that have not settled.[22]

Anxiety is the buzzword, and I am seeing very specific worries in tweens, many of which have been birthed out of the endless talk about death, illness and loss. Kids have a heightened fear of leaving the house, separating from parents, getting sick, germs and the death of a family member or a pet. It's been a lot, and I don't want our kids to get lost in that lot. Sally Williams, a school counsellor in three primary schools and founder of the Kind Mind Project says, 'Post-Sydney lockdown, it's been busy. Struggles are mainly surfacing as anxiety, although I don't particularly like the use of that word. It's become a bit like the word "bullying", everyone is using it – teachers, parents, kids. I get it on referrals. As a psychologist, unless it is diagnosed, the better words would be worried and concerned . . . and most of these worries and concerns are legitimate given what we have just been through.'[23]

One of the greatest gifts we can give our kids is enabling them to make sense of their story without feeling the need to unnecessarily pathologise it. While medical intervention may be necessary for some, if mild symptoms of poor mental health arise, a life coach, mentor or youth counsellor might be a great starting point.

Between 2018 and 2020, before COVID-19 hit, psychological distress in children was already on the rise with an increase from 20 per cent to 25 per cent.[24] Research regarding post-pandemic effects are just starting to emerge, and they are strongly indicating that our tweens are a vulnerable population that need our focused intervention. Social isolation, cancellation of milestone events, family pressures, increased screen time and lack of physical activity have hit our tweens hard. We must realise that the day-to-day impact on them is more significant because of their age and developmental needs. The brilliantly articulated research paper 'Tweens are not teens: the problem of amalgamating broad age groups when making pandemic recommendations' states, 'As we continue to manage and recover from this crisis, we need to consider tweens as a unique population differentially impacted by the choices we make and the strategies we use today. What we do now will have long-lasting impacts on the lifelong trajectories of these youth.'[25]

Chapter 11
THE ROAD TO INDEPENDENCE

Key Message: If our tweens don't feel safe and secure, their hearts won't stay open to our guidance.

For 10 whole years, our son wanted a goodnight tuck (and lengthy chat) before he went to bed each night. It was an essential, non-negotiable part of our evenings. At the time, it felt like it took *forever* to get through that nightly ritual, but no matter how tired my husband or I felt, we would diligently follow through. Then one day I heard a conversation between my husband and our son that stopped me in my tracks. 'Need a goodnight tuck?' my husband asked. 'No, I'm all good dad,' my son replied. Without the slightest pause, my husband responded, 'I'll be in soon.' Who would have thought that we would be fighting to keep the routine alive?

When tweens begin to struggle for independence, they ask the question, 'Who am I without my parents?' Doesn't that question sound preposterous? It's totally out of sync with their current reality because without us they wouldn't even remember to pack their lunch box! However, think of it like this – because it is such a big question, they need to wrestle with it for many, many years before they can sit comfortably with the answer. If your tween begins to casually chat about moving out of home, dating or getting their first job, know that they are beginning to entertain the idea of growing into their own person.

I remember a cute conversation I had with my youngest son when he was about 10 years old. He asked me if he could eat whatever he wanted for dinner when he was an adult. I explained that yes, he would make all those decisions himself. 'Good,' he answered. 'I'll be eating Tim Tams and ice cream every night!'

In my survey I asked parents to tell me how they anticipated their relationship with their tween would change as they grew. As you can see in the comments below, many anticipated their child would display an increased desire for independence and control over the choices they made. I imagine many of the comments below were actually parents' recollections of their own adolescent journey. Our own struggle for independence is something that we, or our own parents, rarely forget!

> **Survey responses from parents when asked, 'How do you expect your relationship with your tween to change as they become a teenager?':**
>
> ◢ I expect he will distance himself from me in adolescence
>
> ◢ Become more independent and not talking to me as much
>
> ◢ Hormones, her fighting hard for things as a teen

- ◢ More resistance to parent guidance and less communication
- ◢ I'll expect he'll look for more independence – he already is!
- ◢ Disconnecting
- ◢ He will become more independent and self-reliant
- ◢ There are going to be times when she hates us as parents as we may say 'no' to something she would like to do
- ◢ Not to be as close. Him pulling away and not listening
- ◢ Having a stronger opinion. Possibly yelling at me like I did my mum.

Developmental psychology indicates that there are two key stages where children are most likely to struggle for independence – toddlerhood and the teenage years. During the tween years, your kids are only just beginning to scratch the surface of this. Most kids won't feel confident in their decision-making skills until the late teen years. Up until then you might notice they push against your ideas while simultaneously needing your help to process their own mind and thinking. This in itself is confusing for parents! What they are in search of is the skill to determine their own thoughts, feelings and behaviour, so they can grow into adults who don't feel the need to be controlled by other people or external forces.[1]

To be able to differentiate themselves from you, they must begin to see you as humans with faults. You don't have to help this process along – trust me, it will happen all by itself. As they move towards the teenage years, they will begin to question your values, and they'll want to develop independent attitudes and beliefs rather than simply accepting yours. They are likely to begin to push boundaries and show a strong preference for their own choice in clothing, music, or even political and social beliefs. Normal, normal stuff.

It Might Start with the Socks

When tweens begin to seek independence, it usually surfaces in the smallest of issues, at the oddest times, but parents notice it like they notice their child's first pimple. Kane, dad of 9-year-old Jack, tells a gorgeous story, saying, 'It's my job to do the boys' hair in the morning. I had combed Jack's hair neatly back as usual, but he immediately went into the bathroom and pulled it down over his forehead. I said, "What are you doing, mate?" and he goes, "No offence, Dad, but it's *my* hair."'

In my home, it began with the socks, before it cascaded into every nook and cranny of our lives. I distinctly remember the day my husband and 12-year-old son had their first big show-down. It started with my husband asking my son to pick up his socks, which my son had dumped on the floor, yet again. My son responded, 'I'll pick them up when I want to pick them up.' Needless to say, things went from one to 100 (plus) very quickly. The Mitchell house turned into a volcano of emotion with voices raised and frustrations in full flight. My son couldn't understand why he couldn't make his own decisions, and my husband couldn't understand why his simple request wasn't being respected. My son stormed off to his room and my husband to the TV room. I heard two doors slam simultaneously. The socks still lay on the floor, looking at me. So, I picked up the damn socks!

What I witnessed that day was something I had never seen before. My son who had just turned 12 decided to stand up to his dad as a young man who was backing his own ideas and beliefs about the critical things in life – *socks*! He was almost 6 feet tall at the time. He wore size 12 men's shoes. His voice was starting to deepen. He was exercising his right to be his own person, with his own ideas and opinions, and to decide when he wanted to pick up his own socks (in the house we paid for of course).

As our kids grow, they have moments where they cry out (really loudly) over the weirdest things. It usually has nothing to do with the issue at hand, and it's all about being seen and heard. The first thing we have to acknowledge is that they have a voice, regardless of how immature we feel that voice is. They are starting to see themselves as leaders of their own destiny, and that is a great thing. As parents, we have the great opportunity to coach their voices to maturity, and to lead by example.

If I wanted to raise kids who were strong enough to embrace their struggles and courageous enough to express themselves, I had to be prepared to hear my son's 'man's voice', which said, 'This is who I am, right now, in all my mistakes and immaturity. Hear me and my voice.' PS: Hearing their man's voice doesn't mean you have to pick up their socks, but that day I chose to. There may be times when you choose to do the same. This doesn't mean you are allowing them to get away with poor behaviour. It simply means you are extending a little graciousness their way – trust me, they notice your wise choice of battles.

I distinctly remember when my son puffed out his chest in defiance, I would say quietly to myself, 'I can hear his man's voice. It's coming around the corner. It's a little rusty around the edges. It needs a little work. It will take some time to mature, but there it is – his man's voice.' It gave me a way to reframe things before I responded, and I think it also helped me accept that he was growing up! Without this deliberate acknowledgement, you may unknowingly push against it, punish it, refuse to accept it, or be hurt by it – all of which puts further strain on a child who developmentally needs to emerge as their own person.

If you notice the door slam just a little harder than usual, make a mental note. If your tween adds an exclamation mark that wasn't previously needed, you know things are on the turn. You might notice a little more sass, moodiness or turn of the heel stomp-offs when they don't get another bowl of ice cream or their preferred car seat. They may begin to push away when they usually would want to be close. The parents I spoke to particularly noted that their child began to ask, 'What are you wearing tomorrow?' as if to check the suitability of their parents' clothes for the morning school drop-off. One mum told me that she had asked her son if he wanted her to be a helper at a school camp, to which he said, 'No way, Mum!' The good news is, when we hear their 'voice' we know they are developmentally right on track.

In my interviews with parents, I heard so many relatable stories, especially from parents whose kids were almost teen-agers. Kids who were in Year 7, or who had recently made the transition, definitely were bringing more friction to the home! I've chosen four to share with you below as a reminder that you don't face these issues alone.

Family outings. Shannon, mum to 12-year-old Josh, explains how he has become fussier about family outings, which is very common for older tweens. She says, 'He wants to interrogate me before every outing, whereas before he was so compliant. He wants to know who is going, how long are we going to be there for and what we are doing when we get there. I can tell he has other more important things on his mind, like gaming. He is weighing everything up, to make sure the cards are stacked in his favour. We had to start to give him some choice, realising not everywhere we went was essential for him.'

School holiday activities. Natalie, mum to four kids ranging from 6 to 13 years old, explains how planning school holiday outings became tricker. She says, 'Things we once used to do, and had such value doing together, were met with negativity, which took the fun out of our family activities. So, I decided to change tack. I allowed each of our kids to choose a part of the day they wanted to have ownership over. I wanted them to be involved and to participate rather than just have to endure it. Once they had ownership, they started to get excited. One wanted ownership over lunchtime and where they ate. The other wanted ownership after the afternoon session and where they swam. This helped get that childlike excitement back again.'

Bedtimes. Anne-Marie, mum to a 12-year-old, spoke to me about sleep and bedtime, and the thoughtful approach she is taking with it. She says, 'There is no such thing as a simple negotiation with a 12-year-old! If his bedtime is later than his brothers and sisters, but they stay up later than their usual bedtime, he wants the same amount of extra time on top of his normal bedtime. They don't think grey, they think black and white, which doesn't allow for a lot of flexibility when we negotiate with him. When everyone is tired, that's when it is hard. I have to really ask myself, what is driving the emotional response from him and from me? At the end of the day, my son wants to be seen as older and to be seen as having privileges. He wants to be heard.'

Bike helmets and phones. Kylie, mum to another wonderfully strong-minded 12-year-old, talked about the very specific things her son is starting to dig his heels in about, and the importance of her picking her battles. She explains, 'In the past, my son has been happy to go with the flow. He has just started to become argumentative about particular things and he has to be right. He has found a chin-up bar that is a 5- to 10-minute bike ride from here, but he refuses to wear a helmet, so we have said no. We are quite relaxed with a lot of stuff, but the two things we are firm on – no phone in the room at night, and you must wear your helmet. He insists that he's a good enough cyclist and doesn't need a helmet.'

Kicking the Can Down the Road

Almost all parents are stricter with their eldest child. We are wrestling with the fear of the unknown. Karen, mum to first-born Olivia, who is 12 years old, explains, 'I don't see all the other mums worrying. They are like, here is your phone, no problem. You want to go hang out at the shops for five hours, sure! Every now and then it gets in my head. Am I being too controlling? If she falls into a bad group, do I need to let go and let her work it out? But I have this constant thing of wanting her to be with friends who bring the best out in her.'

Your child might be asking to do things that they haven't previously asked to do. The first sleepover at the house of someone you don't know very well. The first invitation to a party that doesn't come from the parents. The first real 'interest' in a girl or boy. The first social media account. The first time they catch public transport alone. The first movie or shopping centre trip with friends. Firsts aren't necessarily dangerous, but they are new. As parents, we need to realise that our own brains find it hard to distinguish between the dangerous and new because they can produce the same overwhelming feelings within us.

Increased freedom is necessary as our kids grow, but I encourage you to let the rope out slowly. You can dip your toe in the water and get used to the temperature. What might feel freezing cold at first may become quickly tolerable with some exposure to it. My advice is to test and measure, and then test and measure some more. With every new freedom comes responsibility, accountability and feedback. Letting go is often harder for us than them, and the journey can be less difficult if we practise letting go in safe and small ways.

Most will grapple with what is too strict and what is reasonable at some point. At what point do we take our cues from other parents, and when do we follow our gut instinct? Know that being on the stricter or more lenient side doesn't make you a good or bad parent. Neither of these options assures you that your tween or teen will always make safe choices or stay away from risk-taking behaviour. Isn't that an important thought? If you are unsure of when to step in, ask yourself, 'Is my child experiencing a safe struggle or an unsafe struggle?'

Please remember that your fears are not meant to captain the ship – *you are*. When we lead with fear, it is possible to restrict our tweens *too much* and delay their development in an unhelpful way. This can lead to their development becoming condensed, unfolding unusually quickly or in overlapping succession at a later stage. Understand too that the opposite can happen – if our kids' experiences are earlier and faster than they are developmentally ready for, they can become equally unstuck. One of the greatest things we can do for our tweens is allow them to develop at their own pace, without the external pressure to be beyond or behind where they are at.

It's easy to 'kick the can down the road' a little too often and ignore the struggle for independence. But it needs a healthy outlet! Whenever possible, take the initiative to give freedoms, with age-appropriate accountability attached, before your tween takes it without your consent. This way you can stay on the front foot of things that have the potential to be harmful if tweens go underground with them. As they begin to move, we must start moving with them, which often means we need to revisit our job description, and theirs. In many ways, we become more a consultant than a manager. Consultants ask questions and are on stand-by for much-needed expertise, but they don't make decisions about the day-to-day running of the business.

Check that you are giving your tween plenty of age-appropriate, low stakes opportunities to manage their life, which may include choosing:

- what they wear
- their style of haircut
- what they eat for lunch
- what they do during a family outing
- what time they do their homework (morning or night)
- when chores are done or in what order
- what they do to relax
- which movies the family watches
- what the 'morning song' will be
- who they invite to their birthday party
- which extracurricular activities they participate in
- what they eat for breakfast
- whether they wish to hug extended family members
- whether they wish to talk to a teacher about a problematic issue or not
- how they want to decorate their room
- when they go to bed on the weekend
- which books they want to read
- how tidy or messy their room is

- ◢ how they organise their school things
- ◢ how they organise their clothes.

When It is Not about the Socks

Hi Michelle,

I need your help! My daughter has been caught by my eldest daughter's friend selling vapes at school. I am extremely unsettled by this and don't know what to do apart from talking to her and hoping it goes well. She's only 12 years old and in Year 7. I have caught her lying and being disobedient in other situations lately as well. Is this the sign of worse to come? Or trying to fit in? I am completely lost. Please help, any advice would be welcome.

Thank you,

Johanna

If every conflict was about a low-stakes issue, such as picking up the socks, we'd get through it okay. However, it becomes a bit trickier when our tweens want to make decisions about things that don't align with our family values or things that might jeopardise their safety. Bec, mother of Josh, who is 11 years old, explains, 'It's relentless. They have their eyes set on things that are way beyond their maturity, or things that other kids are allowed to do and you aren't comfortable with. It's even hard to explain to them why some of these things are so dangerous because they just aren't old enough to understand.'

To me, the naive, trusting nature of tweens means they can be even more 'at-risk' than our teens. I could share endless examples of this, but I will always remember the day a 12-year-old girl who was gifted at sport and embedded in a loving family (just so you can ditch the stereotype) visited me at the Youth Excel Centre after sending a nude to an older boy she liked at his request. Because she had no clue of the risks, or even what the motive behind the idea was, she sent a full-frontal image of herself, naked, showing her face. The story gets more tween-ish! She used her mother's phone. Yep, *her mother's phone*. Of course, she deleted the message promptly afterwards but forgot that the boy might text her back on that number! It was incredibly difficult to see her, and her parents, deal with the social, emotional and legal consequences that unravelled.

This is the difference between tweens and teens. I want to strongly emphasise that our tweens are *not* the new teenagers, nor are they some type of mini-teenager, despite the issues that they are confronted with. In the words of Claire Eaton, a youth coach I interviewed who predominantly works with teenagers, 'Our tweens and teens need to be respected and catered for individually. They are in completely different developmental stages, so we need to take the grey out of it.'

In my experience, a 16-year-old girl would be far more likely to send an explicit pic without her face centre stage. I certainly don't think she'd use her mother's phone (do you?), and I guarantee she'd be more prepared to pivot if things didn't go to plan, and she'd be much better at lying! While I'm not for a moment suggesting that this is a good choice for either age group, I feel deeply for tweens who make significant errors in judgement and who have little skill to navigate the damage incurred. I feel even more deeply for those who do not have the loving arms of parents to fall into.

Primary school teachers and principals highlight how difficult it is for parents to stay one step ahead of kids who want to charge ahead into an adolescent world. They also plead for parents to try not to minimise incidents. An inspirational deputy principal in my local area, who is on the front line of reporting self-harm, vaping or sexting incidents to parents of tweens, offered this, 'Parents too often deny or minimise behaviour, telling me that their child doesn't understand what they are doing, or it was just a mistake, or that they are copying their sister, so it doesn't count. I think they are in denial of where their child is really at.'

There is a massive gap between what is best for our kids and what they are reaching for. Standing in that gap isn't easy or straightforward, but it is critical. Don't ever lose sight of the protective role you play in your tween's life. I have found parents sometimes let go a little too early and make decisions that in hindsight they regret. It's not unusual for parents to be the last ones to come to terms with their tween's new interests or behaviour. I have often heard tweens' parents say, 'My child would *never* do that' only to discover that they did! Start to assume tweens will be open to taking bigger risks outside of the home, especially if they are pushing back a bit more at home.

Know that tweens are more likely to take risks in the company of someone older. Our kids tend to idolise anyone and anything that personifies 'grown-up'. Keep a close eye on who they are looking up to, and why, especially when they are online.

Thoughts about Lying

There is something very normal about children fibbing. You might remember telling a 'tall tale' so you didn't get into trouble. You might also remember telling a fantasy lie. Years ago, a Year 1 student told me that his dad was an astronaut and he went to the moon and back the day before, after school. When tweens are on the younger side of development, they are more likely to engage in fantasy lies, saying things such as, 'I am allowed to stay up all night playing Minecraft!' Whenever I hear these types of lies, I smile and think to myself – *You wish!*

Tweens' lies become more sophisticated and well thought out as their cognition, self-control and language develops. You can expect kids to get better at maintaining lies and understanding the nature of polite lies – and to experiment with their 'believability' and people's perception of them. As tweens begin to understand how others think, they also realise the intention behind lies. For example, they might realise the reason their friend didn't tell them where the party was taking place was because they didn't want them to be there. Initially, this can come as quite a shock to them.

In my work I have noticed a considerable uptick in lying when tweens are about 11 to 12 years old, right on the cusp of the teenage years. This can understandably lead to parents feeling more betrayed, hurt and angry. Sophie, mum of a sprightly 12-year-old, shares a very common experience: 'She's started to lie about the weirdest of things. Not only does she lie but when she gets caught, she insists she is telling the truth. She lies about stuff she doesn't even need to lie about, and it seems to have happened overnight.' Remember, development differs for every child, so some tweens reach this point earlier and others later.

Interestingly, I have noticed lying often subsides as they move into the late teenage years. Compared to teenagers, tweens are more likely to be sensitive to the repercussions of getting caught. Tweens might go to greater lengths to cover their tracks, even when it comes to the smallest of fibs. Teens are also more capable of handling consequences, so admitting to trivial lies tends to increase. Although teens can definitely lie about high stakes issues, they are over some of the experimenting they did when they were younger. I remember my son saying to me when he was a teen, 'Yeah, I did it – so what?' In other words, 'What are you going to be able to do about it?' Just a few years prior, he was insistently hiding uneventful things such as not brushing his teeth.

The content of tweens' lies tracks with our kids' developmental needs. In Chapter 1, 'Almost a Teenager', I spoke about the reluctance tweens can have to grow up. Lying can be used to hide emerging teen-ish ambitions, desires and needs in fear that we will stand in the way of them (which we sometimes need to do). You might discover that they are lying about things they never used to – such as playing a computer game instead of doing their homework, stealing a razor to shave or hiding junk food in their room when they know it's not allowed. One dad told me that his Year 5 son went to school and told the class he was having a birthday party on Saturday, which was not true, and they started getting text messages from parents wanting to know what time to drop their kids off.

When asking yourself why a tween is lying, always try to link it to their developmental needs, whether the reason is differentiating themselves from their parents, establishing or trying on a new identity, getting someone's attention or avoiding hurting other people's feelings. The natural drive for independence, mastery and social status tends to dominate tweens' priorities when they are entering high school. It always helps me to interpret their lying as an immature or ineffective way to get needs met or to solve a problem, conflict or consequence they don't want to face.

Besides encouraging honesty, what else can we do to make it easy for our kids to tell the truth?

◢ Breathe a bit. Crazily, there is actually a lot of learning taking place when children lie.

- Try to avoid saying things such as, 'You are a liar' or 'I don't trust you.' Reframe it to say, 'Looks like you are struggling to be honest at the moment.'
- Recognise and make more room for the expression of their developmental needs (and wants). Things that may not have been important to them in the past (such as more independence or pleasing friends) may now be driving their desire to lie.
- Realise that sometimes lying legitimately feels like a tween's best option in that moment, as the skills to fix or problem solve a situation are still lacking. A good example of this is when tweens lie to sidestep homework.
- Remember that tweens work out the payoff for lying, which might be getting attention, avoiding responsibility or getting their own way. If you identify the payoff, you can teach them to ask for what they need instead of resorting to lying.
- Try to keep your focus on who they are growing into. Reinforce and talk about honesty, integrity and trust – and model it every moment you can.
- Getting upset and dishing out extreme consequences is a waste of a valuable learning time. Usually, it only reinforces poor behaviour because it doesn't upskill them with a replacement strategy.
- If the behaviour persists it may be a sign of underlying issues, and professional support may be helpful.

Thoughts about Stealing

I am more regularly hearing about tweens stealing from retail stores. I am told that there are many recurring offenders who have a deliberate plan to 'take and run'. Eunice, manager of a large store in Brisbane, tells me, 'They come in packs. They are about 12 years old and only come up to our hips! They always steal the puffer jackets – the ones that are $100. They are so brazen about it. Sometimes we catch them and sometimes we don't. We literally chase them. When we do catch them, they say, "We didn't steal it" even though it still has the price tag! When they are asked to hand it back, they say, "You can't touch me." Then they threaten to put you on TikTok and start filming with their iPhones. They just don't care.'

Getting in trouble with the law can be a vicious cycle for tweens who may be getting attention from older peers for taking risks. Through my years in alternative learning, I've found that coming down hard on kids, especially those who don't have family support, seldom helps. It only ends up ostracising them further from trusted adults who they need relationships with. I think the missing link here is affordable, age-appropriate supervised services and programs for tweens, especially during school holidays. There seems to be a gap once they are too old for vacation care, which is usually 12 and up. One mum shared, 'I find there are many school holiday programs for younger kids but trying to satisfy the tweenager, early teens, is the hardest.'

Accountability is a must as tweens start to gain more independence. Research tells us that tweens (and teens) are less likely to engage in high-risk behaviour if they are accountable to a trusted adult for their whereabouts.[2] Endless hours in shopping centres unsupervised can be a breeding ground for trouble, especially for kids who have poor impulse control, or peer groups who are pushing the boundaries. When school holidays come, it's very hard for busy parents. These comments from parents show the real challenge it is when we are pulled between work and our young ones. Veronica says, 'We use a mix of vacation care, taking annual leave, scramble playdates, sport camp and grandparents who are in another city. It's a juggle and each holiday I breathe a sigh of relief that we've managed to cover it.' And Kelly says, 'I find it so tricky. I have a 13-year-old son, work almost full time and have no family around. He is very independent in getting himself around and getting what he needs but he is so young, and I feel worried about not always knowing for sure where he is or who he is with. I constantly wonder if I am doing the right thing letting him be out or at home on screens, even with software I can monitor. It's all a worry.'

Stealing can also happen at school or at home in a much more low-key fashion. I often get emails from parents saying, 'Money has been disappearing from my purse and my daughter insists she hasn't taken it, but I'm not so sure' or 'The snacks in the pantry are disappearing!' In the first instance of stealing try to ask yourself what might be motivating that behaviour. Kids can steal for a lot of reasons including not wanting to depend on others to get what they need, getting what others already have, showing bravery in front of friends, or bidding for attention from adults. They may, or may not, be able to articulate the motivation behind the behaviour or what they gained from the experience. That's why asking them, 'Why did you steal?' isn't always helpful. I was reminded of this recently when a group of young people attempted to break in to cars in my neighbourhood during the night. Two of our neighbours have great security cameras, so the next morning we were able to see the brazen group walking around our homes. The youngest couldn't have been more than 12 years old.

Here are a few basic tips if you have found your child has just stolen something that doesn't belong to them:

- By the time kids are 8 years old, they know that stealing is wrong, so you are probably dealing with a heart that already knows they have crossed the line.
- Clearly reinforce why stealing is unacceptable and try and link your explanations to family values.
- If you know your child has stolen, take the lead. Instead of saying, 'Did you steal this?' try saying, 'I know you stole this item. I did that once when I was younger. We need to talk about making this right.'
- Avoid predicting that they will continue to steal in the future. Avoid labelling them a thief or liar.
- Help them craft an apology and make things right. A guide to this can be found on page 284, 'Siblings Who Fight Well'.
- Returning stolen goods is really important, so they aren't benefiting from the theft.
- Once the situation is dealt with, give them a clean slate to start again.
- As with lying, if the behaviour persists it may be a sign of underlying issues, and professional support may be helpful.

Safe and Healthy Rites of Passage

Dr Arne Rubinstein, CEO of the Rites of Passage Institute and author of *The Making of Men*, explains the difference between boy psychology, dominant in children aged 6 to 10, and man psychology, which ideally develops in the tween years and beyond.[3] He expounds, 'Boys need constant acknowledgement, are competitive and want all the power. They can't handle their emotions and think they are going to live forever. They can never be wrong, and they want a mother to do everything for them. Man psychology is very different. Man psychology says my actions affect others. Power is not just for me. I am part of a community. I have to be able to stand with my emotions, and not take them out on others. I need to be able to admit where I am wrong. I am not looking for a mother but a relationship.'

Let's take gender out of the equation. I can see an important application here for all of our kids. Many, many parents haven't understood that they need to help their child pursue independence safely and constructively by initiating activities that stretch their kids and usher them into that next season of growth.[4] Our kids need safe spaces to feel their limits and take risks so they can begin to be the hero of their own story. I see rites of passage as having a very similar function to low-level stressors, which we talked about in Chapter 4, 'Big, Bold Emotions'.

Dr Arne Rubinstein shares, 'Every single one of our kids is going to go through a rite of passage. The question is, are we going to create something positive that works for them or are we going to let them create their own and hope they are going to be okay?' Rites of passage have changed a lot over time. In days gone past, they were physical challenges because of the hunting skills that were required to survive. Today's world is so different, and we must create culturally relevant experiences. When used well, a rite of passage should be a life-changing experience that forces change and moves psychology.

Below I'd like to talk about four areas where we can consider creating a rite of passage.

Physical challenges. In my home, physical challenges were central to my sons' psychological shift. Belonging to a cricket or football team taught them a responsibility to others outside our home. Surfing taught them that the weather did not consider their name, age or fitness level before hurting them. Trips to the emergency department taught them that showing off didn't always pay off and that exercising caution and saying no is not a sign of weakness. Angie explains that for her two girls ballet has been the psychological shifter. She says, 'Ballet has been a big part of their world. Their level of concentration, focus, confidence, endurance and discipline is noticeable compared to other kids. I'm seeing so many benefits – they have to organise themselves well to fit in their school commitments, they have to turn up on time, be committed to the team and encourage others, not just themselves. There were also times when I wondered if it was too much pressure on them, but I'm amazed by the way they have risen to it. Performing has given them a job to do, and they have to get it done.' Angie went on to explain the moments she got to celebrate their hard work, such as buying pointe shoes for her eldest. Apparently, pointe shoes are quite a thing in the ballet world!

Home responsibilities. Many parents think that giving a child an extra chore is fostering autonomy and responsibility, but I see it a bit differently. We want our kids to learn to think, not just do. To stretch them most effectively, they need a sense of ownership. We want them to choose what they have for lunch, not just pack their own lunch. We want them to choose what they wear, not just get dressed in the morning. When we foster ownership, we acknowledge them as their own person, and we hand over the responsibility of those choices with age-appropriate boundaries. Some suggestions might be to:

- ◢ cook a meal once a week or bake snacks for school
- ◢ work for someone else to earn pocket money

- stay at a different extended family member's house each month
- look after a pet
- attend a holiday camp or join a sports team where they don't know anyone
- learn a new physical skill, such as surfing
- help the community by serving in a soup kitchen with you once a month
- contribute in a more significant way on Anzac Day or at other events that have cultural significance to your family
- be responsible for choosing a birthday or Christmas gift for a sibling, or organising a family Mother's Day event.

Expanding their tribe. In cultures around the world, celebrating milestone birthdays is far more than a gift-giving opportunity. They are a rite of passage that comes with a call to grow and an increase in responsibility. One tradition that Stewart, father to Joshua, who is now a young man himself, introduced in his family was a variation of the Jewish bar mitzvah. On his son's thirteenth birthday, he gathered five men to celebrate with them over a barbecue at their home. 'These are the men I want you to turn to if I am ever not here, or if you feel you can't talk to me,' he advised his son. During the celebration, each of the men spoke to his son about what manhood meant to them and how they could be a part of his journey moving forward. They also wrote Joshua a letter and brought him a gift, which I assume was the latest and the greatest electronic gadget they wished they'd owned at his age! If this isn't your style, consider giving your child a list of people they could phone or visit if they needed help. It's a way to open the door to their independence.

Punctuating natural transitions. In Chapter 15, 'Transitioning to High School', we are going to talk about the end of primary school as a rite of passage. Primary school graduations and all the accompanying photos, gifts and goodbyes help punctuate that rite of passage. It's also an opportunity to gift our kids with some meaningful words, in the form of a handwritten note, that they can come back to. I want you to know how much notes amplify your message; you can use them any time you deem a big punctuation mark is needed. They can say what we often stumble over in face-to-face conversations, and they cut to the heart of important matters. Your note might read, 'Things I want you to know before high school' or 'The reason why I'm incredibly proud of you.' Here's a beautiful letter that one family generously shared with me:

> Dearest son,
> You are about to start a new journey in your life.
> I'm so very proud of the young man that you have become, and I can't wait to see what the future will bring! I know we have been through some tough times and life hasn't always been easy for you. You have tried so hard to overcome your challenges! I'm so proud of you. You have come so very far and I wouldn't change anything about you. I have loved watching you grow each year! You are so handsome! I love watching old videos of you when you were little. We watched one of my favourites the other day of you dancing! You have such a great sense of humour and I love how much energy you have. I love watching you play soccer and how happy it makes you. I love listening to your stories about your day or about something funny that has happened. I want you to know that I believe in you and know that you can achieve anything you want. High school is going to be an awesome

adventure. Please remember how much I love you and that I will always be there for you no matter what! I'm so proud of how far you have pushed yourself with your sensory challenges. This should tell you that you can do anything in your life! I'm wishing you the most wonderful start to high school. I love you to the moon and back!

Mum

Chapter 12

BOUNDARIES AND BUY-IN

Key Message: Think about boundaries like a 'playpen' for our tweens to explore life. Ask yourself, What designated space do you want your child to play in *right now*?

There have been considerable shifts within parenting philosophy in the last decade. As a society, we have moved away from focusing on behaviour to emotion. With this shift, I genuinely worry that we have lost the integral role that boundaries play in healthy child development. In this chapter, I want to help you embrace that word 'no' and the depth of love that is behind it. As Dr Michael Carr-Gregg clearly explained in my interview with him, 'I describe parenting like an aeroplane. Your child is one wing, and you are the other. Don't for one minute think that they can navigate this without you.'

Sadly, many parents have to remind themselves that they are in charge and have every right to make parental decisions without endless negotiating. I have had parents ask me if it is okay to ask their kids to get off technology at 8.30 pm at night so they can get ready for bed. 'Hell *yes*,' is my answer. That's why I love statements from parents like this example from Ainsley, who shares, 'Today I decided to go back to the basics and routine. It's not popular here at the moment. You have to have done your jobs and tidied your room, picked two activities to play on your own and go outside, and then you can have tech time at 3.00 pm if you have done all that. We are not talking about gaming until then. Once you let it out it is so difficult to rein back in.' Operative words – *I decided*.

Think about boundaries like a 'playpen' for your kids to explore life. Ask yourself, What designated space do you want your child to play in *right now*? Too small a playpen limits our tween's life experience, adaptivity, social skills and sense of autonomy. Too large a playpen jeopardises their safety and character development. Brad, the father of three kids, offers me a great example of this when he says, 'I understand why my kids pester me every second day about more time gaming, but I just tell them that my answer hasn't changed and that if nothing else, they know where the lines are. They roll their eyes but, hey, that's life and I know they get it.'

The 'feel' of the playpen's edges matters too. Kids don't process words, they process tone. If the edges are too sharp, they can cut our kids' hearts. If they easily collapse, they teach our children that they can't be trusted or relied upon. Our kids will feel the edge of every person they encounter, whether that be a teacher at school, a sports coach or their grandparents. Interestingly, how we describe people (kind, harsh, narrow-minded, generous, soft, pushover, naive, mistrusting, loving, strong, fair) has a lot to do with how they hold their personal boundaries. Everyone has an edge, and that edge is what we remember.

Well thought out and carefully executed boundaries are a gift to our kids, although they are not likely to thank you for them for many years to come. To me, the gift lies predominantly in the messages these boundaries communicate, rather than the restrictions they provide. A child's sense of self and their trust in the world is reinforced every time a parent provides consistency, protection and selfless love. Below, I expand upon four key messages that I believe healthy, well-considered boundaries provide our kids with.

I deeply know you. Boundaries communicate, 'I deeply know you.' Charmaine, the mother of 12-year-old Sophie, provides an excellent example of this when she says, 'She is not on social media at all, but more and more of her friends are. I am not budging on it because she is too fragile for it. She is on SMS group chats and texts. She watches stuff on YouTube quite often too, but I know her capacity at the moment, and social media is not where she is at.' In other words, Charmaine is saying, 'I have completed my parental responsibility and thought about this boundary and how it might impact her life.'

I know who I am in your life. Boundaries communicate, 'I know who I am in your life.' It's our personal self-esteem that allows us to hold boundaries in the face of pressure. If we discard what we really believe in, usually because other parents are okay with it or we fear our children will hate us, we aren't modelling the self-esteem we want our children to carry. We aren't valuing ourselves. When we know ourselves, our kids feel safe and secure in the knowledge that they have predictability and consistency in their lives.

My love has legs. Boundaries communicate, 'My love has legs.' When your tween pushes against a boundary, you both tangibly feel it. There is nothing quite like it, and that's why I suggest that saying 'no' and saying it well is like giving our kids the tightest, most genuine hug possible. You are holding them when they can't yet hold themselves. You are wrapping them in the protective, strong arms that only a parent can provide. It will cost you to do this – time, energy and sometimes a little rejection.

I trust my parenting ability, so you can too. Boundaries communicate, 'I trust my parenting ability, so you can too.' Never replace your own thoughts with those of someone else's unless your whole body knows them to be true. I love this statement from Dr Deborah MacNamara's interview with Rachel Cram, host of the wonderful *Family 360* podcast.[1] She says, 'When you shift into the instincts and emotions that are innate in us to take care of another human being, there is the sense that you are the answer. We are very much wired to take care of each other.' She goes on to explain that no matter what your childhood experience, you can be the key to your child's life if you are able to feel your instincts and move from them.

Clarity Around Decision Making

Now, and in the years ahead, there will be lots of times when you have to say no. No, we can't drive you there. No, we aren't comfortable with that sleepover. No, we aren't spending any more money on takeaway. No, you can't speak to me like that. No, you can't have your phone in your room. No, you can't stay up all night. Gosh, it is relentless! That word 'no' can trigger some really big emotions in our homes. I guarantee mum Brooke is not alone in this experience. She says, 'At the moment it seems that everything Miss 11 asks is so far-fetched and out of the question, saying no is so tough! Some days it is infuriating!'

Over my years working with families, I've found that it's very important that you are clear about which decisions are up to your kids to make, and which are yours. You need to answer the question, Who is the decider? And make the answer very clear. This clarity will see you through the teenage years, and while it won't eliminate tensions, it will provide predictability and a framework to operate within. Many kids assume they will automatically be allowed to make their own decisions, especially once they hit high school. That's why we need to stay in charge of the negotiation process. We want to emphasise that with freedom comes accountability. This particularly rings true when it comes to technology. Tweens very often think the amount of time spent on technology should be their decision, but parents believe it should be theirs.

We cannot teach our tweens everything they need to learn in life. Sometimes we choose not to stand in the way of our tweens' choices because we believe they can handle the life lesson on the other side. For example, you might say to your child, 'If you choose not to do your homework, you will have to face school detention. I won't write a note or bail you out.' Other times, we might choose to step in and enforce doing their homework because we know that their shoulders aren't strong enough to bear the fallout. A good rule of thumb when making decisions: If you don't choose to stand in the way of their decision, don't choose to stand in the way of the consequences.

When it is your decision to make, always remember these three options:

Option 1: A wholehearted, enthusiastic 'yes'.
Option 2: A 'yes', with conditions.
Option 3: Say, 'There is something better,' which is a kind way of saying 'no'.

Option 3 is my cute way of trying to minimise the blow of a 'no' and to show tweens you care. If you have taken something away from your tween, a nice gesture is to offer them something in exchange. Even if your kid declines your offer, the fact that you recognise the impact of your decisions on them is important. If you want your tween to cut back on tech time, ask yourself what you are offering as a replacement. Replacements are a big part in helping tweens 'buy in' to your motive as a parent. I like to think of it as distracting them with love.

Marina Passalaris shared with me an activity conducted at a Beautiful Minds workshop where each member of the family creates a dream board. This dream board is like a wish list of all the things they would like to be, do, see, create or own. As we spoke, I thought about how this could be applied to the boundaries we set with our kids. I realised that tweens often get fixated on things we say no to, but they don't have a visual of all the things we say yes to. I wondered if creating a 'yes' board could be a way of expanding their view of the world and allowing them to see all the things they have to be grateful for.

Remember that boundaries are most effective when they are mutually agreed upon, so keep working on buy-in with your kids and consider using a family meeting to discuss values, boundaries and agreements that you could all benefit from. Buying in doesn't mean they will 100 per cent agree with you, but they have been consulted and can see a legitimate reason for the boundaries. Studies show that teens are more willing to comply with parents when they think the rules are fair, such as moral choices or ones involving safety, but they resist when the rules seem personal or unjust, such as restrictions on how they cut their hair.[2,3] As one parent put it, 'Tanya challenges me the most out of all my kids. One minute she still needs me, the next she is picking arguments just because she wants to prove me wrong! I have to really work on keeping dialogue open instead of saying a blanket "no" every time she opens her mouth. I need to keep helping her with buy-in. Even when she doesn't like it, I want her to understand it.'

When I am assessing whether I've got buy-in from kids, I watch for the 'fair enough' look. I heard a teacher (who was loved by his class) use an incident where tweens scrambled to sit in seats they knew they weren't allowed to as a teachable moment. In a super calm and compassionate tone, he said, 'I will very rarely give you a punishment, but I will help you experience the consequences of choices. If you can't sit in the right place, practising at lunchtime would be a sensible thing to ask you to do.' *Fair enough*, I thought. I also saw a few 'fair enough' looks on the students' faces as they managed to find their correct seats. In our homes this might apply to lunchboxes, hats, dirty clothes, being late for things . . . oh, the list could go on and on! Keep your eyes open for the 'fair enough' look. It's the look a child gives a parent when they are doing their job well. It's the look that says, 'I don't like it, but I slightly buy in to it.'

The Importance of Filters

Parenting well doesn't come out of a textbook. It comes out of the heart, which does its best work when open. It doesn't hurt to have a parenting mantra tucked away within your heart for times when you don't have a clear answer. 'Stand like an oak, bend like the grass' is one powerful mantra that has helped me know when to soften rigid edges, and when not to. When we stand like an oak, we take a strong, non-negotiable position about things that really matter. When we bend like the grass, we consider the lessons our children need to learn as they grow.

I find that tweens need more oak-like parenting, and teens need more grass-like parenting.

Bending like grass encourages parents to look through the lens that allows them to see their child's needs before setting boundaries. Without this perspective, it's possible to offer expectations that are rigid, unhelpful and disconnected. The ideal is for us to first see and then to respond to our kids. We need to be mindful that our own history can leave us with emotional weak spots that stop us from seeing. Our own damage can stand in the way of our ability to instinctively see what tweens need us to see.

If we don't see tweens accurately, we can do damage that we later regret. Jacqueline offers her life experience as an example when she says of her daughter, 'As a child, she wasn't placid or easygoing and we were hard on her. We felt we damaged her sense of self, and we are reparenting that side of her now. If only we had been less strict and let her be herself. Star charts and sad face stickers were making a big impact on her, and she would say, "I don't like myself because I always get sad faces." We have done the right thing in lightening up, and once we realised where we were going wrong, we have started to change the way we spoke to her, with positive language.'

This seems like a sensible place to again emphasise how different each of our kids are. They have a unique neurological profile that means we need to set boundaries in different places for different reasons. Their unique development cannot be reduced to a number, and in fact the number of candles on our kids' birthday cakes means very little. I've seen many 12-year-olds whose development puts them squarely in the 'almost a teenager' category we talked about in Chapter 1.

Here are some common-sense filters to pass your daily parenting expectations and requests through.

Filter 1: Are they tired, hungry or thirsty? It is normal for tweens' capacity to be irregular. Tired can commonly look like a meltdown or a feisty exchange. Most times, melting down is their way of regulating themselves back to balance. Charmaine explains, 'I don't always pick up on the difference between defiance and him not coping as quickly as I need him to. It takes me a while to clue in to it being something else, like the pace of his life. Sometimes I find myself saying, "You are driving me crazy!" And then I realise that he has been out for three days in a row, and no wonder he's falling apart. I have to adjust my expectations.'

Filter 2: How strong is their current resilience? We know that it is not always defiance that drives difficult behaviour. Most behaviour, even the most baffling, frustrating, infuriating parts of it, can be explained by our kids' resilience. How strong their mental health is may impact their ability to live up to expectations. They may have had a particularly bad day at school that we need to take into consideration. Tony explains, 'There were some years where things were pretty tense, and we felt it was unrealistic to be able to be consistent all the time. He just needed a break and we had to accept that.'

Filter 3: What limitations do they have? Each child's strengths and weaknesses need to be taken into consideration. For example, if you want to come off as fair, you can't expect a child who struggles with organisational skills to be as tidy as other members of the family. It's just not realistic. Michelle, mum to an 11-year-old girl, explains, 'I've just had to accept that some things are what they are. No matter how much they frustrate me, they are what they are, and I can't keep comparing her to the others.'

Filter 4: *What is their motive?* Whenever I talk about being flexible with a difficult child, there is always one parent who asks me if that is teaching them that they can get away with bad behaviour. To this I say, yes, it can. That is why we have to consider our kids' motives too. If a child is taking advantage and testing you, stand firm. If they are being unsafe, definitely stand firm. If they are lacking the ability to handle a responsibility, stand firm. This is what Ainslie was doing when she shared, 'It's hard when I have to stand my ground. Every day I try a new tactic, but it is exhausting. He has been angry and refuses to go out to places with us. I'm trying not to lose that connection, but I need to stand my ground.'

Filter 5: *What are their priorities?* I recently got an email from a mum of a 12-year-old who had been caught vaping. Her daughter had started hanging out with a new group of friends at school and within months her attitude and behaviour had completely changed. When her mum tried to talk about the incident, she aggressively responded with the words, 'I don't care.' Hmm . . . very 'almost teenage-like'. When a child tells you that they don't care, don't argue with them – believe them. Don't wish it away – accept it quickly. In this case, I encouraged the mum to quietly make a mental note of her daughter's strong desire to fit in, which is so typical in the teenage years, and to lovingly, firmly and compassionately step up to safeguard her. If you are looking for accurate information on vaping, drugs or alcohol, I would recommend Paul Dillon, who has been working in the area of drug education for more than 25 years and who has an excellent podcast called *The Real Deal on Drugs*.

Stepping into the Boxing Ring

Emotional eruptions happen in every home – no exceptions. Lael Stone, a childbirth educator who has a passion to see parents raise emotionally intelligent humans, calls these eruptions 'beautiful meltdowns' because on the other side our tweens come back into balance. In her appearance on an episode of the podcast *The Imperfects*, she says, 'Our children are either in balance or out of balance. When they are in balance they play, they say no worries and they respond favourably. When they are out of balance they walk into the room and they kick the dog, they don't want to set the table.'[4] So true!

When our kids are having a meltdown, it's easy to wade into immature waters. It's tempting, but it is a mistake to step into the boxing ring with a child and treat them like our opponents. Why? It's not a fair fight. They are not prepared. They don't have the right protective gear. An injury is inevitable and sometimes irreparable. You put them in a position where they have to rage to be heard and seen because, despite their natural efforts, they are unable to win against you. You hold the balance of power.

The boxing ring might not be a physical fight. It might look more like a blaming, shaming, ear-bashing moment when you lose your cool. You might find yourself saying, 'You are always the last to get into the car!' or 'I can't believe you forgot your assignment again!' or 'Do you expect us all to wait around while you just take your time?' Our hearts sink the moment these words leave our mouths because we know we have moved into the boxing ring.

When tensions are high, I think our kids deserve to receive some grace to compensate for the uneven playing field that puts them at a disadvantage. Parents who fight fair offer a crash-free (shame- and embarrassment-free) 'out' when emotions are running high. Anything that slows things down and grounds the discussion back in what is most important will help. There are lots of ways parents can graciously offer this 'out', but here are a few suggestions, all of which highlight the fact that vulnerability is the only way out of conflict.

When you are met with strong resistance from your tween, try to:

Be playful. This is my favourite strategy. This next story is a great example of playfulness in action. James, his wife Helen and their daughter 12-year-old Joanna set off on a morning walk together. Joanna wanted a latte at the beginning of their trip, to which her dad had said no. For the whole 5 kilometre walk, she went on and on and on about how unfair his decision had been. Instead of snapping at her, James started turning the whole affair into a game called 'spot the latte that Joanna doesn't have'. He'd say, 'Look, Joanna, that person has a latte.' Playfulness gives movement to kids' emotions. Admittedly, it can antagonise them too much if taken too far, but it can also communicate your love for them.

Redirect the intensity. You could try asking your child to write down their point of view in a letter to you. The simple act of journalling and slowing their thoughts down can help them access more rational thinking. Remember that tweens' language skills often don't enable them to keep up with the pace of their emotions. Say to your tween, 'Can you write this in a letter to me, so I can really understand how you feel? Then we can come back and talk about it again.'

Offer unexpected gestures of kindness. You might interrupt an argument with a comment like, 'You know I just adore you.' Those words embody so much that they are hard to replace with

250

anything else. I think they always sit best with a deliberate pause at the end of the sentence. My guess is that your tween will smile a confused smile and respond, 'That's not the point. I know you love me.' As a mum, that response means the world to me. The 'flip me off' way they say it makes my heart leap because they are acknowledging, 'That's assumed knowledge, Mum . . . duh!' As they get older, keep saying 'I love you' in creative ways even when they roll their eyes. You can also offer unexpected gestures such as bringing them their favourite snack or making them a hot chocolate.

Ask for a hug. You might also interrupt an argument with a request like, 'I need a hug.' This one might sound crazy, but it was my favourite strategy with my own kids and has lasted me well into their young adult years. My eldest was 6 feet tall when he was 13, which was quite intimidating for a 4-feet-11-inches mum like me. So, I decided to make sure he knew that I needed his softness and compassion just as much as he needed it from me. It was my way of anchoring the relationship in what mattered. I'd often see him look at me as if to say, 'My poor mum needs some reassurance right now.' With a big eye roll, he would walk over and wrap his goofy, long arms around me, and say, 'Seriously, Mum.'

Suggest a do-over. Offering a second take, sometimes called a do-over, is another way we can gently correct our tweens while still letting them know they have crossed the line. Try saying, 'That doesn't sound like your usual self. Want to try again?' Of course, there are only so many do-overs you can offer, but giving them a second chance extends trust in their ability to make good choices. It also gives them a moment to assess this situation and step back to see things from your perspective.

Put it on your shoulders. When you have to hold a boundary, fully owning that decision becomes of paramount importance. I interviewed Dr Vanessa Lapointe, a Canada-based developmental psychologist and founder of the Wishing Star Lapointe Developmental Clinic, who speaks beautifully about this when she advises parents to calmly restate the boundary and remind their tween that the answer is no, without putting an ounce of guilt on their shoulders. She suggests saying, 'This is nothing to do with you, my love. This is all about me and the decision I have to make as your parent.'

When You Stuff Up

If you know you are reaching your limit, do whatever you need to in order to buy yourself some time. Tell your tween that you've got to call grandma, or take a work call, or feed the cat or go to the bathroom (that's a stock-standard timeout strategy!). If you don't catch yourself early enough and you find you are the one having a meltdown of toddler-like proportions, be kind to yourself. Nothing is irreparable. In those moments you can model emotional ownership. You can press reset in your mind and heart, and externally communicate your thought process to your tween. You might say, 'That wasn't an acceptable way to talk, and it doesn't represent our family values. I'm sorry. I need to try that again.' I absolutely loved the perspective of Chantalle, a mum who shared these graceful words with me: 'I love opportunities where I can tell her that I was wrong. Those conversations seem to work the best for me and my teen. We are learning together.'

252

In-charge Energy and Trust

I learnt a lot about setting boundaries very early in my career when teaching life skills at alternative learning centres (education programs set up for young people who had disengaged with traditional education because of social or behavioural challenges). The atmosphere was always chaotic, and I often had a security guard accompanying me to classes. Class sizes were deliberately small – usually limited to 12 students, with an understanding that on a good day 8 would show up.

Very early in the piece, I noticed a strong link between poor behaviour and a lack of trust in adults. Many of the students I taught had experienced a lifetime of power misuse and struggled to take adults' lead. To me, it was obvious that no amount of control or power (even if it included a police uniform and jail sentence) could compensate for it. In a practical sense, it meant I had to know each of my students. It meant being fair and consistent in my responses, without expecting them to reciprocate that consistency. It meant I had to unwaveringly demonstrate my ability to manage my own emotions and behaviours, even when I was offended, hurt or triggered at my core. This is emotionally draining, challenging work.

I like to use the term 'in-charge energy' to describe the presence you need in order to be a responsible adult. For me, this term conjures up images of parents whose batteries are 'fully charged'. In the face of terribly disruptive behaviour from my students, in-charge energy enabled me to end my requests with a big, bold statement like, 'The only response I will accept right now is, "*Yes*, Miss."' 'Yes, Miss' eliminated unnecessary options. It created a clear path forward, which made it easier for young ones when emotions were high. It enabled me to slam dunk my request all the way to the finish line.

There was always a split-second moment when I wondered, *Will they allow me to guide them? Do they trust me enough to follow my lead? Will they push back?* To my surprise, even the toughest students responded to an adult with in-charge energy. In my home, and I'm sure in yours, there are lots and lots of times when we have heated conversations and debate and discuss ideas with our kids, but there should be a few times each day when 'yes' is the only response parents will accept. I tell my kids upfront, 'I am about to give you a "yes, Mum" request.'

Your tween needs to deeply trust you in order to follow your lead. If our tweens don't feel secure, their hearts won't stay open to our guidance. We can't overinvest in building trust, which is the simple belief that you have their best interests at heart. This becomes increasingly important when you draw on that trust to make safety decisions. In my interview with Dr Justin Coulson, co-host and parenting expert on Channel 9's show *Parental Guidance*, we spoke about a specific conversation he had with one of his teenage daughters, which had required him to draw on trust. She wanted to attend a party that he deemed to be unsafe. He deliberately led the conversation with, 'Do you trust me? If you trust me, I need you to trust me now. I forbid you to go, and there will be consequences if you do go. I don't ever imagine having to do this again, but I need to now.'

For many of our kids, following a parent's lead isn't easy. When they don't get their own way and anger turns to tears, there is a sinking feeling of being at the mercy of someone else. Trust and vulnerability are so deeply linked. I have never worked with a family that has been able to move through conflict without first becoming vulnerable with each other – it is the *only* way through disagreements and tensions. Remember, vulnerability is a two-way street that both you and your child may walk down at different paces. Dr Vanessa Lapointe explains,

'When children are the alpha or have had too much to bear, they become defended against vulnerability. They find it impossible to trust an adult's lead.' We see our kids 'defended against vulnerability' when they attack rather than work cooperatively with us. If our children allow us to be in control at a moment when they feel out of control, we get to do the heavy lifting for them. If they don't, we must focus on reinforcing and repairing trust, even when it feels counterintuitive. Part of our job, and our priority in these moments, is to meet their nervous system's need for calm, security and understanding, so it stays in a 'soft and squishy' teachable place.

To help me, I literally imagine a 'trust room' that I invite my child into. It's a space in my heart where I do my best parenting work. I can feel when I have arrived there. It affects every ounce of my body – from how I stand to what I think and to the tone of my voice. It is the place where I stop flapping, yelling and fearing, things that come so much more naturally to me. It's a place where I can hold my own sense of self, and respect that my kids are building a container to hold theirs. Only from this place can I be the selfless, brave adult my kid needs. Only from this place can I truly love.

There are three key messages I try to consistently give my children when we are in the 'trust room'. Firstly, they can trust I have their best interest at heart, even if they don't like my decisions. Secondly, they can trust I will hold my own emotions and boundaries, while they are working on theirs. Thirdly, they can trust I've got them when they fall. If I get these three things right, I know I'm on the right track.

If you ever have a rough time parenting, a good fallback position is trust. Trust acknowledges that tweens have a choice and a mind of their own. Trust provides space for tweens to grow with their ideas and feelings. It acknowledges that their life

255

comes with its own life lessons, and we can't rush, manufacture or schedule those lessons. You will need to assess your posture often in the upcoming years as you continue to see your child advance into the world on their own. I loved this statement from Dr Justin Coulson, who says, 'You can forget autonomy until you have the relationship right. That may take a day, a month, a year. This is the starting point . . .'

Looking After You

You never know what is around the corner in life or what demands your big shoulders will need to carry. But one thing you can count on – tweens will always look to you to lead the way. The nature of parenting is that everything goes better when adults are one step ahead. Which is easier said than done when we have birthed creative, strong-willed children who are insisting on taking the reins. The more we deliberately care for our own needs, the easier it will be to show up with that in-charge energy that keeps our homes humming. For me, self-care is working on the basics, which takes a lot of discipline. It's getting to bed on time, making sure you eat well and stay hydrated, and allowing time to escape into adult play. It's giving yourself what you desire to give your kids – I find that a good benchmark to strive towards.

Chapter 13
THE GIFT OF LANGUAGE

Key Message: If there's ever a time to clear the runway to your child's heart, it's now.

To your child, the word 'home' is interchangeable with your name. Yet you are a soul, not a physical structure. You are a sanctuary, not a building. What you build is not bricks and mortar. Words are like the framework we use to hold up our relationships. I don't always think we realise how powerful words are, or what they have the potential to build. I heard a breathtaking statement by Dr Alex Koefman, neurosurgeon and researcher. Considering all of his work with the human brain, I find it remarkable that he says, 'Words are still more therapeutic than any operation I can do.'[1]

The most consistent and prominent finding in research over the last few decades is that the emotional content of parental discourse is the most significant predictor of children's social and emotional functioning.[2] Evidence has shown that the way parents speak to their kids is a stronger predictor of children's social and emotional outcomes than a parent's general behaviour toward their children, demonstrating that parent–child discourse provides important context for how a child learns to make sense of their experiences.[3] Basically, words not only move our kids' hearts towards us but also shape their capacity to interact and experience the world around them.

As I write this chapter, I am challenged to offer you insights that will help you wisely use the gift of language. I want you to know that deeply close relationships can be developed in the face of imperfection, sickness, trauma or change in family structure. No matter what your situation, each family deserves the tools to experience a deep and lasting connection. If our homes become a performance of care, rather than a heart-centred expression of love, we fall short of what is possible. You might relate to these words from Casey, mother of Josh, who is 10. She says, 'What matters most to me is that there is transparency and honesty, and that my kids know they can come to me about anything and I'll take it on board with an open mind and provide some support, answers and assistance.' It's a glorious end point to strive towards.

Without exception, every parent I spoke to while writing this book expressed a desire to have a close, open relationship with their child. The love we have for our children will motivate us to grow up and take responsibility for communicating well, as few other relationships will. Breaking poor habits can be hard work. In moments where you are tempted to give up and throw a tantrum, remember you are a pattern maker. Children subconsciously follow patterns. The more predictable we can be, the easier it is for them to follow us. The more consistently we handle difficult conversations well, the more confidently we will go there again. Our kids don't need perfect parents, just invested ones. Among the sometimes-overwhelming chaos of life, we must remind ourselves that words that are spoken within the secluded four walls of our homes shape our children. They will be lodged in their hearts forever.

Recognising Sticky Language

History matters when looking forward. Our own early childhood experiences have built our neural capacity for things like self-regulation, self-control, trust and empathy. The more we get in touch with our own childhood baggage and areas of pain in our own lives, the more we tap into the stuff that unconsciously impacts the way we connect with our tweens. Hannah beautifully explains her journey when she says, 'I've had to do a heck of a lot of self-reflection, humbling myself and apologising at times to be a person who responds rather than reacts to my very emotionally volatile 8-year-old. My biggest prayer is that our relationship stays soft and close through these years so that when she's an adult, she sees me as a soft place to fall and not someone she can't trust with tricky conversations for fear of how I will behave (like I am with my own mum at times). So, I'm on a personal learning journey through parenting a child who is just like me. I think I've changed a lot as a person as a result of having to parent a mini-me.'

Our parents (and their parents) were influenced by a parenting methodology called behaviourism. The early 1900s gave rise to researchers such as Watson, Pavlov, Skinner and Bandura, who all genuinely believed that shame was an effective way to ensure children chose socially acceptable 'good' behaviour. They promoted the use of harsh punishment, high expectations and the withdrawal of love and affection to ensure kids were kept on the straight and narrow. Karen Young, who we met in Chapter 1,

'Almost a Teenager', helps by explaining the background of these ideas. In our interview, she said, 'Behaviourists built ideas on studies done with animals. When they made animals scared of something, the animal stopped being drawn to that thing. The big difference is that children have a frontal cortex (thinking brain) that animals and other mammals don't have. With a thinking brain comes incredibly sophisticated capacities for complex emotions (shame), thinking about the past (learning, regret, guilt), the future (planning, anxiety), and developing theories about why things happen.'

Shaming is a hangover from behaviourism that uses 'sticky' language to try to modify children. Sadly, sticky language is like superglue that clings to anything it touches and gets easily lodged in kids' hearts. Once there, it's hard to remove. The impact of shaming language was consistently reinforced in my interviews with parents, grandparents and tweens themselves. I consistently heard about the deep and authentic wounds these methods had caused. All interviewees were able to recall moments, with clarity, where shaming language genuinely squashed their sense of self.

I'd like to share a story from one mother who, in her adult years, was diagnosed with autism. Her experience represents so many in the neurodivergent community as she explains, 'I grew up being told to suck it up and just get on with it, but that meant a lifetime of invalidation. My undiagnosed or unacknowledged sensory issues meant that I had significant challenges wearing my blazer and eating certain foods. That's why as a mum now I always try to validate the child's experience, regardless of whether I understand it or not. I don't think we are ever going to fully understand our kids, or our kids us. The main thing is that we don't dismiss what they are trying to communicate.'

Our language becomes particularly important during vulnerable moments, including when our kids make poor decisions. I'd like to highlight the sarcastic, snippy comments that were characteristic of past generations of parents. Even though some of them go over kids' heads, they deeply feel the tone of them. Karen Young again offers insights, saying, 'Shame drives an internal collapse – a withdrawal from themselves, and the world around us. For sure it might look like compliance, but we lose influence. We can't teach them ways to do better when they are thinking the thing that has to change is who they are. They can change what they do – they can't change who they are.'

Shame-based language doesn't leave room for self-correction or wiser choices. I'd love for us to guide our children to know how to handle guilt well, without feeling the need to shame themselves or others. When tweens mess up and act out of character, it's our job to encourage them to go back to their standards and our family values. Small shifts in how we use our words are actually giant leaps when it comes to our children's experiences.

Instead of sticky language, try saying:

- 'Mistakes won't ever change how much I love you.'
- 'I don't have to fully understand to be able to listen to you.'
- 'I can see how sorry you are about it.'
- 'I know that wasn't your best moment.'
- 'That's out of character for you.'
- 'I'm glad we can start again tomorrow.'
- 'How could you respond differently next time?'
- 'How can you make things right?'

Family Communication Principles

Communicating well under pressure involves a lot of very complex skills, which very few adults have mastered, let alone children. As we guide our kids, let's keep our expectations of kids in check. They often don't know as much as they (or we) think they know. Just because they can do stuff, look grown up or are the eldest child doesn't mean they know how to wisely express themselves.

Remember that tweens rarely do things just to irritate or hurt us, and they, like us, are a work in progress. The conflict is rarely with you – it's with them and the skills they don't have at that moment. Sally, mother of 10-year-old Mia, explains this well when she says, 'She's not a bad kid but she just loses it. Like really loses it. She has worked out that she can dig her heels in and plays on that so well. She has the death stare going too. You certainly know when she is not happy. I guess it's just her not knowing how to put emotional boundaries in place, so I need to do it for her.'

Below are my most treasured communication principles. They guide me as much as they guide my kids, and I find that we revisit them when tensions are high or when disagreements are not easily resolved. I can imagine these being a guiding force in homes, especially as children start to grow, stretch and reconstruct what they know of each other.

Misunderstandings are normal. We want our tweens to normalise misunderstandings and to understand that each person's perception of reality is different from anyone else's. Instead of becoming defensive, we want them to open-mindedly think, 'I can't expect everyone to think the way I do. I wonder what they are thinking?'

Words and hearts can say different things. Too often arguments are about who said what and about who is right and wrong. There is a big difference between hearing words and hearing someone's heart. Being curious about someone else is a skill that we can practise. When people feel safe, their ears are more open to hearing their heart's language, and the hearts of those around them. Instead of focusing on someone's language, we want them to ask, 'What is behind the frustration?'

Always speak the truth. We want to encourage our children to share their truth as deeply and genuinely as they can. For someone to express their doubts and insecurities, they have to be comfortable with being less than; that's a big, brave move that needs practice and support. For someone to listen to another person's truth often means they must be prepared to not react but hold space for that honesty. Instead of reacting, we want them to ask, 'How can I make it easy for someone to talk to me?' and 'How can I be honest and clear?'

Everyone needs self-control. In the heat of any argument, self-control protects us and others from hurting each other. The Gottman Institute is famous for scientifically calculating the exact behaviour that ruptures and ruins relationships. According to John Gottman, there are four habits that we should be on the lookout for avoiding in our communication – criticism, contempt, defensiveness and stonewalling.[4] All of these things can be replaced by kindness, which is loaning someone your strength instead of reminding them of their weakness.

Know your limits. Part of the lens of vulnerability is knowing that we have limits and that there are some things we can't do anything about. The first thing we need to determine is if we are someone's decider or if they are their decider? This extends into every relationship in our lives. Instead of taking control, we want our tweens to ask, 'What is my responsibility and what is theirs?' or 'What can I control and what can't I control?'

I am responsible for me. Ultimately, we want to manage our home in a way that minimises threat energy and creates psychological safety. That, in itself, teaches our kids a lot about what relationships should feel like. It is not selfish or misplaced for our children to ask themselves what they need and want, or what a relationship is teaching them. Instead of ignoring their needs, we want them to ask, 'What do I need' and 'What am I learning about me?'

Getting Rid of Emotional Clutter

I want to ask you an unusual question: Is your child in a close relationship with you yet? If you put yourself in their shoes, do you feel they are all-in, or hesitant, separated and untrusting of your lead? I ask you this because I want to make sure you have established a strong platform of trust before their teenage years. You are going to need it. If there's ever a time to clear the runway to your child's heart, it's now. Our kids are complex, soulful humans whose minds and hearts and more likely to mimic and follow those whom they trust. That means connection is at the very core of what matters – always.

By the time our children are 12, there may be a bit of emotional clutter that stands between us and them. It's pretty normal for clutter to accumulate over time, so don't be alarmed if you find yourself stepping over debris from time to time. This debris acts as interference and surfaces in big feelings – insecurity, inadequacy, comparisons with siblings, fear of harsh judgements or separation. You have to be able to take the lead and sniff out the fears that make it easy for them to detach from you. Similarly, you may also be aware of unresolved issues in your heart. Parents often put resentments or dissatisfied feelings down to personality clashes or their child having a challenging temperament.

Now is a great time to take stock of your relationship and the communication habits that dominate your home. If tweens even remotely believe that there are conditions and expectations associated with your love, it will impact them. Left unchecked, that belief provides an opportunity for a child to disconnect at a time when they need us by their side. Now is the time to build an understanding of the set-in-stone, fixed, immovable, unchanging love you have for them, and in doing so safeguard your relationship with them and create patterns of communication that are healthy.

In our interview, Natasha graciously shared her parenting journey with me. They went to a psychologist to get 'help' for their anxious daughter. Natasha was surprised to find that the first few sessions were about her husband and herself, not their daughter. What eventuated was a deep and lengthy discussion about how their parenting reflected their own upbringing, and how those things transfer to our unhealthy expectations of our children. They had identified conflict as being due to a personality clash, when in reality it was far deeper rooted than that.

Natasha's daughter felt like she couldn't do anything right. Her mother explained, 'As a 10- or 11-year-old you don't know how to rationalise criticism – it becomes a personal reflection of not being good enough and that can quickly escalate.' What they decided was that they needed to let go of the little things. Picking the right battles is important. We need to identify which things are important to consistently send our kids messages about. Otherwise, we would be constantly correcting and directing. We don't have to relentlessly pick on them for the little things, or use a critical or demoralising tone.

Natasha started applying the 80/20 rule. About 80 per cent of your conversations should be enjoyable, even if that means parking your parental frustrations or choosing your battles. No more than 20 per cent of your communication time should be used for instructions, direct requests and corrections. Think about the benefit of the 80/20 rule practically. If your conversations revolve around disagreements or modifying behaviour, without any spark of humour or fun, your kids will be on a one-way train out of there. Applying this rule means you may have to stop verbalising disappointments. If your daughter chose an outfit you didn't think matched, let it go. If your son picked his nose in public, don't comment. Some children challenge us to let go of more things than others do! Try swapping correcting time for connecting time, which means letting go of unhealthy and unreasonable expectations.

If you find your relationship with your child difficult, I don't want you to focus on the cracks or areas that look damaged, but appreciate the relationship for what it is. We don't want to minimise or miss the gift that they already are. Remember these wise words of Thomas Merton: 'The beginning of love is to let those we love be perfectly themselves, and not to twist them to fit our own image.'[5] Otherwise, we love only the reflection of ourselves we find in them.

Investing Now for the Years Ahead

> **Survey responses from parents when asked, 'Are you doing anything to prepare for the teenage years?' Parents could select multiple answers:**
>
> ◢ Encouraging positive friendships – 87.86%
> ◢ Talking about puberty and sex – 56.46%
> ◢ More solo time with them – 55.94%
> ◢ Carefully choosing a high school – 50.78%
> ◢ Upskilling my parenting – 44.44%
> ◢ Nothing as yet – 4.01%
> ◢ Other – 2.33%

Each time we open the door to connection, we invite our children to walk through it. It's very likely that if we show up consistently, they will too. Kerry shares her experience with her son: 'When you have three kids it's hard to get personal time with them. Every Thursday night I go grocery shopping with my eldest. We drive to the shop together, so we aren't face-to-face . . . he is helping, so his self-esteem is up. We have all those life skills conversations, and he is very much open to talking. He loves it, especially because he is away from his little brother and sister. I ask a lot of questions, and he loves to answer them. One night he asked me, "What is the difference between guilt and shame?" He absolutely loves one-on-one time with his dad too. When we take him to the basketball court on his own he lights up.'

If you want to deepen your relationship with your child, start by finding something you both enjoy and a regular, designated time and place to enjoy it. The key is to make sure we are fully present in those moments – make them count. I know I am fully present when there is no one in the world who matters except the person I am talking to – when there is no background noise. Screen-free, distraction-free, pressure-free headspace results in authentic connection. Try never to make this time an interrogation session – just be with them. As our kids get older, they become resistant to our probing!

Sometimes the connection between two people is like a dwindling fire that needs another log thrown on it to keep it going. A fresh idea can change everything, or at the very least it can show that you are making a concerted effort. Below you will find a list of connection-focused activities that families have shared with me. They may inspire and prompt your own creativity!

▲ We have a secret goodbye handshake routine, and we spent ages working it out and what each one of the moves mean.

▲ I have started reading the same book and talking about it together with my daughter. I do the same thing with TV shows she is into. I read and watch it separately and then we get together to talk about it.

▲ I take both kids out for a 'family date', and then I take each one out individually for a 'parent date'.

▲ Friday Fun Day where kids take turns to choose what we do.

▲ I always take time off work for birthdays, so we can do something special together – just the two of us.

▲ I sometimes pretend to be a restaurant and give them a menu to order from. They find it fun, and I even have a chef's hat!

▲ Notes are a great way to keep up with the business of the daily life. Keep those letters going back and forth.

- I love living room picnics instead of sitting at the dining room table. It chops things up a bit.
- We came up with a list of things in January of '22 things to do in '22'. Many of them were new things for our family. It's been so much fun. We even included things like trying new restaurants and finding something new on the menu. One of my daughters is autistic so we feel that trying new things with her is extra important.

Some connection activities have the capacity to grow with your kids. For my family, summer walks have always been a doorway to connection, as have special family dinners that last longer than normal . . . no phones are present, and we all sit and talk and then clean up together. We practise these routines over and over again, and they become cues for our minds and hearts to come together. And although the time and place may change as our children grow older, the framework that was built when they were young will always be present. While I know regular sit-down meals are not possible for every family, even if they are only scheduled for once a week, they are well worth the effort. If your mealtimes have become a little chaotic, argumentative or whingy, try adding some structure. Create a purpose that is broader than simply eating together.

Here are some dinner-table conversation prompts that are perfect for this age group:

- Everyone shares a high and a low from their day.
- Everyone shares something good, bad or interesting.
- Take turns to answer: What went well today? What are you proud of? What was something that felt peaceful today? What was something you enjoyed? Who is someone you are thankful for?

◢ Come to the table ready to tell a joke or an imaginary story.
◢ Come to the table dressed in your favourite outfit.
◢ Keep a gratitude jar and read one of the entries together each night.

Here are some interesting sentence starters that you could also use:

◢ I was in my element when . . .
◢ I am looking forward to . . .
◢ I am secretly afraid of . . .
◢ One person I couldn't live without is . . .
◢ I would never . . .
◢ I find it hard to . . .
◢ It makes me angry when . . .
◢ This week I hope to . . .
◢ I often look forward to . . .
◢ I feel my best when I . . .
◢ I fear that . . .
◢ I find it hard to admit . . .

Creative Communication

Folded Wisdom is one of the most beautiful and inspiring books a parent could ever read about communication. In its pages, Joanna Guest shares the notes her father Bob wrote and drew for her and her brother Theo every day for nearly 15 years. Bob's morning ritual was to wake up early (when he was his best self), walk the dog and then sit down at the kitchen table with paper and coloured markers to create notes for his two children. When they were young, he left them word games and puzzles, with a splashing of thoughts about life woven in between. As they got older his notes morphed into thoughtful guidance and reflections about success, failure, happiness, sadness, frustration, praise and love for one another.

Here is the beautiful note Bob wrote on 21 October 1999, when his son was 8 and in third grade: 'You are my son. I am your dad. Nothing can ever change that. But I do not own you . . . you are not a "thing". I cannot make you into someone you are not. I can only love you. Whoever you are. I will always love you! Dad.'[6]

Among the chaos of family life, we are often forced into conversations at times when we are at our lowest and don't get to express the fullness of our love to our kids. I wonder if there is a way of capturing your enthusiasm and love for your child in your 'best self' moment? Recording a voice memo, writing a note, drawing a comic with stickmen or texting them might be a way of seizing the moment. Communication can come in many forms and sometimes it's the unexpected methods that give conversations that little extra zing! If communication with your tween or teen is getting a tad boring, try changing it up. Introducing a shared journal, a question box or a 'note of the week' might all help.

In the years to come your gestures will matter and be treasured. This is straight from a mother's email, and it mirrors messages I have read time and time again. She writes, 'A couple of times a week I text my children a quote connecting to something we have discussed together or something that is motivating or thought-provoking. I received a birthday card from my 15-year-old where Mr 15 had printed from his phone some of the quotes I had sent him over time. How the small things really do matter.' Another similar story from Joey shows exactly how powerful our communication can be. Her daughter wrote in a card, 'Happy Birthday Mum, Thanks for everything. The front of this card is covered with some of the most recent morning quotes you sent me. I love this about you so much and it always puts a smile on my face. Love from Joey.'

Chapter 14
SIBLINGS WHO FIGHT WELL

Key Message: I couldn't love either one of you more.

Like most families with multiple children, we went through a stage where my eldest began to assert his dominance over his younger brother. He went from being a loving playmate to a bossy tyrant overnight. Although my youngest's feelings were considerably hurt, he wasn't giving up without a fight. In a desperate move to salvage the relationship, he placed a photo of them playing together on his brother's pillow. He wanted to remind him of the good times they'd had together. Oh, my heart! What a wise little man. It was the perfect opportunity for me to talk to my eldest about what having a brother was all about.

Your tween may be the pesky little one or the dominant eldest, or any number of variations in between. The age gap between those in your care, the number of them, their personalities, interests, gender and whether they are biologically related or not are all variables that impact sibling relationships. Regardless of the dynamics, the tween years are a life-altering transition that will change the way our kids relate to each other. It is a time when relationships can easily become dislodged, so we want to do everything we can to safeguard them.

In my survey, 36.16 per cent of tweens identified conflict with siblings as their biggest challenge, as opposed to 22.57 per cent who identified friendship dramas as their biggest challenge. That tells me that home is the centre of a tween's world. When home doesn't feel safe, their world doesn't spin the way it should – and neither does ours. Research on bullying clearly tells us that the closeness of the relationship determines the depths of the impact. In the research paper 'Sibling Bullying and Risk of Depression, Anxiety, and Self-harm' we see that bullying within our homes can open the door to real and lasting damage in our kids' lives.[1]

Survey responses from tweens when asked, 'What are the biggest challenges in your life at the moment?':

◢ Getting along with brothers and sisters – 36.16%
◢ Fighting with friends – 22.57%

The endless comments tweens left in the survey also confirmed that sibling rivalry was something on their mind. Although the classics featured (brothers teasing them and little sisters being annoying), each comment carried a unique tone. For some, it sounded like they were desperate to tell someone about their frustrations. I've included some of the comments below, just to remind you how normal your family is if any of these comments seem familiar. If your kids fight often, please know that our goal is not to stop them from fighting but to help them fight well, without damaging each other.

Survey responses from tweens when asked about their relationship with siblings:

- ◢ Sometimes my brothers can be super annoying and they find it fun to annoy me. Sometimes they can be nice and play handball together but we mostly fight.
- ◢ My older sister, she is in grade 10 and we talk about high school, music and sports. We have only just started getting along well and I think it's because we have more in common now I'm in high school.
- ◢ She's 6 and so annoying. It's draining when she is playing games that I don't really like because we are different ages. I can't back out of it when Mum and Dad are busy. If I stop then she just carries on so I am stuck on it.
- ◢ She steals my stuff, and then Mum doesn't do anything about it. I get really angry and then I get into trouble and not her.
- ◢ When we have been put on warning, I try and tell her to stop, and then it usually ends up with shut up because you don't have to lose a privilege. When she makes trouble, I react and get into trouble and she goes off scot-free.
- ◢ When she and I are doing something, we have different ideas, and it's hard to find ways to cooperate and get along. Sometimes I use words that she doesn't understand, and it is hard to clarify what I mean, and then it just turns into war.

Evidence-based Must Do's

One dad shared with me a story about his two daughters. After a hectic morning of bickering, the girls were finally in the car ready for their dad to take them to school. The youngest was disgruntled about not being able to sit in the front seat, which her older sister got to first. 'She's looking out of my window!' the youngest screamed. 'Your window?' the dad patiently enquired. She said, 'Yes, she gets the front seat, so I get my own window. And she's looking out of it!'

Like you, I strive to send my kids the message that I couldn't love each of them any more than I already do, even if I split myself in half. However, I know that equality is harder to execute among the competing needs that arise in everyday life and in the different seasons that our children face. Each child's life's highs and lows can come at different times. They can easily compare their own down-season with their sibling's up-season. Although it's not a fair comparison, they don't have the experience to know that life is swings and roundabouts, and no one gets out of their share of difficulties.

I'd like to start by talking about 7 evidence-based 'must do's'. They will make the most difference to sibling relationships in the long term, so we can't afford to ignore them. Our kids have the rest of their lives together, so keep your eyes fixed on the end game. Time is one thing that is on our side when it comes to dynamics in our homes.

We must make time for them individually. The biggest predictor of how well children get along with each other as they grow older is their individual relationship with us.[2] When you safeguard your relationship with each of them, kids have a foundation that meets their needs. This is a big challenge for parents, especially when we have more than two children, or when one child has outstanding needs (such as ongoing health challenges, a disability or demanding extracurricular commitments), but we must try. If you can't look in your calendar and see where one-on-one time fits in, don't delude yourself into thinking that it is going to happen incidentally.

You might try saying to your tween:

▲ 'No matter how much your little sister gets, there is always enough for you.'
▲ 'I could never love them any more than I love you.'
▲ 'What would you like to do together, just you and me?'

We must sell the benefits. Something simple, but powerful, is selling the benefits of sibling relationships. When parents talk about siblings in terms of having 'built-in friends' and 'people in your corner', we prime their minds to see the positives in the relationship.

You might try saying to your tween:

▲ 'Siblings stick together.'
▲ 'Although it is normal to be irritated by each other, no one will replace your sibling.'
▲ 'What do you appreciate about your sibling?'

We must acknowledge the challenges. Dr Laura Markham, author of *Peaceful Parent, Happy Siblings: How to stop the fighting and raise friends for life*, says, 'If we aren't prepared to validate their experience, we deny them the opportunity to talk about it, rather than act on it.'[3] This resonated with me! We might feel a strong instinct to shut down how our kids feel, but we must allow them to feel it, and even to share it with us, no matter how difficult that is. Remember too the story they tell themselves about their sibling doesn't have to always be positive, but we ideally want it to be accurate. Some pretty big misunderstandings can arise between siblings, especially when one is going through a hard time that others don't have the maturity to understand.

You might try saying to your tween:

▲ 'You can always talk to me about how you feel, even if it's hard for me to hear.'
▲ 'I know it's really annoying when she takes your stuff or comes into your room without knocking.'
▲ 'Jealousy is a normal feeling. I wonder if he feels jealous about some things too?'

We must stay on neutral ground. As a general rule, try not to come into a room looking like the judge and jury who is going to sentence someone to their bedroom. Take a breath and normalise what is going on, because it is so normal! ABBA's smash-hit song 'The Winner Takes It All' sums up what happens when we don't stay on neutral ground. When it comes to sibling rivalry, there is often a perceived winner and loser – someone standing tall and someone standing small. The one who wins will feel loved, protected and empowered. The one that lost, won't. Try to protect both children so they each feel heard. Be conscious of where your body is placed during the conversation. Try to physically touch both children as you communicate.

You might try saying to your kids:

▲ 'This sounds like a tricky problem to solve. I want to hear from both of you equally.'

- 'Sounds like you both might need a hand to sort this out.'
- 'Let's start by listening to each other.'

We must create positive memories. Research tells us that the more positive memories our children have of each other, the more likely they are to get along as they grow up, even if they hit some roadblocks along the way.[4,5] Memories are anchors for our kids, so we must commit to making them. Admittedly, it can be hard for siblings to find common ground as they grow, especially if the age gap is significant. We must act as the bridge that joins them.

You might try saying to your kids:

- 'When was the last good memory you have of each other? What were you doing?'
- 'Did you see how she lit up when you played with her? She looks up to you.'
- 'What is something that you might both enjoy?'

We must live by values, not feelings. Family values provide a compass to find the true north for our thoughts, feelings and behaviours. Dr Gordon Neufeld, a world-famous developmental psychologist, says, 'Without culture, we are lost. Our kids need a script for what it means to be a parent, grandparent, sister, brother, uncle, aunt, and caregiver.'[6] When family values are in our kids' DNA, they provide them with a script that makes hard life decisions (like how they should treat their brother or sister) easier for them. Without a clear true north, how can we expect our kids to find their way back to acceptable behaviour? True north gives our kids an anchor point to return to when they mess up or when we can't be there to guide them.

You might try saying to your tween:

▲ 'What type of family do we want?'
▲ 'Why is home meant to feel safe for everyone?'
▲ 'What are our non-negotiable "won't do's"?'

We must know the power of our voice. One of the reasons that our kids want to talk to us or text us when they feel overwhelmed is because they have a basic need for safety and love. With the threat of separation, all hell can break loose in their nervous system, and in our homes. These needs are even more heightened in moments of crisis. Before they look for the courage to tackle life's challenges, they look to feel calm. It's from a sense of calm that courage can emerge. The sound of your voice is literally soothing for them. As our kids try to settle their anxious brains, they often need our reassurance.

You might try saying:

▲ 'You always have my ear.'
▲ 'We will work this out together.'
▲ 'You and I are a team.'

The Eldest

Each of our children has a unique perspective, but let's zoom in on life in the shoes of our eldest child. Eldest children often feel overly responsible, have a heightened awareness of their parents' needs and don't know how to use their position in the family wisely. Throughout the COVID-19 lockdowns, when we were homeschooling and working from home, many of our eldest kids carried adult pressures that were beyond their skill set.

I interviewed eldest child Tasmin, who is 9, turning 10, and who was gloriously articulate. I felt that each of her words was important, so I have included them below. This is her side of the story:

I have a sister who is 6 years old and very annoying. It's draining when she is playing games that I don't really like because we are different ages. She does things that only little kids find amusing. I can't back out of it when Mum and Dad are busy. If I stop then she just carries on, so I am stuck on it. I spend a lot of time with her every day. When I am trying to focus on something, and she is trying to get my attention in a bad way, I know if I react, I will get into trouble. Some days I feel like she is just lonely and wants my attention and she will do anything to get it (she will take something of mine, she sprays the perfume I hate in my room, or kicks me under the table) and then other days I think she just likes seeing me get into trouble. I think it is a bit of a game to her. It's a game for both of us. Who can try and get the other person into trouble without getting into trouble themselves? It is happy for the person who is not getting into trouble. But overall, it is a sad game that's not helpful. It doesn't help at all. It puts me in a bad mood for the rest of the day.

Importantly, I want to offer her mother Annaliese's side of the story too. She says, 'It sounds like my husband and I are just lolling around on the couch while I let her look after her sister! I can reassure you, we aren't! There is a fierce love between them, but because of their age difference, it can be hard for them to find common ground. She tries very hard and it's beautiful to watch them try so hard, but some days she gets super frustrated. It's got its lovely parts. We have to find better ways of dealing with and responding to it all.'

My first question to this family was, 'What's the plan?' Besides reacting and fighting, what other options do they have? Creative brainstorming is often essential to get through times when there is a natural imbalance of power. These are some practical ideas this family was able to come up with:

- ◢ Ensure Tasmin has regular timeouts.
- ◢ Schedule designated one-on-one time for both kids with mum and dad. Bedtimes were the natural opportunity to allow space, so Tasmin went to bed half an hour later than her sister so she had one-on-one time with her mum. 'That's my only quiet time without her,' Tasmin explained. 'Reading during that time helps calm me down.'
- ◢ Make room for the girls to have separate adventures. The hope was that they would miss each other in the process. The family allowed Tasmin to stay at her grandparents' house once a month while they took the youngest out for ice cream.
- ◢ Plan special, structured, shared activities. The family often brought some extra toys, cooking ingredients or craft items like playdough to aid this.
- ◢ Encourage and appreciate kindness. From Tasmin's perspective, playtime is often a deliberate gesture of kindness, rather than her preferred option. Tasmin explains, 'A few weeks ago, I painted a portrait of her, and she really liked it. Then I asked her if she wanted to play shops with me, and she really got into it.'

In the Heat of the Moment

When I ask tweens what they fight about with their siblings, the issues are usually not major. They are petty things such as who gets to use the bath, who touches their stuff, who eats all the food and who is cheating in a game – and then there is the roughhousing and rumbling that goes too far. I can tell tweens know how petty these things are because they offer a giggle and a knowing smile when they share them with me, which I probably find more adorable than you do! Karen Young again offers a helpful explanation when she says, 'Arguments in a family are a sign that everyone is having their say, even if the final answer isn't the one they want.'

When conflict happens, regardless of how petty the issue, the ideal scenario is that our children problem solve their way forward. Although problem-solving can happen in the heat of the moment, it is more likely to happen once we have regained calm. The first question you want to ask is, 'What will help right now?' The honest answer to that is, sometimes spending time apart or having hot chocolate together is the best way to relieve big emotions. Don't feel pushed towards problem-solving in a moment if kids aren't ready for it. However, the secret to happy homes is repairing damage to a relationship as soon as possible.

Some families find formal family meetings to be an effective way to help kids problem solve because children have a middleman to help them articulate how they feel. It can give tweens the chance to express themselves in a safe, supportive space where they know tensions will not escalate. If you choose to have a family meeting, always identify what the conversation aims to achieve. If we are unable to do this, we can fail to stay on task towards a positive outcome.

During a family meeting, we can offer three things that our kids' immature problem-solving skills are unlikely to work out without our help – the opportunity to express needs, the opportunity to own behaviour and the opportunity to develop a plan forward. If we can achieve these things without our kids name-calling, blaming or belittling others, that's a massive win! Remember too that our kids are practising relationship skills within our homes, and they learn so much from each other in moments of tension. You might lead with questions such as:

- ◢ 'Can you tell your brother how you feel without calling him names?'
- ◢ 'It is important that you hear how your behaviour is impacting others. What did you hear your sister say?'
- ◢ 'How could we handle things better next time?'

As I write this, I think it is important to mention that you don't have to problem solve with kids every time they fight. In fact, I would recommend that you don't. Children do need to learn to repair their own relationship ruptures, so only step in when you see a teachable moment where you can have maximum impact, or when things are escalating to a point of harm.

Solid Apologies

I am very sure that many families hit moments when their children's behaviour crosses the line, either verbally or physically. I get a lot of messages about tweens' rage, and how much it frightens younger siblings. These moments impact everyone in the family and can create a lot of shame for a child when they don't know how to repair things. Belinda shares, 'It gets quite physical with my kids, which is hard for me to handle, and I want my kids to have a good relationship. My 13-year-old son is almost as tall as me and probably stronger, so can be quite intimidating when he gets into a rage.'

When poor behaviour harms others, apologies are an essential part of the way forward. Without repair, conflict often leads to survival-based reactions that fuel more fights and bad habits. However, solid, meaningful apologies don't always come naturally. I remember insisting that my teenage son say 'sorry' after a fight with his brother. I was terribly disappointed with his efforts. My heart knew he was deeply remorseful, but in that moment, he was unable to convey it genuinely. It's easy to assume that the sorrier they are, the more convincing their apology will be. I have found that the more embarrassed, uncomfortable or upset a tween or teen feels, the more likely they are to apologise poorly. It's really hard to be vulnerable when you already feel at risk of judgement.

I use a four-step structure to teach kids how to apologise well. These are skills they can fall back on at any moment that repair is needed – at school, on the sports field, at the neighbourhood park or at home. Here are my four steps to a good apology:

Step 1: I am Sorry

These are the magic words that get things moving in the right direction. You can help your child understand that their tone of voice and body language can say sorry too. Encourage your child to never add a 'but' at the end of these magic words. Instead, think 'full stop'. Example: *I am sorry.*

Step 2: Take Responsibility

Solidly owning poor choices can be really uncomfortable. This discomfort often stops our kids from communicating exactly what they are sorry for and recognising its impact on the other person. Encourage them to be specific and clear. Example: *I am sorry. The way I spoke to you was wrong. I shouldn't have yelled at you like that.*

Step 3: Make Things Right

Always ask the other person, 'What can I do to make things right?' This is the part of the apology that seals authenticity. However, warn your child that this can be hard to do. Ask them to imagine open-heartedly saying this to their teacher or sibling and accepting their response, whatever it may be. Example: *I am sorry. The way I spoke to you was wrong. I shouldn't have yelled at you like that. What can I do to make things right?*

Step 4: Change Behaviour

Once you damage a relationship, it's your job to rebuild trust. When you are truly sorry, you will do your best not to repeat a behaviour. This intention is important to communicate and may mean they need to negotiate a plan to avoid a similar incident in the future. Example: *I am sorry. The way I spoke to you was wrong. I shouldn't have yelled at you like that. What can I do to make things right? Next time, I will do my best to take some time out if I am feeling heated.*

Chapter 15

TRANSITIONING TO HIGH SCHOOL

Key Message: If you've quietly whispered to yourself, 'I'm not sure I am ready for this!', you have probably grasped the gravity of what is about to come.

How many emotions did you experience on your child's first day of school? Hundreds? Well, the first day of high school is going to be no different. When parents see their tween wearing a high school uniform, complete with an accompanying hat, shiny shoes and oversized backpack, they know life is about to change – for everyone. If you've quietly whispered to yourself, 'I'm not sure I am ready for this!', you have probably grasped the gravity of what is about to come.

In Australia, where I live, many kids are 11 years old when they enter high school. 'Too young' is the feedback I often get, especially from parents of tweens who have special needs or who are neurodivergent, which can make transitions a greater challenge. Helen, whose son recently started high school, explains, 'I found that my son entered Year 6 knowing that this was his last year as a kid. Entering high school was not just an education change for us. It came with the expectation that he would grow up and become a different person, and it brought a lot of other decisions along with it, like whether to buy him a phone or allow him to catch public transport to school.'

The high school you choose will have a great impact on the scope of your child's transition. As a baseline, most tweens will move from having one teacher, and the same classmates they spend 30 hours a week with, to juggling different teacher expectations, a larger student cohort, changing class sizes, timetables, new learning tools and computer software, and different textbooks. If they are moving to a new school location, there will also be the issue of finding their way around a new environment and establishing new friendships, which they may have not had to do for many years.

While some schools have developed innovative, well-thought-out transition programs, many haven't. I love schools who do a good job of tempering academic expectations, organising special activities for the first week, and not giving students homework until mid-term. When schools deliberately use the first few weeks to put wellbeing and relationships first, they are streaks ahead when it comes to lowering anxiety and creating a safe learning environment for students. If tweens feel too much pressure from the very beginning, or if the serious business of high school is used as a threat to make them grow up, it may overshadow the joyful energy they should be experiencing during this time.

The scope of the transition, combined with the uniqueness of your child, makes for a different high school experience for every student. Mum Lisa shares with me, 'So far, we are going ok, so much better than expected. He seems happy enough for now. I do expect maybe struggles to come along when the workload increases.' Karen, a mum who is also a teacher, adds, 'My 12-year-old son started high school this week and had an almost instant yearning for independence and smart-alec comebacks (lol). As a teacher, I've got the tools, but as a parent, nope.' At the other end of the spectrum, dad Justin says, 'It's been a disaster. It's week five and she still hasn't made any friends.'

Try not to oversell the transition to high school to your tween. It can be tough for some kids. Instead of saying, 'You are going to have a fantastic day,' you might consider saying, 'Today is going to be the beginning of a wonderful journey.' That leaves a lot of room for the real ups and downs they may experience. If the first day is rough, remember that it can be all different tomorrow. High school is temperamental like that! Bronwyn says, 'My daughter is in Year 7. It is a big school, and she didn't really know anyone. She was overwhelmed and teary when I dropped her off. It didn't really get any better that day and she ended up reading in the library at lunch. However, today was much better. We had practised questions for her to ask others to help build a conversation. When we spoke, I acknowledged that it is hard so that she felt heard, but I also reminded her of when she has done hard things before. Today she made two new friends and is looking forward to tomorrow.'

Ticking Off the Worry List

There is a difference between our worry list and our tweens'. We have got to be careful not to project our worry list onto them! Dad Henry shares, 'My son started high school this week. A very big transition for him as his primary school included an intermediate, so he's never changed schools before, and secondly, he has started at a private school after getting a sports scholarship. I realised that some of the anxiety I have had, he doesn't have at all. For example, schoolwork has changed from being on a Chromebook to a Windows laptop, and I was feeling apprehensive that learning how those work would be difficult but it's already second nature to him!'

I find that each child's worry list is incredibly different. Tweens can easily become fixated on unusual or small things that might seem insignificant to us. Not knowing exactly where to put their school bag or fearing being refused to go to the bathroom by a teacher can take up all of their attention. I have met some tweens who have heard rumours about mean kids in high school and have become quite afraid that they will cross paths with them. Their perception of high school is also influenced by the many messages they get from television and media, which can ramp up their concerns.

Dr Christopher Scanlon and Kasey Edwards, authors of *Raising Girls Who Like Themselves*, are passionate about ensuring our kids gain a sense of mastery and independence as they grow.[1] During my interview with them, we discussed their own children and how they had been investing in high school readiness well before its due date. I'd like to share our conversation with you by breaking down three core worries and how to tackle them incrementally. When it comes to the transition to high school, Kasey explains, 'The idea is to cross as many things off their worry list as you can before they get to high school. Our reassuring words won't do that. We have to prove to them that they are capable, through their life experience.'

Navigating space. Primary school students move in a cohort. In many schools, they have a buddy system, which means they always have one or two peers with them whenever they leave the classroom to collect tuckshop food or deliver a message.

Some schools go as far as requiring students to be escorted by a peer to the bathroom too! Kids can show up to high school never having had to move around on their own if we don't deliberately create these experiences for them. If you can safely let them walk to the local shop to buy milk, great. If you can't, let them walk to the food court within the shopping centre by themselves. It gives you a chance to talk about what to do if they get lost or stumble across something unexpected.

Speaking to authority figures. In primary school, tweens have one teacher (and maybe a music and a sports teacher) who they interact with regularly. High school presents the opportunity to speak to a variety of authority figures and older students. This can understandably feel scary for tweens. We can help by allowing kids to answer adults' questions for themselves instead of speaking on their behalf. If they visit a professional, empower them with the person's full name before the appointment and allow them to direct the conversation. You might also ask them to call the uniform shop, pay for groceries or order takeaway so they practise interacting with someone they don't know. I remember my mum asking me to call for a pizza when I was about 12 years old. I hung up at least three times before I finally committed to talking to the person on the other end of the line. It felt both exhilarating and terrifying in one single moment.

Looking after belongings. High school comes with more stuff to manage and look after, including a locker, different uniforms, computers and books. When children have never had to take full responsibility for their own belongings, this can be challenging. We can help by not picking up their hats, bags or lunchboxes when they are able to do it themselves. It's so easy to step in because it's quicker and easier than waiting for them to do it, but it doesn't build autonomy. This bleeds into getting kids into the habit of preparing for the morning the night before, which might mean putting their clothes, socks and shoes in one accessible pile, and possibly even choosing what they will eat for breakfast ahead of time. This removes the morning decision-making process that sleepy brains struggle to handle, and also ensures we aren't the unwanted middle man.

Belonging to a Community

There are very few kids (and parents) who don't identify friendships as something high on their worry list! Come high school, what is going to keep kids engaged in school is not the academic learning itself but the feeling of belonging to a community. This sense of belonging is the glue that sticks kids to education. Author Rebecca Sparrow offers this advice: 'The secret sauce of enjoying school is behaving as though you are part of a community. What does that mean in practical terms? It means joining in and making an effort to form positive connections with lots of different kids at school. Lunchtime or after school clubs (ranging from robotics, chess and theatre sports to knitting, book club or a sporting team) are a perfect way to meet like-minded kids. Similarly, when teachers ask for volunteers to help with gold coin drives or to participate in student versus teacher competitions – go along!'[2,3]

In my interview with Sharon Witt, author of 18 books for tweens and teens and a secondary school educator for over 30 years, she said, 'In order to make friends we need to practise being friendly. You can be as isolated as you choose to be in high school. So often we expect that everyone is going to come to us. You have to be prepared to step out of your comfort zone and into your courage zone. Look for places in the unexpected, maybe those who are on their own too. Practise one act of courage everyday – that might just be looking someone in the eye and smiling.' It's the small steps of courage that can be the hardest but the most rewarding.

For those going to a new school, it may be the first time they have had to make new friends in a very long time. Making new friends is a skill we can assume everyone has. But if we think about it, there are a lot of adults who don't know how to do this, let alone kids. Start-up conversations are very different from conversations we have with people we already know and trust. They can feel awkward if tweens don't have their words ready, so we might need to help by rehearsing open-ended start-up questions with them. The moment start-up conversations lead in to meaningful chats, relationships are forged. Meaningful chats require our kids to ask deeper questions and occasionally navigate awkward pauses. They require confidence, a bit of chemistry and being in the right place at the right time.

Close friendships are very hard to find, yet we continue to promote them like it's a standard and necessary part of the high school experience. It's not. The reality is that close friendships might only come along once in a lifetime – good friendships are more common. Michael Carr-Gregg and Sharon Witt's book *Surviving Secondary School: The essential handbook for every Australian family* explains that the best indicator of success in high school is a diverse range of friends.[4] My takeaway from this is that more is better, and one close friend is not always enough to support the high school experience. The biggest change to encourage in high school is that kids embrace a bigger and broader mindset when it comes to friendships.

It can take a while for tweens to accept the buffet approach to friendships, especially if they are used to à la carte. Buffets allow you to enjoy different styles of food, even if you keep coming back to your favourites. They allow you to broaden your taste buds, which is brilliant for developing social skills and resilience. And, most importantly, if the seafood is having a bad day or doesn't want to be eaten, you can choose steak instead! As tweens develop more formal thinking it will help them understand that we can be friends with more than one person at a time without being disloyal.

In my survey, I noticed a big worry for parents was their kids finding an alcohol-free, drug-free, sexting-free, drama-free friendship group. Their kid's safety was at the forefront of their minds. Tweens were more likely to worry about finding friends who 'liked them' and whose company they enjoyed, which I thought was an interesting comparison. The best way you can do this is to get to know their friends. Their social life needs to become your highest priority because it will be theirs. If you can, try prioritising a 'get together' with new friends in the first week or two of the school term. Try saying to your child, 'If there is anyone you want to have over next week, it's okay with me.' That way, if the opportunity arises, you have already eliminated the need for them to ask you. I also encourage families to set up a 'friend's home Friday' routine, or something similar, which sets a time that is suitable for them to plan social activities.

Below I have included an email from a mum who shared with me how they tackled the range of things on their worry list. This family was super prepared!

Hi Michelle,
I have been following your posts about high school. I thought I'd share the ways we prepared for it.

We made a plan for him to meet the couple of boys he did know at a set place for break and lunchtimes, so he wasn't on his own.

We printed maps of the school and stashed one in his pocket and one spare in his bag.

We visited the school the weekend before he started and had a walk around using the maps – this was really helpful.

We organised everything in his bag the day before so the starting morning wasn't too stressful and we allowed heaps of time for photos, etc.

We tried to share examples with him of how we felt when we started high school.

We cleaned up his room properly and got his desk and workspace set up nicely so that he had a place ready to go for homework and would feel better about going there.

We also joined the friends of his school on the Facebook page, which has been incredibly helpful.

Make sure they learn how to tie a tie!

Anything that kind of acts as a trial run is helpful – for example, I realised when I was waiting for him to get off the bus that he might not have realised that he would need to push the button to get the bus to stop at his stop.

We got extra organised with school lunches and home baking favourites, so that lunch had some nice bits, and favourite meals for dinner so that he felt we were thinking of him.

We minimised the amount of out of school stuff happening the first few weeks where possible.

I hope these help some families!

A Word about Play

Come the first year of high school, play equipment vanishes and it communicates a strong message to our kids – childhood is over. Mariana, a high school teacher of 16 years, shares this observation with me: 'A good transition program will help the usual fears and changes, but nothing can replace play that is missing.' When I speak to students, they tell me that the worst part of the first year of high school is the lack of play. They mourn it, saying, 'There is nothing to do at lunchtime, so we just sit around.'

Megan shares, 'I asked my son who has always been super sporty and played at every lunchtime if he was doing that at high school. He had taken a handball with him but said no, they just walked around, so that play has gone too. He said in part it's because of the different uniform, formal shoes, etc.' Tania agrees, 'My daughter has started high school this week and breaks are something that she has commented on. She said there is nothing to do. There is no play time, only eating. Some kind of play, gym or nature area would be great, or the only thing they focus on is the schoolwork.'

Lukas Ritson is the founder of Wearthy, an inspirational company that aims to design, build and educate about all things play.[5] In my interview with him I enjoyed his passion and comprehensive understanding of how play impacts tweens. Of note was the impact that environments have on tweens' behaviour. He shared, 'Play provides a safe place for kids to fall down physically and socially without serious repercussions. When there is no outlet for play, boys especially end up doing silly things like throwing oranges at each other.' Isn't that the truth! When those chemicals are building up in their bodies without anywhere to go, tweens can't focus on learning.

I've been relieved to see some Year 7 coordinators notice and fill this gap. One dedicated high school teacher told me that she created a list of things Year 6 students enjoy and then brought games and play equipment for the students to use in the first few weeks of high school. It made such a difference. In some high schools, first year students are fortunate enough to be offered special lunchtime programs and designated 'newbie' zones and 'buddy' systems. Robyn Hutchinson, Director of Junior Secondary and Primary Partnerships at Pacific Pines State High School, is one of the exceptions. She emailed me to say, 'I work in a large high school and we've just added three new buildings that are dedicated to the Year 7s. We have plans to add ninja-warrior-style play equipment there later this year. We also do an extensive transition program.' Whoo hoo!

Although the swing-and-slide concept may not have the longevity it needs to take kids through to Year 12, it's far from the only or even the best option. I really like the idea of offering students environments they can stamp their own creativity on, understanding that play is at its best when it is directed by children. Lukas Ritson gives an example of this when he says, 'There is a primary school in Logan that dumped dirt on their oval and that began their mountain bike track. From a play value standpoint, the higher the imprint kids put on a space, the higher value to the child.' I look for marks of where students have been in the high schools I visit. Some schools are so neat and tidy you don't get a sense that play is incorporated into their hectic programs. Other times, I see where kids have been – through painted murals, unique seating arrangements, pool tables or music stations – and it's delightful!

Motivation and the Increased Workload

The first year of high school has the potential to be a wonderful experience. It's got adventure written all over it. It's new and exciting. However, most tweens are going to need our help to adjust to the increased workload. That is where routines and systems that bypass their feelings come into play. The more tweens discover the power of doing things regardless of how they feel at the time, the more they are going to be able to lean on the long-term benefits of discipline. Remember, kids don't usually need routines around things that they like, but around things they don't.

Claire Eaton's excellent book *Hello High School* offers a 6-step routine to guide tweens' weekly life schedule. She calls it the 'Sunday set up, and the Wednesday wind up'. The idea is to use a Sunday time slot to think about and organise life, sports and school priorities for the week, and to use a Wednesday time slot to check back on their plan and catch any curveballs, so they can be productive the entire week and relieve needless weekend pressure. She also says, 'Parents need to hold their hand to help teens build this process from the get-go, so they can learn how to plan and maximise routines. We can't expect them to do this on their own. Teens with reliable routines feel more organised and confident, so they procrastinate and stress less, which can only be a wellbeing bonus for high schoolers and parents too.'[6] This is equally applicable to tweens.

When helping tweens establish a work routine, awareness of time will likely be one of their greatest challenges. Time is a complex concept, and that's why younger children rely on parents' prompts and on school bells to direct their next actions. As they get older, they need to learn to allocate the appropriate amount of time to a homework task, so they don't think it is going to take up their whole life. Ideally, I'd like kids to be able to identify what is a 5-minute, 15-minute or 30-minute task.

And this leads me to talk about time spent on procrastination and whingeing, which would be time better spent on something they love. If I could permanently fix anything as a screen saver on a tween's phone, it would be 'just do it'. Getting things done before gaming, watching YouTube, overthinking or getting distracted is the way to go! Procrastination stunts learning and no one wants to be surrounded by half-completed assignments, grades that don't match abilities and deteriorating communication with teachers. Claire Eaton nails it when she says, 'Get the job done and get on your skateboard.'

Visual family planners can help kids understand and allocate time wisely. Many parents swear by visual planners that hang in the kitchen, or even virtual calendars where parents can place their work schedule in an online diary, so children know their parents' whereabouts and who will be transporting them to and from activities. This can be particularly helpful if tweens are living between two homes. You might relate to these words from Leo, a mum who said, 'This week has been full on. Straight into classes, plenty of homework, school photos today, bands and choirs start next week – no easing into it! I think it is possibly a bigger adjustment for me than her. I have had at least three emails from the school every day since Monday.'

Sadly, a curriculum-heavy system means that there will be times when the high school workload feels too much. As a family, you might choose to 'load bear' until a tween finds their feet again. Load bearing is when another family member does a tween's regular chores or part thereof to free up some of their time. You might also choose to drop what is not important, so your tween can continue to enjoy other things in their lives.

Avoiding Labels

Parents often talk to tweens about running their own race, which implies that they have a set lane to run in. Developmental psychology tells us that tweens don't have the capacity to choose a lane when they are 10 years old. Tweens should run in every and any lane. That's exactly what their brain is designed to do – explore widely. You can think of the tween years like the beginning of a marathon. All the athletes are bunched up, shoulder to shoulder. From a distance, it's hard to distinguish one runner from the next, until, at the right time, they each make their move. We don't want them to even see the lines that in the years to come will more easily confine them. Research tells us that curiosity is key, and finding out what promotes or hampers curiosity and wonder in school curricula is essential.[7,8]

During my interview with Madonna King, I asked what her greatest takeaways were while writing *Ten-ager*.[9] One thing she highlighted was how early girls were deciding not to do particular subjects or participate in sports activities because they believed they weren't good at them. In my interview with her, she explains, 'We haven't been able to convince girls that failure is the first step of success. The message hasn't transferred.' Her conclusion is that too many of our kids are putting such a low ceiling on their own ability, from such a young age, which doesn't equate with the growth mindset that will help them become all they were designed to be. I love her proposed remedy – to encourage tweens to put effort into trying rather than achieving. She believes that the more they do that, the more they will achieve later.

The gravitation towards early labels is often driven by the need for certainty rather than growth. Too often children label and pigeonhole themselves at the expense of taking risks or participating in opportunities that come their way. Let's face it, none of us would have imagined ourselves as adults! How much have we changed? It's easy to push kids to pick a lane too early. Many times, this is because we need to see them achieving for our sakes, not theirs. Being conscious of projecting our own unmet needs onto our children is a vital first step in ensuring we don't try to live vicariously through them. Dance groups and sporting fields are full of parents who want their kids to feel the sense of achievement they didn't. Sometimes it pays to stop and ask yourself, 'Is this their dream or is it mine? Why is this so important to me?'

I would like to circle back to my interview with Dr Christopher Scanlon and Kasey Edwards, who I mentioned earlier in this chapter. Their professional work is wonderful, but their personal journey with their 12-year-old daughter really takes my breath away. I'd like to share their words, which I personally found both moving and challenging, as I know the effort it can take to say no to good opportunities in the search for something better. Although their daughter is clearly a capable academic student, they were determined not to label her.

Our biggest hope is that she gets to the end of Year 12 with good mental health, believing she is good enough and maintaining her curiosity. What worries us is the pressure on scores and the end result. If she doesn't get the number, we can fix that. But if she gets to the end of high school and she can't get out of bed, that isn't as easily navigated. If she believes in herself the world is open to her. Every decision we make comes back to that. We have lived this in a very practical way in our home. We said no to the high achievers accelerated learning program, which is a select entry stream of the school. Apparently, we were the only parents who said no to this program but we didn't want 'overachiever' to be a label for our girl, and we didn't feel it would support her mental health. The biggest opportunity our children have is to be children.

I'm not suggesting this would be the right decision for every child or family. What I do want to emphasise is that even positive labels can assign a limiting lane for tweens that can be hard for them to deviate from. Whether our kids define themselves by saying 'I am not smart' or 'I can't do maths' or 'I am a high achiever' or 'I am a pretty girl', we must be mindful that if they hold that title too firmly, it will box them in. I'm more excited to help tweens explore themselves by keeping them curious about their growing self.

Our Highest Priority

A recent Grattan Institute report suggested that as many as 40 per cent of Australian students are consistently passively or actively disengaged in class, and that these students are 1 to 2 years behind their peers in academic performance.[10] The report also identified that the majority of disengaged students do not actively disrupt the class, but rather they tend to be unmotivated and off-task without attracting the teacher's attention. Factors such as academic interest, teacher relationships and a sense of belonging all contributed to engagement. Please watch out for what research terms the 'Year 9 dip', where kids are most likely to disengage from education.[11]

When children transition to high school, many who are not academically wired get lost in the system, especially our boys. Each situation is different, but I'd like to share Ann's story about her son Jay, who had always significantly struggled with maths, yet never got the focused support he needed to feel competent and courageous in spite of his learning difficulties. Ann explains, 'We knew he wasn't good at maths but when I was told he was unhappy it really shocked me. *Unhappy at school*, I thought. *How could I miss that?* That really surprised me because he gets up in the morning and he goes to school. He doesn't fuss and he doesn't argue about it. People always commented on how polite he was, but when I look back there were signs that he wasn't connecting with his peers. There was no interest in hanging out with friends and in his schoolwork. When he was 11, we noticed little changes, but we dismissed them. Because home is the safest place, we don't see him at his worst. When he ended up telling me he was really depressed and hated school, we realised we needed help.'

Because tweens often don't have the language to allow us full insight into their world, they can appear to hit a wall suddenly, when the build-up has actually taken place over some time. As I spoke with Ann, we identified that Jay's easygoing temperament made it really easy to miss the warning signs of his deteriorating mental health. Jay was polite and compliant. Ann explains, 'That word "compliant" almost broke me. My son was this unhappy because he was compliant! Compliant is not what I wanted. A happy child was. Our daughter is more explosive, but she is also competent in other areas too and her language is more advanced, so it's interesting that she has been more confident expressing herself.'

Throughout high school, there will be increased demands on our kids. Some of them will compliantly shuffle through it, but they'll be deeply unhappy, to their detriment. Remember that prolonged periods of poor mental health, when left undetected or untreated, can stunt our children's growth and impact their love for learning. When they have no spark, we need to pay attention.

Emma, whose children struggle with school for different reasons, also shares her story. She says, 'I looked at their report cards this year, and their grades had slipped, and I felt it was my fault. Some things don't happen as well when you have limited resources and there is only one parent to do everything. There are only so many hours in a day, and we are all exhausted from running a business and going through a separation.' So many families get pulled between the internal and the external. Pressing, practical things have to be done and it's easy to get lost in the obligations rather than the art of parenting.

Another mother shared, 'Emotional things are obviously the most important, but the weight is on the practical things. They are obviously the things that are most pressing, and everything gets clouded. If you can't go out and have a milkshake with a child, you don't have a life!' She also says, 'It takes time and space for boys to open up, both of which most parents are often short of. If I don't sit with him alone, by himself, away from his sisters, we will miss it.'

Throughout high school let's not lose sight of what is really important. You might feel you are pushed to participate in programs or spend time in places that aren't going to give your child the best return or end result. We all know that no excellent academic education will give you a relationship with your child, nor will it secure their wellbeing, happiness or ongoing desire to learn and grow. You don't want to be in a position where they are 15 and can't talk to you, and homework and schoolwork dominate your conversations. Make what matters now, matter.

Chapter 16

FIVE MESSAGES FROM YOUR TWEEN

I want to use this final chapter to elevate the words of the tweens who participated in my 2020 survey. In total, 567 tweens chose to answer the optional question, What is one thing you wished all adults knew about life as a tween? If your child was asked that question, how do you think they would answer? They might wish adults knew that kids who were 10 *shouldn't* go to bed at the same time as a sibling who is 7, or that kids who don't like broccoli should *never* be made to eat it. This is the important stuff that characterises much of a tween's headspace!

But I want to probe a bit deeper. Would there be one thing that your child wishes they could tell you, but can't quite manage to communicate? Do you think there is anything that they find difficult to talk about or intentionally hide because of fear or shame? If you take a moment to revisit your tween years, were there important things that you found difficult to communicate to your parents?

Survey responses from tweens when asked, 'What do you want adults to know?':

- ◢ Life is hard
- ◢ Our emotions are changing
- ◢ Listen to us
- ◢ Is that I do love them
- ◢ That, when we are angry and upset 😣, sometimes we say stuff we don't mean. And we are sorry even if it doesn't sound like we are.

Over and over tweens have consistently told me that they want their parents to listen to them – and to hear their fears, thoughts and dreams on a deep level. They struggle to know when to talk to you, among the busyness of life. And when they did talk to you, they wondered if you were really listening. I am constantly reminded of how much gets lost in the translation of daily life. That's why I want to encourage you to be intentional about your time now and in the upcoming years. If you don't make room for quiet, agenda-less time together, meaningful conversation may not happen.

Please be mindful that fear will stop you from asking curious questions with an open heart and mind. Asking questions without responding with correction, teaching or strategies is a big learning curve for parents of tweens. Admittedly, tweens aren't always amazing at articulating their thoughts, and I can often see them looking at me as if to say, 'Am I doing this right?' However, my hope is that by asking, they connect with their inner world.

Below I'll be sharing the findings from my anonymous survey that I hope give you insights into your own tween's inner world.

For ease of reference, I have collated five of the most consistent messages tweens shared with me. I hope their words continue to shed light on their development, needs and inside story.

Message 1: Life is Harder than You Realise

Tweens believed life was harder for them than their parents acknowledged. As you can see in the comments below, they felt their challenges were minimised and trivialised. My concern is that if tweens don't feel understood now, where does that position us as they get older?

Some comments from tweens that caught my attention:

- ▲ It is not how they think it is. Everything is hard.
- ▲ Strange things are happening to your body, mood swings come and go, and you generally don't know what to do.
- ▲ I wish they knew how hard it is to get used to changes and that when we don't know what's happening more things are put on our plate.
- ▲ How stressful it is to have hours of homework. How stressed I am about my grades.
- ▲ that it is not just hard to be an adult it is hard to be a tween as well. When u ask a tween if they are ok they are 9 times out of 10 not. Life is hard and it is never going to get easier.
- ▲ we try our hardest and sometimes our hardest isn't good enough, it's not our fault.

- its harder than you think. even when someone says their good, they might not be. but then when you keep going on saying 'are you okay?' over and over again it makes us feel worse.
- Its harder than it looks. Please, please be patient with us. Please give us time to think about things. Listen to us. That's all I ask.
- they just don't get it
- schools really overwhelming, and I don't know how to tell people
- I'm having trouble telling adults what I am struggling with
- Everything is hard, the simple way to them is not simple to us. It's hard. Friendships are hard, talking about our feeling is hard, it is hard not to react to things, it is stressful, keeping track of everything is hard.

Message 2: I am No Longer a Kid

Tweens voiced a strong desire to be taken more seriously by the world around them, and not to be overlooked or dismissed because of their age. They wanted us to listen to them and to take their thoughts, ideas and needs seriously. I noticed that they felt like teenagers, while only being recognised as children. That's quite a downgrade! My concern is if tweens don't have a meaningful place to contribute now, how will they make a significant contribution as they get older?

Some comments from tweens that caught my attention:

- The teen years have started. We are going through similar things to teenagers, but we have a littler body.
- Most adults think that teenagers are the ones with mood swings and might act moody, but tweens might go through these (my friend felt really down for a while).
- i know stuff and I am important too.
- Sometimes we are treated like ping pong balls and we get pushed around to places that may or may not do something.
- i feel trapped in not being a kid or a teenager.
- i feel caught in the limbo of being little and big.
- we want to be trusted and taken more seriously
- It is extremely annoying when you say no to something that your friends or cousins get to do and you can't.
- parent need to trust me more
- don't want to be called a twelvie anymore
- don't want to be treated like a kid anymore
- roam free
- own decisions
- make my own path
- not trapped at home
- hang with friends without adults

Message 3: You are Missing Stuff

Although it broke my heart, I was not surprised to hear tweens emphasise that their parents were missing stuff. When I walk through a primary school playground, I am often shocked at the 'teenage-like' chatter and themes I hear. I know that parents have no idea of the real content of these conversations and the pressures kids are under to engage in them. My concern is, if we don't keep our eyes open, we may not see those things that are most important.

Some comments from tweens that caught my attention:

- ◢ You think we are okay, but we aren't always.
- ◢ That there's a lot more bad things out their than they think. challenges are getting harder like schoolwork and problems.
- ◢ How many times you hurt your self, It is ALREADY happening to me.
- ◢ its easy to get depressed as a tween. a lot of things, they need to be educated and stop thinking everything is okay or that they haven't done anything wrong while growing up
- ◢ Sometimes, our parents ask us what's wrong and we say 'nothing' but there is something. But we just don't feel like we want our parents to know cause they might judge me

Message 4: We Might Always Disagree about Screens

Technology was a central theme of tweens' frustration. PS: Feelings are often mutual! Emphasis was placed on parents' alleged lack of understanding of how central technology was to tweens' social status and life. As adults, we know there are some very real and legitimate reasons why we say no to screen time. For this reason, I'd like to suggest that we might always have slightly different views about technology. My concern is, if we don't take the lead in this area, they will travel into dangerous waters.

Some comments from tweens that caught my attention:

- ◢ I think, the thing that most parents don't get is, screens.
- ◢ When they were a kid they didn't have the games and the social media apps as we do today and yes they might use them like insta or Facebook but they'll never get what it's like wanting to use those apps as a tween or as a kid.
- ◢ That being on our phone a lot doesn't mean We're addicted. We just want to hang around people our age who get what it's like being a tween in this era.
- ◢ Kids need more screen time. That we aren't addicted to phones.
- ◢ we expect more online privacy.
- ◢ That we need phones.
- ◢ That when you show someone your device and they start looking at things and you grab it off them, that doesn't mean there is something on there to hide, I just don't want people going through my stuff, it's my privacy.

Message 5: It's Time to Start Knocking

When tweens begin to need more privacy, most parents respect and welcome it as a sign of growing up. However, when they begin to desire space from adult supervision, it poses a new range of dilemmas. While our tweens are pushing for all the trimmings that come with being grown up, such as catching a bus on their own or shopping alone with friends, their limited life experience leaves them vulnerable. They still need us. My concern is that if we are not willing to enter into age-appropriate negotiations as they grow, they may begin to hide unsafe behaviour.

Some comments from tweens that caught my attention:

▲ Privacy, safety, and a change of communication style.

▲ How you need a bit more space.

▲ Is that we like to be with friends alone

▲ We need space.

▲ We need our own space and time

▲ Sometimes we are moody for no reason so don't shout at us just leave us alone.

▲ Let us have opinions without arguing or correcting them . . . space to grow up.

A CLOSING THOUGHT

Last year, I overheard this cute conversation between two girls who were seated in the front row of my puberty presentation. The girl seated on the right was gorgeously cheeky and keen to hear everything I had to say. She turned to her friend sitting beside her and, with grand hand gestures, enthusiastically announced, 'Whoo hoo! Michelle is here for *the talk*!' Her friend, who looked far more reluctant to see me, quickly whispered back, 'The talk?' Without even the slightest hesitation, the first girl replied, 'Let me put it this way – goodbye, childhood!'

The countdown is on. In a few short years you will have a teenager on your hands. Right now, you are watching the sun set on an era as a new one begins. Don't waste a minute of this magical view. Now is the time to impress on their hearts who they are, the safe place they belong and an unwavering belief that their voice matters. Although time will go quickly, a lot will happen in the next few years. Liken it to having a 16-year-old who is almost an adult. Another year or two of brain development (and life experience) are going to make a significant difference to the person that they are, so let's honour every bit of it.

If I were to leave you with one thought, it would be that what you invest now will have a great impact on the person that they become in 10 years' time. Not one ounce of the love you offer them will be wasted. Among the tiresome, seemingly never-ending pressures of our current world, don't forget to make memories. Our kids define their relationship with us based on their memory of us. Isn't this significant? When I hear kids tell me that their dad is their cricket coach or their mum reads with them at night, I always think about the beautiful reference point this will be in their future.

I have long talked to parents about choosing connection over comfort. When parenting a tween or teen you are liter-ally stealing hours, often at the expense of things that you once deemed to be essential. Those stolen hours will be spent listening to friendship issues, driving them to social activities, saying no to things they want to do or buy. These are hours you never knew you had but suddenly find because they need you.

As your tween grows into a teenager, the struggle for inde-pendence and the search for belonging will be more tangible. Memories will become increasingly important to anchor them. Beautifully, the images in our hearts and minds tend to lead us back to the people who love us and to the roots of who we are. If your child hits some rocky waters in the teenage years ahead, trust. Trust that those memories will help them follow their inner compass to the safest, most secure place they know – home. When they feel disappointed, lost, afraid or disorientated, it will be the predictability of home that continues to welcome them with open arms and wise words. Home is the emotional shield from all that hurts us, bothers us and tires us. It's a place where love is tangible and where we are cared for in ways that make it easier for us to move back into the world with a soft heart. It's the utopia that we all yearn for and strive towards.

ENDNOTES

Introduction: A Change in Conversation

1 'Understanding suicide, suicide attempts and self-harm in primary school aged children', Headspace School Support; headspace.org.au/assets/download-cards/02-HSP254-Suicide-in-Primary-Schools-Summary-FA-low-res2.pdf (accessed May 9, 2022).

2 Batchelor, Samantha, 'Suicidal thoughts start young: The critical need for family support and early intervention', National Suicide Prevention Conference, Brisbane, 2017.

3 *Kids Helpline Insights 2020: Insights into young people in Australia*, Your Town; yourtown.com.au/sites/default/files/document/Kids-Helpline-Insights-2020-Report-Final.pdf (accessed 10 February 2022).

4 Martin, Graham et al., 'Self-injury in Australia: A community survey', *Medical Journal of Australia*, vol. 193, no. 9, 2010, pp. 506–10.

5 McArthur, Brae Anne, Sheri Madigan and Daphne J. Korczak. 'Tweens are not teens: The problem of amalgamating broad age groups when making pandemic recommendations', *Canadian Journal of Public Health*, vol. 112, 2021.

Chapter 1: Almost a Teenager

1 Tierney, Adrienne L. and Charles A. Nelson III, 'Brain development and the role of experience in the early years', *Zero Three*, vol. 30, no. 2, 2009, PMID: 23894221.

2 The Childhood to Adolescence Transition Study, Murdoch Children's Research Institute; cats.mcri.edu.au/publications/ (accessed 27 December 2021).

3 Ramsey, Helen, Molly O-Sullivan and Lisa Mundy, 'Promoting wellbeing and learning in the middle years: An opportune time for intervention', Murdoch Children's Research Institute, 2020; doi.org/10.25374/MCRI.13146512.v2 (accessed 27 December 2021).

4 ibid.

5 Del Giudice, Marco, Romina Angeleri and Valeria Manera, 'The juvenile transition: A developmental switch point in human life history', *Developmental Review*, vol. 29, no. 1, 2009, pp. 1–31.

6 Tierney and Nelson III, 'Brain development and the role of experience in the early years'.

7 Backes, Emily P. et al. (ed.), *The Promise of Adolescence: Realizing opportunity for all youth,* National Academies Press (US), Washington, 2019.

8 Keenan, Kate et al., 'Timing and tempo: Exploring the complex association between pubertal development and depression in African American and European American girls', *Journal of Abnormal Psychology*, vol. 123, no. 4, 2014, pp. 725–36.

9 Marceau, Kristine et al., 'Individual differences in boys' and girls' timing and tempo of puberty: Modeling development with nonlinear growth models', *Developmental Psychology*, vol. 47, no. 5, 2011, pp. 1389–409.

10 Mundy, Lisa K. et al., 'Adrenarche and the emotional and behavioral problems of late childhood', *Journal of Adolescent Health*, vol. 57, no. 6, 2015, pp. 608–16.

11 Backes et al. (ed.), *The Promise of Adolescence: Realizing opportunity for all youth.*

12 Young, Karen, Hey Sigmund; heysigmund.com/about/ (accessed 6 May 2022).

13 Fuhrmann, Delia et al., 'Adolescence as a sensitive period of brain development', *Trends in Cognitive Sciences*, vol. 19, no. 10, 2015, pp. 558–66.

14 Dow-Edwards, Diana et al., 'Experience during adolescence shapes brain development: From synapses and networks to normal and pathological behavior', *Neurotoxicology and Teratology*, vol. 76, 2019.

15 Wallis, Nathan, Nathan Wallis: Neuroscience Educator; nathanwallis.com/ (accessed 6 May 2022).

Chapter 2: Speaking Tween

1 'Piaget's theory of cognitive development', Wikipedia, Wikimedia Foundation Inc.; en.wikipedia.org/wiki/Piaget%27s_theory_of_cognitive_development (accessed 20 January 2022).

2 Dent, Maggie, 'Leaning in with light for our tweens and teens', Maggie Dent, 29 November 2021; maggiedent.com/blog/leaning-in-with-light-for-our-tweens-and-teens/ (accessed 20 January 2022).

Chapter 3: Tricky Friendship Days

1 'Insights: Youth mental health and wellbeing over time', *Headspace National Youth Mental Health Survey*, Headspace; headspace. org.au/assets/Uploads/Insights-youth-mental-health-and-wellbeingover-time-headspace-National-Youth-Mental-Health-Survey-2020.pdf (accessed 1 July 2022).

2 Hawkley, Louise C. and John T. Cacioppo, 'Loneliness matters: A theoretical and empirical review of consequences and mechanisms', *Annals of Behavioral Medicine,* Vol. 40, No. 2, 2010, pp. 218–27.

3 Pickering, Leanne, Julie Hadwin and Hanna Kovshoff, 'The role of peers in the development of social anxiety in adolescent girls: A systematic review', *Adolescent Research Review*, vol. 5, no. 10, 2020.

4 Channel 9, *Snackmasters*, 9now; now.nine.com.au/snackmasters (accessed 10 April 2022).

5 Ury, William, *The Power of a Positive No*, Bantam, 2007.

6 Harter, Susan and Bonnie Buddin, 'Children's understanding of the simultaneity of two emotions: A five-stage developmental acquisition sequence', *Developmental Psychology*, vol. 23, no. 3, 1987, pp. 388–99.

Chapter 4: Big, Bold Emotions

1 Nook, Erin et al., 'The nonlinear development of emotional differentiation: Granular emotional experience is low in adolescence', *Psychological Science*, vol. 29, no. 8, 2018, pp. 1346–57.

2 Nook et al., 'The nonlinear development of emotional differentiation', pp. 1346–57.

3 Dent, Maggie. 'The only three rules that matter: KISS parenting', Maggie Dent; maggiedent.com/blog/three-rules-matter-kiss-parenting/ (accessed 10 May 2022).

4   Taylor, Paul, Mind Body Brain Performance Insitute; mindbodybrain. com.au/ (accessed 6 May 2022).

5   Sinek, Simon, *Leaders Eat Last: Why some teams pull together and others don't*, Penguin, 2017.

6   Keller, Matthew C. et al., 'A warm heart and a clear head: The contingent effects of weather on mood and cognition', *Psychological Science*, vol. 16, no. 9, 2005, pp. 724–31.

7   Lansdowne, A. T. and S. C. Provost, 'Vitamin D3 enhances mood in healthy subjects during winter', *Psyhcopharmacology*, vol. 135, no. 4, 1998, pp. 319–23.

8   Jennens, Scott and Andrew Wicking, 'Connected, protected, respected', Resilient Youth Australia, 2021; https://static1.squarespace. com/static/5850e095414fb5946daf8f2c/t/602db6a850e228599394 72bc/1613608682937/ResilienceSurvey4PageBrochure_NoBleed.pdf. (accessed 1 July 2022).

Chapter 5: Sturdy Self-esteem

1   Bialecka-Pikul, Marta et al., 'Change and consistency of self-esteem in early and middle adolescence in the context of school transition', *Journal of Youth and Adolescence*, vol. 48, no. 8, 2019, pp. 1605–18.

2   Pinquart, Martin and Helena Block, 'Coping with broken achievement-related expectations in students from elementary school: An experimental study', *International Journal of Developmental Science*, vol. 14, no. 1–2, 2020, pp. 9–17.

3   Jelic, Margareta, 'How do we process feedback? The role of self-esteem in processing self-related and other-related information', *Acta Psychologica*, vol. 227, 2022.

4   'Social comparison theory', Wikipedia, Wikimedia Foundation Inc., 17 March 2021; en.wikipedia.org/wiki/Social_comparison_theory (accessed 10 January 2022).

5   Brandtstädter, Jochen and Werner Greve, 'The aging self: Stabilizing and protective processes', *Developmental Review*, vol. 14, no. 10, 1994, pp. 1003.

6   Pinquart, Martin, Julia C. Koß and Helena Block, 'How do students react when their performance is worse or better than expected? An analysis

based on the ViolEx model', *Zeitschrift für Entwicklungspsychologie und Pädagogische Psychologie*, vol. 52, no. 1–2, 2020, pp. 1–11.

7 Pinquart and Block, 'Coping with broken achievement-related expectations in students from elementary school: An experimental study', pp. 9–17.

8 Pinquart, Koß and Block, 'How do students react when their performance is worse or better than expected?', pp. 1–11.

9 ibid.

10 Jelic, 'How do we process feedback?'.

11 Pinquart, Koß and Block, 'How do students react when their performance is worse or better than expected?', pp. 1–11.

12 Taylor, Paul, '7 Body-brain Vitality Rituals with Paul Taylor at Happiness & Its Causes 2018', YouTube, 11 October 2018; youtube.com/watch?v=7RKUAglmhrE&t=574s (accessed 20 May 2022).

13 Buckingham, Marcus, *Love + Work: How to find what you love, love what you do, and do it for the rest of your life*, Harvard Business Review Press, 2022.

14 Damour, Lisa and Reena Ninan, 'E64: How do I build my kid's confidence and self-esteem?', *Ask Lisa: The Psychology of Parenting*, 13 September, 2022.

15 Guasp Coll, Marian et al., 'Emotional intelligence, empathy, self-esteem, and life satisfaction in Spanish adolescents: Regression vs. QCA models', *Frontiers in Psychology*, vol. 11, no. 1629, 2020.

Chapter 6: Talents, Interests and Abilities

1 Manning, Lee, 'Erikson's psychosocial theories help explain early adolescence', *NASSP Bulletin*, vol. 72, no. 509, 1988, pp. 95–100.

2 McArthur, Brae Anne, Sheri Madigan and Daphne J. Korczak, 'Tweens are not teens: The problem of amalgamating broad age groups when making pandemic recommendations', *Canadian Journal of Public Health*, vol. 112, 2021.

3 Gardner, Howard, *Multiple Intelligences*, Little, Brown US, 2006.

4 'Meet the mastery team', *Ph360 Edu*, 2021; education.ph360.me/edu-meetthemasteryteam/ (accessed 12 August 2022).

5 Plomin, Robert, *Blueprint: How DNA makes us what we are*, Penguin UK, Great Britain, 2019.

6 Plomin, *Blueprint*.

7 Buckingham, Marcus, *Love + Work: How to find what you love, love what you do, and do it for the rest of your life*, Harvard Business Review Press, 2022.

8 McArthur, Brae Anne, Madigan and Korczak, 'Tweens are not teens'.

9 Damour, Lisa, *Untangled: Guiding teenage girls through the seven transitions into adulthood*, Ballantine Books, 2017.

10 Mylett, Ed, *The Power of One More: The ultimate guide to happiness and success*, Wiley, 2022.

Chapter 7: Sex and Other Tricky Topics

1 McCrindle, Mark and Ashley Fell, *Generation Alpha*, Hachette Australia, 2021.

2 Pariera, Katrina and Evan Brody, '"Talk more about it": Emerging adults' attitudes about how and when parents should talk about sex', *Sexuality Research and Social Policy*, vol. 15, no. 2, 2018, pp. 219–29.

3 Brizendine, Louann, *The Female Brain*, Bantam, UK, 2008.

4 Brizendine, Louann, *The Male Brain: A breakthrough understanding of how men and boys think*, Harmony, 2011.

5 Brizendine, *The Male Brain*.

6 Brizendine, *The Female Brain*.

7 ibid.

8 Dent, Maggie, 'Kids and gender', *Parental as Anything with Maggie Dent*, ABC, 25 May 2021.

9 Jones, Tiffany, 'Evidence affirming school supports for Australian transgender and gender diverse students', *Sexual Health*, vol. 14, no. 5, 2017, pp. 412–16.

10 Jones, 'Evidence affirming school supports for Australian transgender and gender diverse students', pp. 412–16.

11 Bradlow, J. et al., 'School report: The experiences of lesbian, gay, bi and trans young people in britain's schools in 2017', *Centre for Family Research*, University of Cambridge, UK, 2017.

12 Jones, Tiffany and Lynne Hillier, 'Comparing trans-spectrum and same-sex-attracted youth in Australia: Increased risks, increased activisms', *Journal of LGBT Youth*, vol. 10, no. 4, 2013, pp. 287–307.

13 Ferfolja, Tania and Jacqueline Ullman, 'Inclusive pedagogies for transgender and gender diverse children: Parents' perspectives on the limits of discourses of bullying and risk in schools', *Pedagogy, Culture & Society*, vol. 29, no. 5, 2021, pp. 793–810.

14 McCrindle and Fell, *Generation Alpha*.

15 McInnes, Elspeth and Lesley-Anne Ey, 'Responding to problematic sexual behaviours of primary school children: Supporting care and education staff', *Sex Education,* vol. 20, no. 1, 2020, pp. 75–89.

16 Dr Robyn Silverman; drrobynsilverman.com/ (Accessed 6 May 2022).

Chapter 8: The Chapter You Need to Read

1 'Teens, Social Media and Technology', *Pew Reserach Centre,* 2018; pewresearch.org/internet/2018/05/31/teens-social-media-technology-2018/ (accessed 20 May 2022).

2 'Teens, Social Media and Technology', *Pew Reserach Centre.*

3 *Kids Helpline Insights 2020: Insights into young people in Australia,* Your Town; yourtown.com.au/sites/default/files/document/Kids-Helpline-Insights-2020-Report-Final.pdf (accessed 10 February 2022).

4 'Are they old enough?', eSafetyCommissioner, Australian Government; https://www.esafety.gov.au/parents/skills-advice/are-they-old-enough (accessed 1 July 2022).

5 'Family tech agreement', eSafetyCommissioner, Australian Government; esafety.gov.au/parents/skills-and-advice/family-tech-agreement (accessed 1 July 2022).

6 Warburton, Wayne A., Sophie Parkes and Naomi Sweller, 'Internet gaming disorder: Evidence for a risk and resilience approach', *International Journal of Environmental Research and Public Health*, vol. 19, no. 9, 2022, p. 5587.

7 McCrindle, Mark and Ashley Fell, *Generation Alpha,* Hachette Australia, 2021.

8 *The Outsideologist Project Survey*, Claratyne; claratyne.com.au/the-outsideologist-project (accessed 16 May 2022).

9 Kumar Jha, Amrit, 'Understanding Alpha Generation', Indian Institute of Technology Kharagpur, 2020.

10 Twenge, Jean M. et al., 'Underestimating digital media harm', *Nature Human Behaviour*, vol. 4, no. 4, 2020, pp. 346–8.

11 Gámez-Guadix, Manuel et al., 'Risky online behaviors among adolescents: Longitudinal relations among problematic internet use, cyberbullying perpetration, and meeting strangers online', *Journal of Behavioral Addictions*, vol. 5, no. 1, 2016, pp. 100–7.

12 Warburton, Parkes and Sweller, 'Internet gaming disorder', p. 5587.

13 ibid.

14 Marshall, Brad, Wayne Warburton and Maria Kangas, 'Internet gaming disorder (IGD) in children: Clinical treatment insights', *Annals of Case Reports*, Macquarie University, vol. 7, no. 2, 2022, pp. 816–26.

15 Werling, Anna Maria et al., 'Problematic use of digital media in children and adolescents with a diagnosis of attention-deficit/hyperactivity disorder compared to controls. A meta-analysis', *Journal of Behavioral Addictions*, vol. 11, no. 2, 2022, pp. 305–25.

16 Twenge, Jean M. et al, 'Underestimating digital media harm', *Nature Human Behaviour*, vol. 4, no. 4, 2020, pp. 346–8.

17 Dresp-Langley, Birgitta, 'Children's health in the digital age', *International Journal of Environmental Research and Public Health*, vol. 17, no. 9, 2020, p. 3240.

18 ibid.

19 Von der Heiden, Juliane M. et al., 'The association between video gaming and psychological functioning', *Frontiers in Psychology*, vol. 10, 2019, p. 1731.

20 Schneider, Luke A., Daniel L. King and Paul H. Delfabbro, 'Maladaptive coping styles in adolescence with internet graming disorder symptoms', *International Journal of Mental Health and Addiction*, vol. 16, no. 4, pp. 905–16.

21 Hale, Lauren et al., 'Youth screen media habits and sleep: Sleep-friendly screen behavior recommendations for clinicians, educators, and parents', *Child and Adolescent Psychiatric Clinics of North America*, vol. 27, no. 2, 2018, pp. 229–45.

22 Wahl, Siegfried et al., 'The inner clock – blue light sets the human rhythm', *Journal of Biophotonics*, vol. 12, no. 12, 2019.

23 McKee, Alan, 'Yes, your child will be exposed to online porn. But don't panic – here's what to do instead', *The Conversation*, 17 November 2020; theconversation.com/yes-your-child-will-be-exposed-to-online-porn-but-dont-panic-heres-what-to-do-instead-149900 (accessed 16 May 2022).

Chapter 9: Building Body Confidence

1 'Body image of primary school children', *Longitudinal Study of Australian Children's 2013 Annual Statistical Report*, Australian Institute of Family Studies, Growing Up in Australia, 2013.

2 Ricciardelli, L. A. and M. P. McCabe, 'Dietary restraint and negative affect as mediators of body dissatisfaction and bulimic behavior in adolescent girls and boys', *Behaviour Research and Therapy*, vol. 39, no. 11, 2001, pp. 1317–28.

3 Gugliandolo, Maria C. et al., 'Adolescents and body uneasiness: The contribution of supportive parenting and trait emotional intelligence', *Journal of Child and Family Studies*, vol. 29, no. 10, 2020, p. 1007.

4 Allen, Karina L. et al., 'Eating disorder symptom trajectories in adolescence: Effects of time, participant sex, and early adolescent depressive symptoms', *A Journal of Eating Disorders*, vol. 1, 2013, p. 32.

5 ibid.

6 ibid.

7 Ferfolja, Tania and Jacqueline Ullman, 'Inclusive pedagogies for transgender and gender diverse children: Parents' perspectives on the limits of discourses of bullying and risk in schools', *Pedagogy, Culture & Society*, vol. 29, no. 5, 2021, pp. 793–810.

8 Brumfitt, Taryn, Body Image Movement; bodyimagemovement.com/ (accessed 10 May 2022).

9 Harper, Craig, Craig Harper: Keeping shit real; craigharper.net/ (accessed 2 May 2022).

10 Harper, Craig, *The You Project Podcast*; craigharper.net/podcast (accessed 2 May 2022).

11 The Butterfly Foundation; butterfly.org.au/ (accessed 6 May 2022).

12 Sanders, Jessica, *Love Your Body,* Five Mile Publishing, 2019.

13 Damour, Lisa and Reena Ninan, 'E64: How do I build my kid's confidence and self-esteem?', *Ask Lisa: The Psychology of Parenting*, 13 September 2022.

14 Brumfitt, Taryn, Body Image Movement; bodyimagemovement.com/ (accessed 10 May 2022).

15 Rogers, Rachel F. and Tiffany Melioli, 'The relationship between body image concerns, eating disorders and internet use, part I: A review of empirical support', *Adolescent Research Review*, vol. 1, pp. 95–119.

16 Hosseini, Seyed Alireza and Ranjit K. Padhy, *Body Image Distortion*, StatPearls Publishing, 2022.

17 Richardson, Jodie, *Well, Hello Anxiety*; drjodirichardson.com/podcast/ (accessed 16 May 2022).

18 Richardson, Jodi, *Anxious Kids*, Penguin Life Australia, 2019.

19 'Body image report – Executive summary', Mental Health Foundation; mentalhealth.org.uk/explore-mental-health/articles/body-image-report-executive-summary (accessed 1 July 2022).

20 Neumark-Sztainer, Dianne et al., 'Family weight talk and dieting: How much do they matter for body dissatisfaction and disordered eating behaviors in adolescent girls?', *Journal of Adolescent Health*, vol. 47, no. 3, 2010, pp. 270–76.

21 King, Madonna, *Ten-ager: What your daughter needs you to know about the transition from child to teen,* Hachette Australia, 2021.

22 Fischetti, Francesco et al., 'Gender differences in body image dissatisfaction: The role of physical education and sport', *Journal of Human Sport and Exercise,* vol. 15, no. 10, 2019.

23 ibid.

24 ibid.

25 'About eating disorders', The Butterfly Foundation, butterfly.org.au/ (accessed 16 May 2022).

26 ibid.

Chapter 10: Mental Health and the Path Less Travelled

1 Damour, Lisa, 'What is mental health?', Instagram, lisa.damour.

2 McArthur, Brae Anne, Sheri Madigan and Daphne J. Korczak. 'Tweens are not teens: The problem of amalgamating broad age groups when making pandemic recommendations', *Canadian Journal of Public Health*, vol. 112, 2021.

3 'Insights: Youth mental health and wellbeing over time', *Headspace National Youth Mental Health Survey*, Headspace; headspace.org.au/ assets/Uploads/Insights-youth-mental-health-and-wellbeing-over-time-headspace-National-Youth-Mental-Health-Survey-2020.pdf (accessed 1 July 2022).

4 Mundy, Lisa K. et al., 'Adrenarche and the emotional and behavioral problems of late childhood', *Journal of Adolescent Health*, vol. 57, no. 6, 2015, pp. 608–16.

5 ibid.

6 *Student Wellbeing, Engagement and Learning across the Middle Years*, Australian Government Department of Education, 24 October 2018; dese. gov.au/quality-schools-package/resources/student-wellbeing-engagement-and-learning-across-middle-years (accessed 16 May 2022).

7 Nehmy, Tom, *Apples for the Mind: Creating emotional balance, peak performance & lifelong wellbeing*, Formidable Press, 2019.

8 Nehmy, Tom, Healthy Minds; healthymindsprogram.com/ (accessed 14 September 2022).

9 Maté, Gabor, *When the Body Says No: The cost of hidden stress*, Wiley, 2019.

10 Neufeld, Gordon and Gabor Maté, *Hold On to Your Kids: Why parents need to matter more than peers*, Ballantine Books, 2019.

11 Brown, Brené, *Rising Strong: If we are brave enough, often enough, we will fail*, Vermilion, 2015.

12 Mitchell, Michelle, *Self-Harm: Why teens do it and what we can do to help*, Big Sky Publishing, 2019.

13 ibid.

14 Hawton, Keith et al, 'Self harm and suicide in adolescents', *Lancet (London, England)*, vol. 379, no. 9834, 2012, pp. 2317-82.

15 Griffin, Eve et al., 'Increasing rates of self-harm amongst children, adolescents and young adults: A 10-year national registry study 2007–2016', *Social Psychiatry and Psychiatric Epidemiology*, vol. 53, no. 7, 2018, pp. 663–71.

16 Hawton, Keith et al., 'Self harm and suicide in adolescents', pp. 2317-82.

17 Mitchell, Michelle, 'How to talk to a teen about counselling', Michelle Mitchell; michellemitchell.org/eight-different-ways-to-talk-to-tweens-and-teens-about-counselling/ (accessed 1 July 2022).

18 Beautiful Minds; beautifulminds.com.au/ (accessed 10 May 2022).

19 *Kids Helpline Insights 2020: Insights into young people in Australia*, Your Town; yourtown.com.au/sites/default/files/document/Kids-Helpline-Insights-2020-Report-Final.pdf (accessed 8 May 2022).

20 ibid.

21 'Insights: Youth mental health and wellbeing over time', *Headspace National Youth Mental Health Survey*, Headspace; headspace. org.au/ assets/Uploads/Insights-youth-mental-health-and-wellbeingover-time-headspace-National-Youth-Mental-Health-Survey-2020.pdf (accessed 1 July 2022).

22 Baker, Jordan, 'Teachers say pandemic hurt child development, ask for study into chaotic schools', *Sydney Morning Herald*, 1 May 2022.

23 Williams, Sally, *The Kind Mind Project;* https://www.kindmindproject. com.au (accessed 10 December 2021).

24 'Insights: Youth mental health and wellbeing over time', *Headspace National Youth Mental Health Survey*, Headspace.

25 McArthur, Brae Anne, Madigan and Korczak, 'Tweens are not teens'.

Chapter 11: The Road to Independence

1 Soenens, Bart and Maarten Vansteenkiste, 'Antecedents and outcomes of self-determination in 3 life domains: The role of parents' and teachers' autonomy support', *Journal of Youth and Adolescence*, vol. 34, no. 6, 2005, pp. 589–604.

2 Boyer, Ty W., 'The development of risk-taking: A multi-perspective review', *Developmental Review*, vol. 26, no. 3, 2006, pp. 291–345.

3 Rubenstein, Arne, *The Making of Men,* Xoum Publishing, 2013.

4 Karabanova, Olga A. and Nataliya N. Poskrebysheva, 'Adolescent autonomy in parent–child relations', *Procedia – Social and Behavioral Sciences*, vol. 86, 2013, pp. 621–8.

Chapter 12: Boundaries and Buy-in

1 MacNamara, Deborah, 'E60: Attachment, separation & belonging', *family360 Podcast,* 28 February 2022.

2 Altman Klein, Helen and Jeanne Ballantine, 'For parents particularly: Raising competent kids: The authoritative parenting style', *Childhood Education*, vol. 78, no. 1, 2001, pp. 46–7.

3 Slaughter, Charles W. and Alika Hope Bryant, 'Hungry for love: The feeding relationship in the psychological development of young children', *The Permanente Journal*, vol. 8, no. 1, 2004, pp. 23–9.

4   van Cuylenburg, Hugh, Ryan Shelton and Josh van Cuylenburg, 'Lael Stone – Creating emotionally intelligent humans', *The Imperfects*, 13 June 2022.

Chapter 13: The Gift of Language

1   Koefman, Alex and Craig Harper, '#127 Neurosurgery for dummies', *The You Project*, 20 October 2019.

2   Percy, Ray et al., 'Parents' verbal communication and childhood anxiety: A systematic review', *Clinical Child and Family Psychology Review*, vol. 19, no. 1, 2016, pp. 55–75.

3   ibid.

4   Gottman, John, *The Seven Principles for Making Marriage Work*, Orion Spring, 2018.

5   Merton, Thomas, *The Seven Storey Mountain*, HarperOne, 1999.

6   Guest, Joanna, *Folded Wisdom*, Celadon Books, 2019.

Chapter 14: Siblings Who Fight Well

1   Bowes, Lucy et al., 'Sibling bullying and risk of depression, anxiety, and self-harm: A prospective cohort study', *Pediatrics*, vol. 134, no. 4, 2014, pp. 1032–9.

2   McHale, Susan M. et al., 'Sibling relationships and influences in childhood and adolescence', *Journal of Marriage and the Family*, vol. 74, no. 5, 2012, pp. 913–30.

3   Markham, Laura, *Peaceful Parent, Happy Siblings: How to stop the fighting and raise friends for life*, TarcherPerigee, 2015.

4   Francka, Baylee A. et al., 'The relative impacts of sibling relationships on adolescent body perceptions', *The Journal of Genetic Psychology*, vol. 180, no. 2–3, 2019, pp. 130–43.

5   Rogers, Christina R. et al., 'Neural correlates of sibling closeness and association with externalizing behavior in adolescence', *Social Cognitive and Affective Neuroscience*, vol. 13, no. 9, 2018, pp. 977–88.

6   Neufeld, Gordan, 'Making sense of kids', YouTube, April 2018; youtube.com/watch?v=flGFs7NORRU (accessed 3 April 2022).

Chapter 15: Transitioning to High School

1   Scanlon, Christopher and Kasey Edwards, *Raising Girls Who Like Themselves,* Penguin Life Australia, 2021.

2   Sparrow, Rebecca, *Find Your Tribe (and 9 Other Things I Wish I'd Known in High School),* University of Queensland Press, 2010.

3   Sparrow, Rebecca, *Ask Me Anything (Heartfelt answers to 65 anonymous questions from teenage girls),* ReadHowYouWant, 2015.

4   Carr-Gregg, Michael and Sharon Witt, *Staring Secondary School: The essential handbook for every Australian family,* Penguin Life Australia, 2020.

5   Ritson, Lukas, Wearthy; wearthy.co/ (accessed 20 May 2022).

6   Eaton, Claire, *Hello High School: Goodbye drama and stress, 85 tips for high school teens that boost friendships, mindset, productivity and success,* Claire Eaton, 2020.

7   Barbot, Baptiste and B. Heuser, 'Creativity and identity formation in adolescence: A developmental perspective', in M. Karwowski and J. C. Kaufman (eds.), *The creative self: Effect of beliefs, self-efficacy, mindset, and identity,* Elsevier Academic Press, 2017, pp. 87–98.

8   Lindholm, Markus, 'Promoting curiosity? Possibilities and pitfalls in science education', *Science & Education*, vol. 29, no. 9, 2018, pp. 987–1002.

9   King, Madonna, *Ten-ager: What your daughter needs you to know about the transition from child to teen,* Hachette Australia, 2021.

10 Goss, Peter and Julie Sonnemann, 'Engaging students: Creating classrooms that improve learning', Grattan Institute, February 2017.

11 ibid.

ACKNOWLEDGEMENTS

When people ask me what it takes to write a book, I am never quite sure how to answer. For me, each book has demanded something different of me. One thing that is consistent is the support that you need while undertaking it. It's more than a one-man job, and there are so many people that deserve appreciation.

Firstly, thank you to Penguin. I consider publishing this book with you such a privilege. I particularly want to thank Sophie for her genuine interest and support of my work. She's been a cheerleader from our first conversation. Also, to my editor, Shané, who is a divine fit for me. Her gracious manner, attention to detail and quick mind are superb to work with. I can't believe you pick up the phone after 5 pm with such enthusiasm.

Thank you to each one of my team who have picked up some extra 'weight' in my overall business while I wrote these pages. An extra special thank you needs to go to my husband, who not only works with me, but also listens to my grand ideas well after work hours have ended. I adore you. Another special thank you must go to Helen, my research assistant. Her enthusiasm for this age group has been a joy to share. Helen, you are such a beautiful soul, and nothing has ever been too much trouble for you.

I am surrounded by generous colleagues, all of whom I greatly appreciate. Firstly, I want to thank someone who has had a much bigger influence on my life and career than she may realise – Maggie Dent. Her support, wisdom, care and character always feel close to me and make it a little easier for me to take the risks I need to. Maggie's small gestures have helped me stay focused and continue to give through life's challenges, and she will always be the person in my industry I aspire to be like. Thank you to Madonna King who told to me, 'Just get it done and out into the world' when I was on the final legs of the journey and feeling fatigued. I needed that extra push. Thank you also to Karen Young, my friend, who enthusiastically read my entire book. Given I consider Karen to be the best writer in the entire universe, that felt special.

On a personal level, talking to my young-adult children about their tween years has been a very special part of writing this book. We spent a lot of time reminiscing about their transition into the teenage years. They are now old enough to have an opinion! I want to particularly appreciate my eldest son for reading this book in its entirety and for giving me his like-it-or-not feedback, stories and thoughts. I have loved sharing this experience with him. Thank you to my parents, whose endless support still means as much as it did when I was ten years old, knitting vests and selling lamingtons.

I'm not sure how to begin to thank the community of people who read and follow my work on social media. You won't ever realise how much of a place you hold in my heart. I only get to do this because you are willing to have me in your world. Every time I meet a parent or young person who feel like I have made a different in their lives, it's incredibly special. I feel a deep sense of responsibility to help this generation transition into adulthood. Here's to sharing wonderful tween years, and even better teen ones, with you.

INDEX

abilities, belief in their own 103–4
abstract concepts, making sense of 30–1
acceptance and commitment therapy (ACT) 93
accountability 231
adolescence
 meaning of term xiii
anger management 1
anxiety 1, 9, 195, 196–7, 212
apologies 284
 steps to making a good apology 285–6
assumptions 68
autism 114
autonomous learning 109–13

bedtimes 221
behaviour
 genetics and 107, 108
 nurture, nature of 107–8
behaviourism methodology 259–60
belonging 46, 58, 87–8
bike helmets 221–2
'blueprint' of innate talents and abilities 106, 107–8, 109
bodies, owning their own 144
body confidence 171–3, 175–6
 conversations to have 176–82
 'fat' 176–7
 healthy choices 177
 positive body culture, creating 182
 weight control 172
body dissatisfaction
 boys' experience 173, 174
 early intervention 187
 factors driving 188
 girls' experience 173, 174
 technology, link to 180
 unrealistic body ideals 182
body language 144
body shaming 178
body uneasiness 172
boundaries 239–41
 agreed on, mutually 244
 buy-in 244, 245
 filters for parenting expectations 246–8
 friendship boundaries, communicating 54–6
 healthy child development and 239
 messages behind 241–2
 'no' decisions 242
 options in making a decision 243–4
 who makes the decision 243
boys
 body dissatisfaction 173, 174

boy psychology and man psychology, differences 233–4
 testosterone levels in puberty 122
brain
 adult size, when reached 8
 prefrontal cortex 66, 76
 synaptic pruning in puberty 14
Brizendine, Louann 122
Brown, Brené 2
 Rising Strong 200
Brumfitt, Taryn 175
Buckingham, Marcus 96, 109
 Love and Work 109
bullying 60–2
Burton, Robert 200

Carr-Gregg, Dr Michael 100, 148, 239, 293
Child to Adult Transition (CAT) study 195–6
cognitive development
 tweens, stages experienced 26–8
communication
 being creative with 270–1
 communication principles 262–4
 80/20 rule 266
 habits to avoid in communication 263
 parent-child discourse, impacts 257–9
 shaming language 260–1
comparing themselves to others 83, 85–6
 downward social comparisons 86–7
 lateral social comparisons 87
 upward social comparisons 86
competency, developing 105
 finding an area of 114
concrete thinking 27, 28
 connecting with concrete thinkers 29–32
confidence, lack of 81
conflict with parents 64
consent 1, 124, 140–5
 intuition, listening to 143
 key messages 142–4
 sexual and non-sexual situations 140
contributions, experiences around 118–19
conversation topics, change in 32
Coulson, Dr Justin 254, 256
COVID-19 lockdowns, impacts 211, 212
curiosity, maintaining 300, 301

daily debriefs 30
Damour, Dr Lisa 177, 192
 Ask Lisa: The Psychology of Parenting 97
 Untangled 116
dating 134
 discussion questions 135–6

331

TWEENS

ABOUT THE AUTHOR

Michelle Mitchell is an educator, author and award-winning speaker. She has been termed 'the teenage expert' by the media and is sought after for her compassionate and grounded advice about parenting tweens and teens. Michelle started her career as a teacher, but soon discovered a special interest in wellbeing. She left teaching in 2000 and founded Youth Excel, a 'boutique' health promotion charity that delivered tailor-made life skills programs and psychological services to thousands of young people and their families each year. Today she uses her experience to champion parents of tweens and teens.